Intellectu... but the
world of ... . While
globalisati... s by the
transnatio... gions of
the South ... narkably
little atte... g in the
world of ... ely and
analyticall... critical
overview ... unions
worldwide ... national
period in ... ovement
is itself a... olds out
the hope ... a global
economic

The a... ion and
feminisati... ng them
conscious... alism of
the trade-... g into a
'new' int... common
interest a... ounda-
ries. Dra... ers and
trade uni... trialised
North an... suggests
that we n... Polanyi,
many yea... The im-
plications for workers, trade unions and their transnational corporate
employers could be profound.

ABOUT THE AUTHOR

Ronaldo Munck is Professor of Political Sociology and Director of the Globalisation and Social Exclusion Unit at the University of Liverpool. Previously he held the first post-apartheid Chair in Sociology at the University of Durban–Westville in South Africa, and taught for many years at the University of Ulster in the North of Ireland. He has written extensively on labour issues including *The New International Labour Studies* (Zed Books, 1988), *Argentina: From Anarchism to Peronism. Workers, Unions and Politics, 1855–1985* (Zed Books, 1987) and *Labour Worldwide in the Era of Globalization: Alternative Union Models in the New World Order* (1999, coedited with Peter Waterman). His recent work includes *Marx@2000: Late Marxist Perspectives* (paperback edition, Zed Books, 2002) and *Critical Development Theory: Contributions to a New Paradigm* (Zed Books, 1999, coedited with Denis O'Hearn). He is currently researching labour flexibility and worker organisations in Latin America.

GLOBALISATION AND LABOUR

THE NEW 'GREAT TRANSFORMATION'

RONALDO MUNCK

ZED BOOKS
London & New York

Globalisation and Labour was first published in 2002 by
Zed Books Ltd, 7 Cynthia Street, London N1 9JF, UK,
and Room 400, 175 Fifth Avenue, New York, NY 10010, USA

Distributed in the USA exclusively by Palgrave, a division of
St Martin's Press, llc, 175 Fifth Avenue, New York, NY 10010, USA

Designed and typeset in Monotype Ehrhardt by Illuminati, Grosmont
Cover designed by Andrew Corbett
Printed and bound in Great Britain by Bookcraft Ltd, Midsomer Norton

A catalogue record for this book is available from the British Library

Library of Congress Cataloging-in-Publication Data applied for

ISBN 1 84277 070 5 (Hb)
ISBN 1 84277 071 3 (Pb)

Printed and bound in Great Britain by Biddles Ltd, *www.biddles.co.uk*

CONTENTS

LIST OF TABLES

LIST OF ABBREVIATIONS

ACEs	advanced capitalist economies
AFL–CIO	American Federation of Labor – Congress of Industrial Organisations
AIFLD	American Institute for Free Labor Development
CAW	Canadian Auto Workers
COSATU	Congress of South African Trade Unions
CUT	Unified Worker Central
ETUC	European Trade Union Confederation
EWCs	European Works Councils
FDI	foreign direct investment
FOSATU	Federation of South African Trade Unions
FTZ	free trade zones
GATT	General Agreement on Tariffs and Trade
GDP	Gross domestic product
ICEM	International Federation of Chemical, Energy, Mine and General Workers' Unions
ICF	International Federation of Chemical and General Workers Union
ICFTU	International Congress of Free Trade Unions
ICT	Information and Communications Technology
ILO	International Labour Organisation
IMF	International Metalworkers' Federation
IMF	International Monetary Fund
IPE	International Political Economy

ITS	International Trade Secretariat
ISI	import substitution industrialisation
ITO	International Trade Organisation
IUF	International Union of Food and Allied Workers
JIT	'Just in time'
KCTU	Korean Confederation of Trade Unions
MERCOSUR	Common Market of the Southern Cone
MNCs	multinational corporations
NAFTA	North American Free Trade Agreement
NGO	non-governmental organisation
NHS	British National Health Service
NICs	newly industrialising countries
NIDL	new international division of labour
OPEC	Organisation of Petroleum Exporting Countries
RILU	Red International of Labour Unions
SAPs	structural adjustment programmes
SEWA	Self-Employed Women's Association (India)
SID	Danish General Workers' Union
SME	Small and Medium Enterprise networks
TINA	'There is no alternative'
TNC	transnational corporation
TUC	Trades Union Congress (UK)
TWN	Third World Network
UAW	United Auto Workers (USA)
UN	United Nations
VTSIOM	All-Russian Centre for the Study of Public Opinion
WCCs	World Company Councils
WCL	World Confederation of Labour
WFTU	World Federation of Trade Unions
WTO	World Trade Organisation

For Santiago, the engineer

PREFACE

In the speeded-up, globalised postmodern world we live in we are moving into a time of flux and uncertainty – in short, a time of transformation. This is a process of change unleashed by powerful economic forces but it also reflects a growing social movement of contestation. Just over a decade ago, socialism seemed to evaporate before our eyes and the world order declared by the managers of global capitalism looked set to last a thousand years. The discourse of 'globalisation' appeared to capture well the de-embracing totalising logic of the new order where the rather ludicrous slogan 'There is no alternative' (TINA) actually seemed to make sense for a while. Yet just a decade after the collapse of the Berlin Wall in 1989, the disruption of the World Trade Organisation (WTO) Ministerial Meeting in Seattle in late 1999 signalled the beginning of a new logic unfolding. There was an alternative globalisation 'from below' seeking to rein in the forces of globalising neo-liberalism. This book seeks to tell the story of workers and their organisation in the era of capitalist globalisation and their potential to construct a democratic alternative.

Chapter 1 sets the scene by examining some of the most salient transformations of our era, including the decline of the nation-state (deterritorialisation) and the Brazilianisation (or Thirdworldisation!) of the West as the world becomes more integrated. A global labour force is emerging and, at least potentially, workers are emerging as a new (yet 'old') global social movement. What potential does the post-Seattle movement for a globalisation 'from below' have and what role might workers and their organisations play in this process?

To understand the 'new' global capitalism, we also need to go back to the 'Golden Era' of post-war capitalism. We examine Fordism as a way of producing goods but also as a social order and a means to regulate capitalism. In the South this was the era of the 'new' division of labour as manufacturing emerged in once mainly agricultural or extractive economies. Towards the end of the 1960s this model entered a crisis, which led not to the collapse of capitalism but to its re-emergence as 'globalisation' in the 1980s.

Thus the scene is set to grasp the era of globalisation in Chapter 3, which seeks to take us 'beyond the buzzword' to understand the complexity and contradictions lying behind this new discourse of domination. We see how after a period in the doldrums in the 1980s workers' organisations have begun to contest the new order since the 1990s. There are several 'matters arising' from this process that we need to consider, including the 'flexibilisation' and 'feminisation' of labour worldwide but also the crucial 'social clause' debate, which centres around the pros and cons of including labour rights in world trade agreements. This last issue shows the enduring differences between labour in the North and labour in the South.

Chapter 4 examines the main aspects of labour's condition and social dynamics in the countries of the relatively prosperous North during the era of globalisation. The new flexible financial capitalism is explored, as is the sometimes neglected topic of regionalisation. This leads us to examine the new post-Fordist labour processes and social regimes of accumulation typical of the epoch. This is the period in which socialism collapsed and the East rejoined (or tried to) the capitalist North. The implications of the world historical transformation are still uncertain. However, trade unionism in the North has been reconfigured in the last decade.

In Chapter 5 the narrative and analysis shift to the global South, that part of the globe once known as the Third World. This is the main site of 'informalisation' (or Brazilianisation) whereby 'non-standard' forms of employment become prevalent. However, women working worldwide have not only contested this labour regime but have been at the centre of innovative trade-union responses to globalisation in the South. We take up again the issue of the 'social clause', central to post-Seattle debates, which is viewed by many in the South as a protectionist measure by Northern markets.

Having examined the era of globalisation in relation to workers North and South we turn to attempts by workers to develop transnational solidarity networks and activities. The labour movement was born in the nineteenth century as an internationalist movement and there are signs that in the twenty-first century it may be reborn with a globalist perspective. Chapter 6 examines aspects of the 'old' pre-globalisation internationalism. It traces the emergence of internationalism as the world of nation-states in the West took shape. It also critically examines the negative practice of trade-union imperialism vis-à-vis workers in the South. Further angles are the campaign in the 1970s by some international trade unions to establish labour 'counter-vailing power' in relation to the transnational corporations (TNCs) and the issue of 'development solidarity' in relation to South Africa, for example.

In Chapter 7 we turn to the 'new' internationalism or global solidarity practices, where we see a decisive move beyond the confines of the nation-state. What are the challenges posed by globalisation and how can an alternative social agenda be developed? How can labour interact with the 'new' social movements around gender, environmental and human rights issues in constructing global solidarity? From development solidarity (Chapter 6) we move towards global development as a framework for analysis and action. Finally, what are the complex relations between the local and the global in building resistance to neo-liberal globalisation?

Chapter 8 reconsiders the results for labour of the processes of globalisation and its prospects in the period now opening up. What is the basis of the 'new order' we all live under and what are its contradictions? If we believe there are alternatives to the status quo we need to specify what life 'beyond competition' would mean? What future awaits the world's workers and what are the social transformations occurring in the world of work? Labour is being reinvented in the era of globalisation but is also reinventing itself. The question of agency is recentred in our analysis in the belief that globalisation can be (and must be) democratised socially, politically and culturally to the benefit of all the world's workers. This is necessary to complete the second great transformation in world history.

ONE

LABOUR IN THE GLOBAL

Globalisation appears to be the new 'great transformation' of our time, a striking expression used by Karl Polanyi (Polanyi, 1957) to describe the massive dislocation caused by the rise of industrial capitalism. This introductory chapter examines some of the crucial aspects of the new great transformation, such as 'deterritorialisation' (the decline of the nation-state) and the 'Brazilianisation' (the rise of the informal labour sector) of the West. It goes on to examine the rise of a new global labour force, because we must stress that globalisation is productive, and what it produces above all are more workers. We need to consider whether this is giving rise to a global labour market, however, because workers are simply not as mobile as capital. A third section considers the emergence of labour as a global social movement. Has the labour movement 'risen from the ashes' of the defeats inflicted by neo-liberalism and begun creating a new transnational democratic force? Finally, we consider the prospects of a globalisation 'from below' to match that 'from above' run by the transnational corporations and legitimised by free-market fundamentalism. Could the power of solidarity post-Seattle create a countervailing power to that of global capitalism, as the perspective developing Polanyi's insights would lead us to believe?

TRANSFORMATIONS

Karl Polanyi wrote his neglected classic *The Great Transformation* (Polanyi, 1957) during the Second World War due to a deep concern (as much Christian as socialist) over the relationship between the market and society. For Polanyi, the notion of a self-regulating market was a dystopia; it 'could not exist for any length of time without annihilating the human and natural substance of society', and if not controlled 'would have physically destroyed man and transformed his surroundings into a wilderness' (Polanyi, 1957: 3). Today, the free-market gospel of the World Trade Organisation (WTO) and the neo-liberal economists promoting 'freedom' for the market would do well to ponder Polanyi's warnings. Polanyi also believed, however, that society took measures to protect itself. This he called a 'double movement' whereby ever wider extension of free-market principles generated a counter-movement of social regulation to protect society. Against an economic system that creates 'a dislocation which attacks the very fabric of society' (Polanyi, 1957: 130) the social counter-movement is based on 'the principle of social protection aiming at the conservation of man and nature' (Polanyi, 1957: 132). More than fifty years after Polanyi developed this understanding of the dynamic of social transformation, it remains more valid than ever, I will argue. The 'Polanyi problem' of reconciling the demands for 'free' markets and the need for minimal social cohesion is a very current one for the global elites. Opponents of globalisation seem too pessimistic in their views if they do not recognise the contradictions posed by this problem highlighted by Karl Polanyi.

The 'great transformation' that Polanyi wrote about was the Industrial Revolution of the eighteenth century, which saw 'an almost miraculous improvement of the tools of production, [but] which was accompanied by a catastrophic dislocation of the lives of common people' (Polanyi, 1957: 33). What we may call the Globalisation Revolution of this turn of century is also characterised by a seemingly miraculous development of capitalism, but also by an equally profound dislocation of the lives of ordinary people across the globe. As in Polanyi's time, it is clearly the state which has itself created the so-called self-regulating market. Also as in Polanyi's time, a crucial counter-movement involves 'the most immediately affected by the deleterious action of the market ... the working classes ... using protective legislation, restrictive associations [i.e. trade unions] and other instruments of intervention as its methods' (Polanyi, 1957: 132). So we see that one of the fiercest debates at a global level is over the advisability of tying the free-trade principles of the WTO to a 'social clause' which would protect the basic rights of workers across the trading nations.

Today's international trade-union leaders seek to introduce a 'social clause' into trading agreements while protesting their adherence to free-market principles. They seem silenced by the neo-liberal economists who have argued since the 1970s that trade unions are 'protectionist' institutions which conspire against the free operation of the market. Yet Polanyi was able to see that labour was not a commodity like any other, as if it was it would have to be permanently on strike to achieve a better price. Polanyi is refreshingly blunt in arguing that 'social legislation, factory laws, unemployment insurance, and, above all, trade unions' had precisely the function 'of interfering with the laws of supply and demand in respect to human labour, and removing it from the orbit of the market' (Polanyi, 1957: 177). This is another theme we shall be developing: namely, the counter-hegemonic logic of the labour, ecology and other social movements' protests following the successful disruption of the WTO meeting in Seattle in late 1999. Of course, Polanyi can only provide inspiration; his times are very different from ours in at least two ways, which we shall now examine, namely 'deterritorialisation' (decline of the state) and the 'Brazilianisation' (informalisation) of the West.

Once upon a time the great corporations of capitalism were seen as 'national champions', inextricably linked with the national interest. It was not mere bravado which led Charles Wilson to declare in 1953 that for him 'What was good for our country was good for General Motors and vice versa' (cited in Reich, 1992: 48). This particular brand of economic nationalism was the dominant theme of twentieth-century governance, and the welfare state of the North was an unambiguous institution. Nations competed with nations and their workers were the foot soldiers in that war. Today the situation is different. Robert Reich (who went on to become US Secretary of Labor in the Clinton administration) argues that there is a worldwide trend whereby 'National champions everywhere are becoming global webs with no particular connection to any single nation' (Reich, 1991: 131). The much-vaunted 'American' corporation may be partially Japanese controlled and it is, at least, part of a corporate world-wide web, where its interests now lie. This basic economic transformation means that, put simply, 'national savings increasingly flow to whoever can do things best, or cheapest, wherever located around the world' (Reich, 1991: 133). Not only does the traditional notion of 'national competitiveness' lose its purchase but the very notion of a nation-state is itself drawn into question.

David Held and his co-authors have argued persuasively that, 'As economic, social and political activities are increasingly 'stretched' across the globe they become in a significant sense no longer primarily or solely organised according to a territorial principle' (Held et al., 1999: 27–8). Globalisation, in the shape of its prime economic agent the great corporation, does indeed cut across political frontiers in a way which leads to deterritorialisation. While corporations have headquarters in particular nation-states, they are effectively disembedded from these societies by their economic logic. It is, of course, in the 'financialisation' of contemporary capitalism, whereby financial transactions become autonomous from material economic processes, where this deterritorialisation is most extreme. The managers of money seek the best return for their investment wherever that may be, and its political ramifications are not their concern. However, as with many of the processes of globalisation, there are also counter-tendencies. The 'new' localism and the 'new' regionalism, whereby cities and regions are seen to renegotiate globalisation, are but one example of reterritorialisation. At a cultural level, as well, we have seen a resurgence of territorial ties and a return to the indigenous in the face of a cosmopolitan globalism.

Another widespread tendency created by the new capitalism is what is known as 'Brazilianisation', by which is usually meant the spread of production patterns and social relations typical of the South to the advanced industrial societies of the North. Ulrich Beck writes of how 'The social structure in the heartlands of the West is thus coming to resemble the patchwork quilt of the South, characterised by diversity, unclarity and insecurity in people's work and life' (Beck, 2001: 1). Beck bases his analysis on the spread of temporary, insecure and 'informal' employment in the cities of the North. This is seen to be the result of the neo-liberal free-market utopia unleashed by globalisation, which is creating great social disruption. By Brazilianisation we mean a turn towards the pattern of employment which has always been typical in Brazil and most of the South, namely a preponderance of 'informal' and precarious forms of work. Now this pattern has become generalised as capital turns the globe into one integrated labour market to be exploited at its pleasure. Brazilianisation can thus be seen as a 'Thirdworldisation' of the North.

I believe that while Brazilianisation is a powerful image and does reflect certain tendencies of globalisation, we must be wary in our use of the term. First, it tends to operate with a fairly mythical view of full employment, jobs for life and general social stability in the North, which probably never existed. Second, it inevitably has a certain pejorative or negative view of the South, now seen to be 'infecting' the North. In general, the stress on insecurity is presented in a somewhat deterministic fashion. That is to say, the social transformations of the world of work currently under way are not always necessarily negative. For example, labour 'flexibility', while generally deleterious for workers, can be seen to have possible positive connotations. The diversity and lack of clarity to which Beck refers are not necessarily negative phenomena and may just reflect the decline of modernism as an organising principle for society. Work has always been unstable for the majority of the world's workers, and now this reality has become generalised due to globalisation.

Returning to Polanyi as inspiration we can start with his argument that 'only when the economy is re-embedded in society … will individuals regain a sense of purposefulness which is rooted in the culture and creativity of the people' (Mendell and Sallé, 1991: xxiii). Indeed there is today considerable debate on the extent to which the transnational corporations (TNCs) are 'embedded' in society and not simply freewheeling economic agents. All the disparate social movements promoting a 'globalisation from below', as opposed to that from above created by the TNCs and governed by the WTO, also reflect the enduring dynamism of different cultures which refuse to be homogenised by the market. Polanyi's writing on noncapitalist societies (see Dalton, 1971) also shows him surprisingly attuned to today's concerns with indigenous knowledge, cultural creativity and sustainable development. We can see that there is, indeed, life beyond the 'competitivity' preached by the free marketeers and there is a need for economic institutions to be embedded in society if they are to lead to sustainable development. Certainly, the contradictions between market and society are even more acute today than in Polanyi's day precisely because of the almost total worldwide dominance of capitalist market mechanisms.

The enlightened globalising elite is acutely aware of the problem 'of adjusting the still nationally based political governance of world politics and society to the rapidly growing globalising economy' (Group of Lisbon, 1995: 121). They understand the need for global governance on a stable basis and the implications for social stability of a deepening 'Brazilianisation'. The requirement of good governance is in direct contradiction to fundamentalist free-market ideologies. This dimension brings to the fore the workings of the 'double movement' whereby society seeks to protect itself from the dislocations created by the market. As with Polanyi's 'great transformation', the one being created by 'globalisation' is not a natural phenomenon as some of its more fervent supporters seem to believe. I would agree with Barry Gills, who seems to be in the spirit of Polanyi when he argues that 'globalisation is a contested concept, not a received theory' and when he goes on to reject 'the idea that neo-liberal globalisation is either historically necessary or inevitable' (Gills, 2000: 6). Polanyi, as Marx before him, leads us to historicise the great transformation of our time which we call globalisation.

I believe that labour and other social movements should be neither for nor against globalisation but, rather, see the issue as one of understanding the complexity of globalisation as a process of social transformation. At the level of global development theory, it was early in the 1980s that the World Bank signalled a decisive move away from development as a process of national economic growth to embrace a vision of development as equal to participation in and integration with the capitalist market. The globalisation project thus replaced the post-Second World War modernisation project in a paradigmatic shift with huge economic, political, social and cultural implications. At a political level it was of course the collapse of 'actually existing' socialism after 1989 which paved the way for neo-liberal globalisation as a new master narrative. Sociological pessimism had already led to widespread belief in the 'death of the working class' (Gorz, 1982) and now its strategy for social transformation had imploded on itself. For perhaps a decade, until Seattle 1999, it seemed that capitalist globalisation was, indeed, the 'only game in town', hegemonic in all respects. But what if, as Marx predicted in his own era, this dynamic new capitalism on a global scale was producing its own 'gravedigger'?

GLOBAL LABOUR FORCE

It is important to start off with a very clear understanding that 'Globalisation in its modern form is a process based less on the proliferation of computers than on the proliferation of proletarians' (Coates, 2000: 256). If capital is understood as a social relation (between the owner of capital and the proletariat) then clearly its

TABLE 1.1 GROWTH OF THE WORLD WORKFORCE

Region	1970 (million workers)	1985 (million workers)	2000 (million workers)	Annual growth rate 1985–2000 (%)
OECD*	**307.0**	**372.4**	**401.3**	**0.5**
United States	84.9	122.1	141.1	1.0
Japan	51.5	59.6	64.3	0.5
Germany	35.5	38.9	37.2	–0.3
United Kingdom	25.3	28.2	29.1	0.2
France	21.4	23.9	25.8	0.5
Italy	20.9	23.5	24.2	0.2
Spain	13.0	14.0	15.7	0.8
Canada	8.5	12.7	14.6	0.9
Australia	5.6	7.4	8.9	1.3
Sweden	3.9	4.4	4.6	0.3
Developing regions*	**1,119.9**	**1,595.8**	**2,137.7**	**2.1**
China	428.3	617.9	761.2	1.4
India	223.9	293.2	383.2	1.8
Indonesia	45.6	63.4	87.7	2.2
Brazil	31.5	49.6	67.8	2.1
Pakistan	19.3	29.8	45.2	2.8
Thailand	17.9	26.7	34.5	1.7
Mexico	14.5	26.1	40.6	3.0
Turkey	16.1	21.4	28.8	2.0
Philippines	13.7	19.9	28.6	2.4
South Korea	11.4	16.8	22.3	1.9
USSR	**117.2**	**143.3**	**155.0**	**0.5**
World*	**1,596.8**	**2,163.6**	**2,752.5**	**1.6**

* Totals include some countries not listed in table.

Sources: Johnston, 1991: 117. For OECD nations except Germany: OECD, Department of Economics and Statistics, *Labor Force Statistics, 1967–1987*; US Bureau of Labor Statistics; The World Bank, *World Development Report*, 1987. For developing nations and Germany: International Labor Office, *Economically Active Population, 1950–2025*; The World Bank, *World Development Reports*, 1987.

worldwide expansion will inevitably spell a global expansion of the working classes. This is not just a quantitative expansion; it also entails a series of qualitative shifts in the nature of work and the global labour force in both social and spatial terms, as we shall see in Chapters 4 and 5, on workers in the North and South, below. Globalisation has not just occurred because capital suddenly became more mobile in the 1980s. It also responds to the needs of the capital accumulation process not only to expand but to subsume more and more workers under the capital/wage-labour relation. The key ballpark figure is that the global proletariat doubled in numbers between 1975 and 1995 to reach 2.5 billion workers. It is the particular nature of this expansive process which we now need to examine to consider whether a global labour market is emerging.

It is interesting to see how the transnationalised corporate elite now argues that, 'Just as managers speak of world markets for products, technology and capital, they must now think in terms of a world market for labour' (Johnston, 1991: 115). A decade ago William Johnston argued categorically that 'The globalisation of labor is inevitable' (Johnston, 1991: 126). The logic was a simple one: to make the best of all resources, including 'human resources' (labour), wherever they might be. The underlying facts we need to consider to assess this argument are those of a growing world workforce, as outlined in Table 1.1.

Perhaps the most salient fact to be derived from Table 1.1, apart from the accelerated overall expansion of the labour force after 1985, is the differential between Northern and Southern expansion rates: while the Northern (i.e. OECD countries) labour force expanded by one-third between 1975 and 2000, that of the South (i.e. 'developing countries') nearly doubled over the same time period. This Southern workforce is much better educated and trained than it was twenty or thirty years ago and so more attractive to capital. It is also not necessarily trained in the ways of the 'old' industrial capitalism and is thus more able to adapt to the needs of the 'new' informatised capitalism. It is also, literally, a 'young' labour force compared to the 'greying' workforce of the North, where in 2000 only 40 per cent of the working population was under the age of 34, compared to 55 per cent for the 'developing regions' of the South.

The gender composition of the global labour force has also been changing rapidly with its expansion, as we can see from Table 1.2. We

TABLE 1.2 WOMEN IN THE WORLD'S WORKFORCE

Country or region	Working women* (million)	Female share of workforce (% of total workforce)	Female labour force participation (% of females age 15–64)
Developed regions‡	**156.5**	**40.9**	**58.6**
United States	53.9	44.1	66.0
Japan	24.3	39.9	57.8
Germany	11.1	39.3	51.3
United Kingdom	11.7	41.4	62.6
France	10.2	42.5	55.2
Italy	8.9	36.9	43.4
Spain	4.8	32.6	37.5
Canada	5.7	43.2	65.4
Australia	3.1	39.7	54.1
Sweden	2.1	48.0	79.4
Developing regions‡	**554.2**	**34.7**	**48.6**
China	267.2	43.2	75.5
India	76.8	26.2	32.3
Indonesia	19.8	31.3	38.0
Brazil	13.5	27.2	32.2
Pakistan	3.4	11.4	12.1
Thailand	12.2	45.9	74.8
Mexico	7.1	27.0	31.1
Turkey	7.3	34.0	47.4
Philippines	6.4	32.1	39.2
South Korea	5.7	34.0	42.2
USSR*	**69.2**	**48.3**	**72.6**
World†	**790.1**	**36.5**	**51.3**

* For developed regions, 1987 figures were used; for developing regions and the USSR, 1985 figures.
† Totals include some countries not listed in table.
‡ Developed and developing regions as defined by the International Labour Office.
Source: International Labour Office, *Economically Active Population, 1950–2025*, Table 2.

see that by the mid-1980s more than half of working-age women across the world were in paid employment. Women represented more than one-third of the total labour force, and considerably more in the North, although we may question the validity of the data on female paid employment in the South to some extent. The implications for the economy of an increased entry by women into the paid labour force are considerable. Johnston argues, for example, from a management perspective, that 'If other conditions are favourable countries with many women ready to join the workforce can look forward to rapid economic expansion' (Johnston, 1991: 118). From the point of view of women workers these economic transformations may have significant impact on their role in the wider gender division of labour in society. Of course, like any broad process of social transformation, what is referred to as the 'feminisation' of the workforce has a mixed impact. Thus, as Brigitte Young argues, 'The flexibilisation of the labour market has produced greater equality between educated middle class women and men while creating gender inequality among women' (Young, 2000: 315). For every professional female post there are probably quite a few more 'menial' female posts created.

Returning to the question of a global labour market we may now reconsider the verdict that we have a global labour market. Analysts such as Johnston seem to work with a fairly unilinear scheme whereby 'what was once a local labor market became regional, then national, and finally international' (Johnston, 1991: 123). This extension has been much more uneven than this modernising perspective implies, both in spatial and in temporal terms. That is to say it ignores, for example, the question of unfree and semi-free labour in the South (but in the North as well); nor can any but a small minority of today's lead sector workers be part of a truly global labour market. Manuel Castells is undoubtedly correct to argue that 'Labor markets are not truly global, except for a small but growing segment of professionals and scientists' (Castells, 1998: 93). Castells also goes on to argue, however, that 'labor is a global resource' in so far as corporations may go anywhere in the world to seek the labour they want, highly skilled labour will be imported from anywhere in the world by these same corporations, and, lastly, workers are driven by economic necessity, war and famine to seek work across the globe (Castells, 1998: 93). Maybe we *are* moving towards a global labour market.

What we probably can agree on is that globalisation sets new parameters for the labour force today and that there is a tendency towards the creation of a global labour market. We live and we work in an increasingly integrated global economy. Certainly labour is not as mobile as capital, but the former is certainly not immobile and the latter is still embedded in national societies. The labour process is also increasingly part of an integrated transnational network, as are the corporations that create them and recruit workers to them. Some leading sectors of the labour market – for example, in information and communications technology (ICT) – are already part of a unified labour market. Others are increasingly affected by the operations of a global capitalism that constantly seeks to devalue labour power. This process has even in one key country, the United States, helped to break the national unity of US capital and US workers in pursuit of the imperial interest. A sensible conclusion on the global nature of workers' horizons is that of Mihály Simai, who argues that 'Workers and their unions ... have come to the understanding of the internationalisation of the main processes influencing employment, wages and conditions and social policies' (Simai, 1995b: 27). Gains that may have been achieved on the national terrain will, increasingly, be lost or maintained within the parameters of the global capital/wage-labour relation.

It is important to understand that a labour market is not simply an economic institution. Polanyi understood clearly that 'Not only conditions in the factory, hours of work and modalities of contract, but the basic wage itself, are determined outside the market' (Polanyi, 1957: 251). Labour is simply not a commodity like any other in so far as it reflects a human capacity. Its 'price' is determined socially and involves the state, trade unions and other public bodies in its regulation. The ideology of neo-liberalism behind the drive towards globalisation has portrayed its policy of 'free' market forces as one where capital is no longer restrained by government. In fact, what it has sought is to free capital from any social and public restraints, while at the same time removing any social protection for labour rights. We also need to understand, however, that the distribution of the social product also depends on the ongoing bargaining, conflict and compromise between capital and labour. The political economy of the labour market implies that another determinant of wages is what used to be called the 'class struggle' and is now politely dubbed the 'social contract'. The neo-liberal ideological offensive notwithstanding, this element has not disappeared.

More or less at random, if we look across the world, we see workers taking action to defend themselves from capital's continuous offensive. In the first few months of 2000 there were at least six general strikes against the effects of neo–liberal globalisation. Significantly, most of these were in semi-peripheral, semi-industrialised countries like Argentina, South Africa, South Korea, India, Uruguay and Nigeria. All occurred in different contexts and had different causes but they were unified in some way by globalisation. This indicates again, I think, the tendency towards a global labour market. It also points towards the integral element of labour resistance within capital's new mode of operating. Hardt and Negri point to how 'the globalisation of economic and cultural relationships ... means that the virtual centre of Empire [as they dub the new era of globalisation] can be attacked from any point' (Hardt and Negri, 2000: 59). As capital spreads its global networks so it becomes more vulnerable from the multitude of social forces it constructs and exploits. The 'virtual centre' of the new age of imperialism can be accessed anywhere, so that its strength is also its weakness.

Finally, in any consideration of the global labour market it is important to understand how much labour is part of international political economy. Antonio Gramsci recognised in the 1930s that international hegemonic regimes had an economic component (Gramsci, 1971b). Thus, a political regime if it is to be hegemonic (i.e. achieve consent and not just domination) needs to hold sway over the world of work. This perspective allows us to have an integrated analysis of how, for example, the global power of the USA rests on a particular politics of production in the USA, as well (of course) as military power and so on. Mark Rupert, in an interesting pioneering look at 'Producing Hegemony' (Rupert, 1995), shows how US global power was shaped by the way in which production was institutionalised within the workplaces of that country. So, mass production under the labour process known as Fordism (see Chapter 2) was an integral element in the expansionist neo-imperial US policy overseas. Likewise, today, as the era of Fordism gives way to an as yet unspecified post-Fordism, based on 'flexible specialisation', so a new role for labour in the system of global governance can be expected.

Much of the literature on globalisation, critical as much as adulatory, seems to assume that capital has all its own way and that labour can only negotiate the terms of its surrender. Capitalist triumphalism may, however, be misplaced. As Richard Walker notes, 'it is misleading in so far as it partakes of the myth of capital's perfection and potency and says nothing of capital's limits and contradictions' (Walker, 1999b: 18). The common picture of capital's worldwide expansion as an unstoppable, if not benign, process ignores the profitability problems of most capitalist countries and the stagnant wages in most countries of the North (not to mention the South). The success stories of Japan and the Southeast Asian 'Tiger' economies have all been tarnished in recent years. Yet there is always somewhere else which is doing better. Once we begin to think of globalisation as a specific epoch of capitalism, perhaps, but still sharing all the problems of capitalism (as well as, undoubtedly, its technological dynamism) then we can see, as Polanyi did for the first 'great transformation', that there is always an alternative.

GLOBAL SOCIAL MOVEMENT?

From the International Confederation of Free Trade Unions (ICFTU) to the smallest local union, there is now an established understanding that globalisation represents one of the severest challenges to the labour movement since its inception. Yet workers' rights are now firmly on the globalisation agenda, which is not being fulfilled quite according to plan. At its sixteenth World Congress held in 1996, the ICFTU's main position paper argued that 'The position of workers has changed as a result of globalisation of the economy and changes in the organisation of production' (ICFTU, 1997a: 4). So, at the very centre of its strategic concerns was the question of globalisation and the need for transnational action, once the lonely call of far-left groups on the fringes of the labour movement. Now the ICFTU – still bureaucratic, but with a new post-Cold War identity – could state quite categorically that 'one of the main purposes of the international trade union movement is the international solidarity of workers' (ICFTU, 1997a: 51). Perhaps symbolically marking the entry of the ICFTU into the era of globalisation and the information society, the 1996 Congress also saw the launch of the organisation's own dedicated website.

'International solidarity must become a natural reflex throughout the union movement' was the bold proclamation of ICFTU general secretary, Bill Jordan. When Jordan, a cautious (not to say conservative) ex-leader of the British Engineering Workers' Union, states that international labour solidarity (not just on May Day) is the order of the day, something has changed. I believe it is mainly that the objective conditions created by globalisation demand a concerted international trade-union strategy. Furthermore, in terms of the 'organisation of production' mentioned above, the ICFTU has become aware that the Western, urban male, full-time, permanent worker is no longer the only, or even the core, member of the trade unions. The ICFTU now proclaims a new orientation towards women workers and young workers. It addresses the issue of the informal sector, both in developing countries and in the advanced individual societies. The ICFTU has even begun to understand that it must work with far less traditional NGOs (non-governmental organisations) and campaigning groups on issues such as that of child labour. There are, of course, limitations to this sea change in traditional ICFTU policies and practices, but the shift is a comprehensive one.

The International Trade Secretariats (ITSs) have for a very long time played a strong international role. These organisations trace their origins back to the turn of the last century and embrace national unions in a particular sector – for example, transport, the food industry, mining. One of the ITSs, the International Federation of Chemical, Energy, Mine and General Workers' Unions (ICEM), has recently addressed the whole issue of globalisation and workers' actions in a comprehensive study (ICEM, 1996). The basic argument is that the dramatic level of internationalisation over the last decade or so now demands a coherent international labour strategy. The move towards international trade-union action should not be seen as a last resort (when action at the national level has failed); rather, 'action has to be planned on the international basis right from the start' (ICEM, 1996: 55). Fire fighting, or wheeling in the international dimension when all else fails, is simply seen as an inadequate trade-union response when capital has become so mobile in its activities. The ITSs are also keenly aware that their members, for example in the food industry, exist in commodity chains stretching from the supermarket through to the fields of the developing countries.

The ITSs also have their weaknesses, however, as pointed out by Dan Gallin, himself a former general secretary of an ITS, the International Union of Food and Allied Workers (IUF). Whilst Gallin believes that the ITSs are the most effective international trade-union organisation around, for him their weaknesses include: being based on national unions which think in national terms, their financial and personnel constraints, and the fact that 'they hardly ever co-ordinate, do not communicate much and rarely co-operate' (Gallin, 2000: 7). In the past this lack of co-ordination was partly due to hostility between the ICFTU and some of its national affiliates who were jealous of what they saw as its lack of constraints on the ITSs. If the ITSs were now to join the ICFTU (a proposal made as far back as the 1920s), with its Cold War preconceptions behind it, these turf wars could cease. It is still important to remember that, compared to the re- sources of a TNC, the average ITS has a small contingent of fifteen to twenty staff members co-ordinating global strategy from Geneva, albeit with an increased outreach potential due to the communications and transport revolution of the last twenty years.

At the regional level, trade unions are increasingly beginning to develop a coherent joint strategy. This is necessary and not surprising given that one of the main effects of globalisation is, in fact, an in- creased regionalisation. The so-called Triad of the USA, the Euro- pean Union and Japan has increased the importance of the regional dimension in all three areas. Thus in 1973, the once fervent Little Englanders and rejectionists of all things 'continental' in the British trade-union movement became enthusiastic supporters of the European TUC concept. There is, of course, considerable debate on the effective- ness of this body. For one it is dependent on the Commission of the European Union for three-quarters of its budget, which hardly augurs well for its independence. Likewise, the European Workers Councils initiative is highly questionable (see Wills, 2001). Yet even if a pale Europeanism based on semi-mythical notions of social 'dialogue' or partnership prevails over internationalism, there has been a significant cross-national union co-operation across Europe in the last decade.

In North America, there was a fierce trade-union debate in the USA, Canada and Mexico on how to respond to the North American Free Trade Agreement (NAFTA) in the 1990s. Nationalist responses by the three labour movements moved, albeit partially and hesitantly, closer to a common position in relation to this major step towards capitalist rationalisation. Establishing a community of interests among the workers of North America was not easy and it did not do away with particular national interests. The US union orientation towards 'upward harmonisation' of labour rights and standards in the region was by no means unambiguously welcome in Mexico, where different priorities might prevail. However, it is also noticeable that the Canadian unions, which previously knew little about labour conditions in Mexico, developed a remarkably sophisticated and sensitive policy towards transnational co-operation with Mexican workers and unions. Careful study of this whole experience can help move us beyond the sterile counterposition between the globalisation blues and an abstract internationalism. Some of the ambiguity (and hopefulness) of the new transnational labour discourse can be discerned in the statement by American Federation of Labour – Congress of Industrial Organisations (AFL–CIO) president Lane Kirkland that 'You can't be a trade unionist unless you are an internationalist. You can't be a real trade unionist unless you think of workers wherever they happen to be, and unless you realise that substandard conditions and poverty anywhere in the world are a threat to good conditions and comparatively good standards anywhere in the world' (cited in French et al., 1994: 1). The conflictual but ultimately productive interaction between US, Mexican and Canadian trade unions over NAFTA may yet prove to be a watershed in terms of international labour solidarity, or, to be more precise, labour transnationalism.

National union centres are also changing under the impact of globalisation. The limitation of nationalist, economistic and corporatist strategies are plain to see. In Denmark, the General Workers' Union (SID) has not only expanded greatly to embrace around a quarter of the country's workers but has put forward a remarkable programmatic statement (SID, 1997). The Danish union calls for a bold 'new global agenda' which argues that 'We must use our global strength to force TNCs to have much more moral and ethical standards, to respect workers' rights, to have codes of conduct and to accept the establishment of international workers' councils' (SID, 1997). There is a keen awareness here of the pressing international political issues raised by globalisation. There is a feeling that this statement reflects more than just pious declarations, as many ICFTU statements seem to be. That is because the Danish union does not think in purely trade unionist ways and recognises, for example, that 'NGOs are an important voice in civil society. As trade unions we must be more open to enter into strategic alliances not only with our political allies, but with NGOs such as women's and youth organisations, social welfare, development and human rights, and environment and consumers' organisations who share our general objectives' (SID, 1997).

It is not only in social-democratic Denmark where these changes are occurring but also, significantly, in the United States within the once arch-conservative, pro-imperialist AFL–CIO. The new director of the AFL–CIO's International Affairs Department recently argued that 'globalisation is here to stay, but the neo-liberal model of globalisation is not pre-ordained. In fact, it is within organised labour's collective ability and responsibility to radically change the dangerous course we are now on' (Mantsios, 1998: 279). It would seem that the trade-union movement of the most powerful capitalist economy on earth is now seriously reconsidering its strategic political alliance with 'its' capitalist class. New AFL–CIO president John Sweeney has declared that 'Labour has finally awakened from a long deep sleep' (Sweeney, 2001). Its international strategy would be a litmus test of the new orientation. Yet we also see significant changes in domestic policy towards more open forms of organisation and an overdue orientation towards women and 'people of colour'. At the very least this reorientation should warn us against a historical view which does not recognise how the labour movement can change over time.

So the question now arises as to whether these labour organisations constitute social movement, let alone a global social movement. For Manuel Castells, in his authoritative three-volume study of the new capitalism, 'Torn by internationalisation of finance and production, unable to adapt to networking of firms and individualisation of work, and challenged by the engendering of employment, the labour movement fades away as a major source of social cohesion and workers' representation' (Castells, 1997: 354). The rest of this book will seek to demonstrate that while the challenges to labour are well specified, the prognosis is at the very least outdated. It ignores the way a social movement can, by definition, learn and change to meet new situations. It assumes that capital and labour live in two watertight compartments, one in real-time fluidity, the other on boring clock-time stagnation. This is clearly not the case. At the other end of the spectrum we have the 'inevitabilism' of those such as Brad Nash, who introduces an important electronic debate on labour internationalism with the words: 'Rapidly globalising capital obviously calls for the need for a global labor movement' (Nash, 1998: 1). That small word, 'obviously', points to a long tradition of 'necessitarian' social theory on the left, which sees the 'subjective' inevitably 'catching up' with the 'objective' conditions. This, again, is simply not the case.

What I think we can say, following Dan Gallin (ex-official of an important ITS), is that the global labour movement is a 'virtual reality' (Gallin, 2000: 5). For Gallin this is a negative prognosis based on his diagnosis of the ICFTU as an organisation which 'drifts along without an ideology, without a policy and without a program' (Gallin, 2000: 5). Today, this verdict is simply incorrect, whatever one may think of the effectiveness and even sincerity of the ICFTU's 'turn to struggle'. However, we can also make a more positive reading of the notion of a global labour movement as virtual reality. If, as I believe, globalisation can open doors as well as close them, then the transnational labour movement can move from aspiration to reality, from pious congress declaration to practical solidarity. Certainly it is virtual because it does not have, and possibly could never have, the institutional solidity of the big corporations. But the simple germ of the idea of 'global solidarity' can materialise and spring up across the world, however fleetingly and however mixed up with other motivations. I would also argue that there are many tendencies indeed impelling local, national and regional trade-union movements to develop a 'global outreach' perspective.

GLOBALISATION FROM BELOW?

It has now become commonplace to counter the dominant globalisation 'from above' with a popular or anti-capitalist globalisation 'from below'. But what precisely does this mean and how might it inform concrete struggles by workers and others? Jeremy Brecher and colleagues, in a forceful twenty-first-century 'globalisation from below' manifesto, declare that, 'Just as the corporate and political elites are reaching across national borders to further their agendas, people at the grassroots are connecting their struggles around the world to impose their need and interests on the global economy' (Brecher et al., 2000: 10). Thus globalisation from below is seen as a counter-movement beginning in diverse parts and around different issues. It could be 'global warming', the 'debt crisis', genetically modified food, consumer movements or identity politics which brought people into action against globalisation or, at least, its effects. Brecher et al. recognise that 'much of the convergence [between these movements] is negative' in so far as they face the same market-driven process, but argue that 'there is also a growing positive convergence around common values of democracy, environmental protection, community, economic justice, equality and human solidarity' (Brecher et al., 2000: 15). Of course, this would need to be demonstrated in terms of post-Seattle anti-globalisation politics rather than just asserted, but the point is clear.

There is still a left orthodoxy that would deny almost any validity to the globalisation debate and even to the movements contesting it. Thus Ellen Meiksins Wood, in a special issue of *Monthly Review* celebrating labour 'rising from the ashes' in the age of 'global' capitalism, firmly rejects 'the assumption that the more *global* capitalism becomes, the more global the *struggle* against it would have to be' (Wood, 1997: 9). Keen to demystify the globalisation rhetoric, this orthodox Marxist perspective would take us back to standard nation-state-era politics. Rejecting the 'completely abstract internationalism' implicit in much anti-globalisation protest, Wood makes a plea for a return to the state 'as a target of anti-capitalist struggle' (Wood, 1997: 15–16). This is seen as a timely corrective to a mood on the left which would concede to neo-liberalism the inevitability of globalisation. This is a conception of solidarity as beginning 'at home' within the parameters of a given nation-state, and which ultimately refuses to give credence to globalisation as the parameter of current and future labour struggles. Its backward-looking nature and its almost reactionary nationalist and statist outlook make this particular form of orthodoxy a poor substitute for whatever sketchiness, exaggeration or polemical overstatement the globalisation-from-below approach articulates.

In considering the debates around globalisation and its contestation since Seattle we might start by questioning a hierarchy of strategies which assigns some special quality to action from 'below'. Globalisation itself would appear to be multifaceted and complex, even to some extent dissolving traditional conceptions of 'levels' in society and political processes. So, why would labour, for example, prioritise actions 'from below'? An intervention from 'above', say, in relation to the WTO can sit easily with a grassroots labour-environmentalist campaign, for example, against the Rio Tinto Zinc corporation. In between, the national 'level' would continue to be important in terms of dictating the level of the 'social wage', for example. Nor can we neglect the city as a framework for much labour activity and there are also vital regional and subregional repertoires of labour activity. These facets of labour action may combine in different ways and their interrelationship may not always be harmonious. But to assert a debilitating binary opposition – globalisation 'from below' versus globalisation 'from above' – does not seem to be a credible basis for a transformative labour politics in the twenty-first century.

An underlying, not always explicit, assumption in the globalisation 'from below' arguments is that the key actors will be the 'new' social movements around environmental, gender and peace issues, for example. Brecher et al. are open in their belief that 'Globalization in all its facets presents new problems that the old [social] movements failed to address. That is part of why they declined so rapidly' (Brecher et al., 2000: 17). The 'new' social movements are seen to represent a qualitatively different form of transformative politics and, in embryo, a new societal paradigm. They stress their autonomy from party politics and prioritise civil society over the state. Power itself is re-defined not as something to be 'seized' but as a diffused and plural element woven into the very fabric of society. The very notion of power is redefined and the limits of state politics are clearly exposed. However, we should not draw too stark a counterposition between bad/old social movements and good/new ones. While a certain type of trade-union and labour politics may well be defunct, the workers' movement has been at the forefront of many 'new' movements for change. Nor have the 'new' social movements, such as the environmental campaign, escaped the problems of routinisation and bureaucratisation which have bedevilled the labour movements at certain points.

W might also want to question the assumption made in many activist milieus that one is either 'for' or 'against' globalisation. At many conferences of labour and other social movements concerned with globalisation we find a simple 'for or against' choice. I, for one, think globalisation is an ongoing process and that to seek to 'halt' it is simply misguided and a strategic cul-de-sac. To understand this process critically, to demystify it, to seek out its contradictions and weak points is another matter. Certainly globalisation is more vulnerable than either its supporters or critics can see, if we take a Polanyian perspective. Furthermore, at a theoretical level the globalisation debate seems to suffer from what Roberto Mangabeira Unger calls 'necessitarianism' (Unger, 1998). That is to say, necessitarian assumptions imagine us as puppets in a social world constructed through law-like forces which are the inevitable and inescapable framework of social action. Certainly, as Marx showed a long time ago, we do not make history in conditions of our own choosing, but we need to avoid a 'false necessity' approach that sees us with no choice when faced with a process like globalisation that is not law-like or a fact of nature.

For me, the basic dispute underlying the post-Seattle globalisation debates is, indeed, the very 'old' one between 'reform' and 'revolution' as strategies for social transformation. The 'revolutionary' strategy would suffer from 'necessitarianism' and is usually based on a 'deep-structure' social theory which 'treats the formative institutional and imaginative frameworks of social life as indivisible units, each of which stands or falls as a piece' (Unger, 1997: 83). The political approach taken by a positivist social theory will, instead, advocate incremental social reform. What Unger advocates from a radical anti-necessitarian theoretical perspective is a strategy of 'radical reform' as a type of transformative politics in which 'Reform is radical when it addresses and changes the basic arrangements of a society: its formative structure of institutions and enacted beliefs' (Unger, 1998: 18–19). A radical reform perspective might allow us to reimagine the presuppositions that are made about globalisation and the possible role people may play in constructing a different, more democratic, future. Better than an 'all or nothing' perspective – reflected in the 'fix it or nix it' slogan from Seattle – the revolutionary reform political outlook refuses binary oppositions and opens up exciting vistas of social transformation.

A better understanding of the 'globalisation from below' perspective might well start with a more nuanced understanding of the 'Battle of Seattle' itself. First of all we must question the durability or even depth of the labour-environmentalist *entente* established at Seattle and encapsulated in the slogan 'Teamsters and Turtles'. Not long after that, the US labour movement made its main campaign the exclusion of China from the WTO, as it returned to its traditional protectionist stance re 'US jobs'. Second, the governments of the South were not totally off the mark when they saw a common Northern agenda, uniting the protesters and the Northern governments, which excluded them from the WTO corridors of power. From a long post-war perspective the main issue has probably been the failure of the South and the labour movement to unite in an anti-systemic alliance. The main point, though, is that the events in Seattle should not be exaggerated or oversimplified to gain short-term advantage. The weaknesses and the limitations of the Seattle events should make us wary of any prognosis that we are now entering a new golden age of anti-systemic movements on a globalisation-from-below course. If Seattle opened up a path to 'civilise' globalisation, that would be an achievement though.

We can go further, and argue that the struggle to democratise globalisation is considerably more complex than the slogan with 1960s' reverberations that we should seek to 'create two, three, many Seattles'. There is now a transnational democratic terrain infinitely more developed than when the United Nations was formed, for example. While it is easy to see how neo-liberal globalisation conspires against democracy, we must also recognise the openings it presents to transformative social movements. The negative features of a particular kind of globalisation have led to the 'democratic deficit', but stronger modes of regulation could make globalisation more 'democracy friendly', in my view. The growing economic/political/social integration of the world caused by the processes of globalisation also creates prospects for transnational processes of empowerment and democratisation. In some areas this new framework for social transformation is particularly clear. Thus in relation to human rights we can note with Anthony McGrew 'the extent to which the traditional notions of sovereign political space and political community are being reconstituted by the nature of the international human rights regime and the activities of transnational social movements in the human rights domain' (McGrew, 1995: 46). If the defence of human dignity knows no frontiers, the same may also become the case for labour rights.

What many of the pro- and anti-globalisation positions alike leave out is a proper understanding of the national diversity of contemporary capitalism. Globalisation, for its more fervent supporters such as Kenichi Ohmae, means we are now entering a 'border-less world' (Ohmae, 1990) which will obliterate national variations. Certainly neo-liberal globalisation has, as we shall see in Chapter 3, cut down on the space for manoeuvre by national states. However, as the 'new institutionalists' had shown already in the 1970s, 'the differences ... in the social organisation and the modus operandi of modern capitalist economies were of more than merely aesthetic interest' (Crouch and Streek, 1997: 1). While some convergence has since taken place, the debate on the different national 'models' or paths to capitalism continues. Workers and the labour movement are not disinterested in this battle of capitalism versus capitalism. Technologies and markets do not overdetermine the social and political conditions we live in. There are meaningful alternatives within the wide band of societal forms possible under a 'market' society. In the same way that cultural globalisation has not led to a single 'global culture' (see Tomlinson, 1999), so we may expect that national variations will continue to play an important role in the uneven and combined development of capitalism worldwide.

Finally, while critical of much of the content of globalisation 'from below' approaches, I would like to relate their contestatory tenor to the Polanyian approach I have been seeking to develop. In his own day, Polanyi saw 'an unparalleled momentum to the mechanisms of markets' with the development of world commodity markets, world capital markets and world currency markets, but also 'a deep-seated movement [which] sprang into being to resist the pernicious effects of a market controlled economy' (Polanyi, 1957: 76). Today globalisation is probably an even more intense internationalising process, and the movements contesting it are more diverse. It is not just the labour movement, but a vast range of particularist, even 'fundamentalist', movements which seek to contest globalisation. For Polanyi, workers, representing as they did a large section of society, were 'the only available class for the protection of the interests of the consumers, of the citizens, of human beings as such' (Polanyi, 1957: 235). It is the task of this study to examine to what extent this assessment might be true today. Certainly, in terms of articulating a role for socialism today I find it hard to disagree with Polanyi when he argues that 'Socialism is, essentially, the tendency inherent in an industrial civilisation to transcend the self-regulating market by consciously subordinating it to a democratic society' (Polanyi, 1957: 234).

TWO

THE 'GOLDEN ERA'

Capitalism as a stable mode of production seemed to come into its own in the aftermath of the Second World War. After this terrible, destructive period in human history a new vista of stable capital accumulation and harmonious labour relations seemed to be opening up. When British prime minister Harold Macmillan looked back in the 1950s and told people that 'we have never had it so good' he was not just politicking and he was not just talking for Britain. We need just recall that between 1950 and 1973 output per capita in the industrialised countries rose *three times* faster than the average of the previous 130 years. This new model capitalism created a new mode of regulation, which included Fordist production methods and the welfare state, at least for the advanced industrial societies. The first two sections of this chapter examine the basis of this unpredicted expansion of capitalism and its implications for the workers of the West. This was the heyday of national capitalism and corporatism, of the increased role of the state in economic affairs and in regulating labour–capital relations. But as the third section shows, the so-called Third World or developing countries did not partake of the synergy and apparently rosy prospects of the Golden Age. A new international division of labour incorporated these countries into its global capitalist economy but in a subordinate and uneven manner. The final section of this chapter examines the various versions accounting for the end of the Golden Age some time in the early 1970s. Our interpretation of the making and unmaking of the Golden Era, in the North and South, is specifically in terms of its implications for workers and the labour movement.

NEW MODEL CAPITALISM

The great crash of 1929 and the long Depression of the 1930s provided a salutory shock to the economic and political leaders of capitalism. Free-market forces would have to be tempered by state intervention if capitalism was to achieve a stable form resistant to such shocks in the future. The central feature of this new model 'managed' capitalism was a generalised 'acceptance of the so-called mixed economy – that is, a capitalist framework within which state enterprise was tolerated and the government held responsible for managing the economy'. Equally significant from the point of view of the present text, 'workers obtained certain rights and material benefits' (Armstrong et al., 1984: 193) from this dispensation. At least in the core capitalist countries, workers had jobs and even pay rises, received welfare services and could join trade unions. Economic relations are always mediated through social relations and in this new model capitalism, which consolidated itself in the post-war period, the labour–capital relation achieved a certain stability with consensus over its key parameters. In the so-called developing world, the 1930s' depression at the centre created the conditions for an import-substitution industrialisation for some countries. The post-war period saw the definitive surpassment of colonialism based on direct political domination and in its place the development of a neo-colonialism based on economic domination. The capitalist world was becoming integrated into a coherent whole, albeit unevenly, and excluding those parts of the world under the sway of state socialist regimes committed to endogenous growth.

John Maynard Keynes produced the macro-economic tools to prevent a recurrence of the economic destruction and mass unemployment of the 1930s. The Keynesian toolbox is quite simple: use of monetary policy by the state to slow down or stimulate the economy, use of spending and reverse to achieve the same objectives, and manipulation of the minimum wage/workforce levels (Lipietz, 1987: 38). This mode of regulation of the capitalist economy greatly facilitated the high and stable growth rates of the Golden Era. Keynes had, in his general theory of 1936, laid out the basis for this new institutionalisation of aggregate demand management, but it was only after the Second World War that the approach was actually implemented. The leaders of the capitalist economies in the West had noted a Soviet

Union industrialising strongly during the 1930s while they were in depression. Even the economic success of Nazi Germany was a salutory lesson to the depression-marked capitalist democracies. As Stephen Marglin puts it, 'the Western democracies were put under considerable political pressure to prevent output and employment from being regulated by swings in private confidence' (Marglin, 1990: 5). The 'animal spirits' of the capitalist were going to have to be tamed and the vicissitudes of the market controlled, at least to some extent. Workers in the West had come out of the Second World War strengthened. Unionisation had increased in quantitative terms but there was also a fundamental leap in confidence in the ability of the organised working class to run society for the common good.

It was the spectre of mass unemployment that was to haunt capitalist policy-makers as they moved out of depression and war into the Golden Era of capitalism. Pure laissez-faire attitudes towards employment were not credible after the catastrophe of the 1930s. The new countercyclical economic policies would have to have as a priority the achievement of full employment, or at least the avoidance of mass unemployment. A social compromise between capital and wage labour would have to replace the free-for-all of laissez-faire economic dogma. High growth rates would be matched by high employment rates and rising living standards for most workers in the advanced capitalist economies. Expansionary demand-side policies made sense to the capitalist elites, and workers granted the new 'reformed' capitalism a certain legitimacy. In retrospect, though, the commitment to full employment was storing up problems for the system. Michael Kalecki, the Polish economist who some assert came up with 'Keynesianism' independently from Keynes, had argued that

> The *maintenance* of full employment would cause social and political changes which would give a new impetus to the opposition of the business leaders. Under a regime of permanent full employment, 'the sack' would cease to play its role as a disciplinary measure ... 'discipline in the factories' and 'political stability' are more appreciated by business leaders than profits. Their class instinct tells them that lasting full employment is unsound from their point of view and that unemployment is an integral part of the normal capitalist system. (Kalecki, 1943: 140–41).

This, arguably, would be a factor in the later shift to supply-side and contractionary demand policies.

The international dimension was also crucial in ensuring the stability of world capitalism in the post-war period. This was centred around the so-called Pax Americana, a world system in which political and military hegemony was vested in one power, namely the United States. In the post-war period a return to a pure gold standard for international finance was impossible, so the Bretton Woods Agreement of 1944 established a 'flexible' gold standard. As the US dollar was the only convertible currency, this effectively made it equivalent to gold; as Webber and Rigby note, 'linking the dollar and gold was a boon to trade and the emerging post-war international financial system' (Webber and Rigby, 1996: 27). Restrictions in the full flow of goods would be removed, and trade would reinvigorate the capitalist world system. Bretton Woods created a system of fixed parities among the world's major currencies, to be adjusted through the new international body it set up, the International Monetary Fund (IMF). Though many of the 1944 agreements were never implemented, the Bretton Woods system created a certain degree of international financial stability until 1971, when it was unilaterally scrapped by the USA. The American 'peace' was also ensured by force, which included open or covert military interventions in Iran (1953), Guatemala (1954), Lebanon (1957) and the Dominican Republic (1965). Undisputed hegemony was, however, shattered by the ignominious defeat of the global power in Vietnam (1973), the effects of which were felt in the impunity with which the Organisation of Petroleum Exporting Countries (OPEC) raised the price of oil in 1973, thus hastening the demise of the Golden Era.

Pax Americana also meant an unprecedented expansion of US business interests through the (in)famous 'multinationals': the barely 7,000 overseas affiliates of US corporations in 1950 had risen to over 23,000 by 1966. During the 1950s and 1960s, the growth rate of multinational investment increased dramatically and they became the main agents of capitalist internationalism. The initial wave of post-war international investment originated in the USA, which accounted for more than half of the global total of foreign direct investment. The US corporations invested in and dominated much of the oil industry, mining and agriculture across the world. In the 1960s they also set up behind protectionist barriers to engage in manufacturing – for example, in Latin America. Later, European and Japanese international firms would become major players on the global stage. Thus while the USA remained the largest overseas investor, its share of global foreign direct investment (FDI) dropped from around 50 per cent in 1960 to 25 per cent in the mid-1990s. Though there is the occasional 'multinational' from Korea (Daewoo) and Venezuela (the state oil company) in the 'top 100', the 'vast majority of MNCs and FDI flows originate within, and move among, OECD countries' (Held et al., 1999: 248). It is among the Triad of North America, Western Europe and Japan that real transnational power lies. In the post-war period, the MNCs became the main bearers of capitalist relations worldwide and arguably paved the way for globalisation after the collapse of the Golden Era and the neo-liberalism of the 1980s. They have risen to a position where they dominate the global production and distribution of many goods and services and are at the cutting edge of technological development.

The third pillar of the new model capitalism, after Keynesian macro-economic management and the US-led international financial and investment regimes, was undoubtedly corporatism. Subject to a multiplicity of debates and definitions, theories of corporatism assert that 'unions are organized by the state and that the conduct of industrial relations is structured through a system of compulsory arbitration' (Roxborough, 1984: 3). For trade unions in the West it made sense to seek political representation for labour within state structures. The class struggle could be 'managed' in the interests of labour as much as capital, or so it seemed. Representatives of the working class were at one and the same time fighting the capitalist system and striving for its continued expansion to the benefit of workers. Corporatism in some developing countries also allowed trade unions to 'punch above their weight', as they engaged in political bargaining on the basis of fairly meagre social weight. The state–capital–labour relation took many different forms, and the term 'corporatism' may well be too flexible to be useful. The main point, as Armstrong et al. make in their broad-canvas analysis of the making and breaking of the post-war boom, is that 'the right of workers to organised representation was ... [an] ... important feature of the consensus' (Armstrong et al., 1984: 199). Whether in the form of institutionalised collective bargaining as epitomised by Britain, the co-determination system of Germany, Bolivian miners' co-determination, French indicative planning or Japan's particular labour relations, there was a generalised belief in and consensus around the legitimacy of workers' representation and on the desirability of compromise over conflict.

It is important to note, for the purposes of this text in particular, that corporatism also took an international form. The International Labour Organisation (ILO) was formed in 1919 and was to become an integral element of managing labour–capital relations in the post-war world. At its origins it was a response of the Western powers to the perceived menace of the Russian Revolution. When US President Roosevelt presided over a major ILO conference in 1944 it signalled US endorsement of its role in terms of an international social policy. From its inception, the ILO reflected the principle of tripartite representation, with representatives from government, employers and trade unions sitting down together. Its commitment to trade-union freedom and collective bargaining during the Golden Era was part and parcel of US hegemony over the 'Free World'. Robert Cox, in a significant critical insider account of the ILO, argued that 'Tripartism can now be defined, in the perspective of the United States, as the reality of the corporative state veiled by the still vigorous myth of free enterprise' (Cox, 1996: 427). Parts of organised labour would be allowed to sit at the 'top table' with employers and governments but at the cost of excluding the majority. Corporatism at the international level shifted from an understanding that the class struggle needed to be institutionalised to a quite nonconflictual version of tripartism in which managerial ideologies of production would exist unchallenged. A bitter fruit of this ideology at its most extreme was the long history of the US AFL–CIO as a labour agent of US imperialism, especially in its Latin American backyard.

What the new model meant in terms of the world of work was, in the first place, a vast increase in the number of workers. In the advanced capitalist countries, total employment rose by 30 per cent between 1950 and 1970. This is a significant increase in the size of the working class, but the degree of proletarianisation is even greater if we take into account the decline from 30 per cent to 15 per cent of the self-employed as a proportion of those officially classified as in work (Armstrong et al., 1984: 236). The secular decline of agriculture and the rise of the new services sector marked a fundamental recomposition of the Western working classes. Increased mechanisation and technological development led to increased skill and educational levels. Proletarianisation led to an increase in unionisation as well, with trade-union members in the advanced capitalist countries increasing from 49 million in 1952 to 62 million in 1970 (Armstrong et al., 1984: 238).

Though a crude indicator at best of labour organisation, and not that significant in terms of 'class consciousness', trade unions became social organisations of considerable weight during this period. From there to argue that capitalism was 'creating its own gravediggers', as many Marxists believed, was another matter. The working classes and the trade unions in the West during the Golden Age could only but reflect the ethos of the time. Hardly a social or political movement, let alone a government, however left-leaning, would articulate a project fundamentally opposed to the new model capitalism whatever radical sounds might be made.

If we allow for a lag of a decade for the so-called developing countries, we can see a similar process of proletarianisation. Agriculture, once the main employer by far, declined in the 'upper middle income' developing countries from 50 per cent in 1960 to 30 per cent in 1980 and from 62 per cent to 46 per cent in the 'middle income' countries. The degree of industrialisation was not so marked, yet the percentage of the labour force employed in manufacturing increased between 1960 and 1980 from 20 to 28 per cent in the upper middle income countries and from 15 to 21 per cent in the middle income countries. Though very unevenly across what became known in the post-war period as the Third World, capitalist relations of production were making considerable advances. There were few signs of a 'social compromise' between capital and labour and the process was more akin to the bloody 'primitive accumulation' described by Marx, but it was the development of capitalism nevertheless. As Bill Warren once put it provocatively: 'Whatever the new world being created in Latin America, Asia and Africa is to be, nothing can be gained from a refusal to recognise the existence of the developing capitalist societies already there' (Warren, 1980: 255). With the development of a new international division of labour in the 1960s (see below), this development of a proletariat across the globe shifted from an extensive to an intensive mode. This was probably a necessary prerequisite to the development of globalisation in later decades.

We need to turn now to Fordism, the mode of regulation and the way work was organised during the 'Golden Era'. But first it is necessary to reiterate how uneven this undoubtedly dynamic capitalist period was. It was often in looking back from the bleak neo-liberal 1980s that this era looked more golden than it actually was. In a bold retrospective analysis of the long post-war upturn and its subsequent undoing, Robert Brenner (Brenner, 1998) has questioned in particular the harmonious capital–labour relations implicit in most versions of this history. Across the political spectrum there has been an assumption that workers were accommodated within the new regime of capital accumulation. For Brenner, on the contrary, it seems obvious for example that the post-war boom in Japan and Germany was 'premised upon the suppression of labour and its consequent acceptance of low and (relative to productivity growth) slowly increasing wages' (Brenner, 1998: 42) rather than on the consolidation of some capital–labour accord or compromise. Even in relation to the United States, Brenner is able to bring evidence to show that 'Contrary to received wisdom, there was never anything approaching an 'accord' between capital and labour ... at any time during the post-war period' (Brenner, 1998: 60). So at most we can place the labour–capital accommodation in relative terms (compared to the open class war of the neo-liberal era) and then mainly for Britain and Western Europe outside Germany. There is, of course, another side to the post-war boom, namely the peripheral Fordism of the developing world, usually instigated by highly repressive political regimes committed to no form of accommodation with labour whatsoever.

FORDISM AND WELFARISM

At the heart of the 'new model capitalism' lay the Fordist labour process and the welfare state. When Henry Ford began producing his famous Model T motorcars in Detroit in the 1910s he created a new work method. From the First World War, F.W. Taylor's so-called scientific management was introduced into most advanced industrial societies, based mainly around the separation between planning and execution in the workplace and the 'one best way' to carry out a task. Taylorism, as it became known, only came into its own when it was transmuted into Fordism. Ford pioneered the flow-line principle of the assembly line, where Taylor's 'time and motion' method could be vigorously applied as the machine now dictated the workplace. Ford also introduced a daily wage ('measured day work') to replace piece rates, along with the famous Five Dollar Day, to attract workers to his car plants. Antonio Gramsci, a contemporary observer of Fordism (as Lenin was of Taylorism), noted perceptively that its aim was 'To build up an organic and well-articulated skilled labour force or a team of specialised workers[, which] has never been easy' (Gramsci, 1971a: 312). Fordism was seen by Gramsci as eminently rational, with a trade-off between higher wages and the associated rise in living standards on the one hand, and a new labour process demanding an unprecedented expenditure of muscular and nervous energy on the other. From its inception, then, Fordism was a form of capitalist production but also a mode of consumption. As Gramsci put it in a striking way: 'Hegemony here is born in the factory...' (Gramsci, 1971a: 285). This new logic of social transformation was to have profound effects on the social institutions and wage labour–capital relations during the Golden Era.

Fordism may be taken as an 'ideal type' but clearly it had many variants across countries and across time. Robert Boyer refers appropriately to 'one model, many national brands' (Boyer, 1995: 27) in relation to Fordism. From this perspective he develops a typology of different national Fordisms, in a similar way to Tickell and Peck's model (Table 2.1). What is particularly interesting about this model is that it integrates the particular Fordist accumulation patterns with the Keynesian-welfare modes of regulation for each case. It is also a less Eurocentric model than those usually found in the industrial relations literature, with due attention being paid to 'peripheral Fordism' and the 'racial Fordism' typical of apartheid-era South Africa.

If there was one enduring legacy from the Great Depression it was the welfare state, that 'safety net' to catch those who fell through the formal wage-earning structures of capitalist society. In Britain's paradigmatic welfare state, the post-war Beveridge Report was premissed on the notion of a 'social minimum' of welfare based on compulsory social insurance. While the origins of welfarism can be traced back to the turn of the century, it was in the post-war period that it was consolidated and generalised, in a way that commanded cross-party support. Coverage of previous unemployment schemes was broadened beyond full-time industrial workers. In relation to the Western European countries, Armstrong et al. found that, 'Comparing the situation in 1975 with the year of introduction ... the duration of benefits had doubled ... the delay before eligibility had halved ... and the period of disqualification had halved' (Armstrong et al., 1984: 196). Far and away the most radical innovation was the British National Health Service (NHS) based on need, as of right and universal. Certainly the welfare state never came close to eradicating poverty, even in the

TABLE 2.1 VARIANTS OF FORDISM

Regime	Characteristics	Examples
'Classic Fordism'	Mass production and consumption by social-democratic welfare state.	USA
'Flex-Fordism'	Decentralised, federalised state. Close co-operation between financial and industrial capital, including facilitation of inter-firm co-operation.	West Germany
'Flawed Fordism'	Inadequate integration of financial and productive capital at the level of the nation-state. Archaic and obstructive politics identified by some authors.	United Kingdom
'State Fordism'	State plays leading role in creation of conditions of mass production, including state control of industry. *L'état entrepreneur.*	France
'Delayed Fordism'	Cheap labour immediately adjacent to Fordist core. State intervention has key role in rapid industrialisation in 1960s.	Italy, Spain
'Peripheral Fordism'	Local assembly followed by export of Fordist goods. Heavy indebtedness. Authoritarian state structures coupled with movement for democracy, attempts to emulate Fordist accumulation system in absence of corresponding mode of social regulation.	Mexico, Brazil
'Racial Fordism'	Dualistic workforce. Privileged minority has North American-style working conditions and remuneration levels that rely upon authoritarian state structures and 'super-exploitation' of majority population.	South Africa
'Primitive Taylorisation'	Taylorist labour process with almost endless supply of labour. Bloody exploitation and huge extraction of surplus value. Dictatorial states and high social tension.	Malaysia, Bangladesh, Philippines
'Hybrid Fordism'	Profit-driven expansion based upon modified Taylorism. Truncated internal market, societal segmentation and underdeveloped welfare state. Indirect wage indexation.	Japan

Source: Tickell and Peck, 1995: 362.

advanced capitalist countries. It did, however, fundamentally reform the laissez-faire capitalism of the 1930s and provide it with a 'human face'. To some degree it was only in retrospect as the neo-liberal age developed that the welfare state acquired a more positive connotation. From the perspective of the developing countries, without even a rudimentary welfare state in most cases or at best a formal system which did not deliver, the Western welfare state seemed desirable indeed to workers and their families.

The welfare state was probably not an unambiguous good for the working classes. A critical reading of the Keynesian welfare state, especially in its heyday, argued that it was designed to secure popular consent, to ensure the smooth 'reproduction' of the working classes. It was seen as one of the repressive mechanisms of the state, along with schools, housing departments and the family. It was perceived as part of the state along with schools, housing departments and the family: an 'ideological state apparatus' (see Althusser, 1971) to match the 'repressive state apparatus' of army, police, and so on. These were seen to work hand-in-glove to tame a rebellious working class, a case of an 'iron fist in a velvet glove', as it were. Even when writers did not see the welfare state as an unambiguous offence against libertarianism, there was a tendency (in retrospect) to overstress its negative elements. Ian Gough, author of an influential political economy of the welfare state, could argue as late as 1979 that the welfare state

> simultaneously embodies tendencies to enhance social welfare, to develop the powers of individuals, to exert social control over the blind play of market forces; and tendencies to repress and control people, to adapt them to the requirements of the capitalist economy. (Gough, 1979: 12)

As monetarism began to exert its grip on the Western political imagination, the welfare state began to be seen as an unaffordable luxury. As mass unemployment took a grip, it became harder to see a public health system and a welfare state 'safety net' as somehow repressive social institutions 'taming' a naturally rebellious working class.

If we now add up Keynes, Ford and Beveridge (the welfare state) we get the basic ingredients of the 'Fordist' social compromise which dominated across the advanced capitalist countries in the Golden Era. This KFB model not only dominated the economic scene, working relations and consumption patterns; it also shaped society as a whole and its particular post-war institutional arrangements. As Boyer puts it, 'An unprecedented conjunction of political and social forces led to this new order' (Boyer, 1995: 21). The rebuilding of war-torn societies took precedence over social and political differences, at least to some extent, and temporarily there was a paradigm shift. The Malthusian capitalist became a rational manager. The radical trade unionist took on board 'scientific management' methods. Above these new 'social partners' stood the KFB state setting up the necessary public infrastructure and maintaining the countercyclical economic policy to keep things going. Managers would be allowed to manage by labour, and workers could expect a share of productivity gains as Fordism matured and to be 'looked after' by the welfare state if necessary. The new production methods would be matched by new consumption patterns across the working classes, which helped legitimise the new order. The main point is that the KFB social order was an integrated whole, a seamless package with considerable synergies. As Boyer puts it, in summing up this virtuous circle, 'It can be shown that a rather coherent accumulation regime has been built upon this genuine social compromise' (Boyer, 1995: 22).

One way of taking a broader perspective on the particular post-war social dispensation in the West is via the concept of citizenship. T.H. Marshall, an early theorist of the British welfare state, developed a model based on the elements or aspects of citizenship:

- Civil – such as freedom of speech the right to justice, and the prerequisites for individual freedom.
- Political – involving the right to participate in the exercise of political power through local government and national parliament.
- Social citizenship – 'the right to a modicum of economic welfare and security to the right to share to the full in the social heritage and to live the life of a civilised being according to the standards prevailing in the society' (Marshall, 1950: 10).

The language of Marshall may be a trifle arcane, his Eurocentrism was undoubted, and gender had not entered his discourse (see Lister, 1997). However, Marshall usefully highlighted the limitations of a purely political definition of citizenship. By introducing the social element of citizenship, Marshall recognised that civil and political citizenship under capitalism was at best partial without the essential rights to social and economic welfare. Marshall has been criticised for advancing an evolutionary view of the development of citizenship as some inherent characteristic of capitalism (see Mann, 1987). However, if we take a fluid reading of Marshall's account of the contradictory relationship between political democracy and the free market of capitalism, we can see its relevance in the era of globalisation and understand why oppositional forces in developing countries have adopted similar political paradigms in varied situations.

So how did the workers of the West fare under Fordism? We have already mentioned the quantitative expansion of the Western working classes and the development of trade unionism. Yet, as Armstrong et al. argue,

> The increase in output was out of all proportion to the growth of employment. The number of people classified as in civilian employment rose by only 29 per cent between 1952 and 1973. So most of the extra production represented an increase in output per worker. Annual productivity doubled. (Armstrong et al., 1984: 168)

This great leap forward in productivity was not due to longer hours worked, as these decreased steadily (albeit at less than 1 per cent per annum over this period). It was, rather, the quantity and the quality of the means of production that improved. There was, in essence, a veritable technological revolution during this period. According to Eric Hobsbawm,

> More than any previous period, the Golden Age rested on the most advanced and often esoteric scientific research, which now found practical application within a few years. Industry and even agriculture for the first time moved decisively beyond the technology of the nineteenth century. (Hobsbawm, 1994: 265)

The language used by Hobsbawm to describe the Golden Age equals that of Marx and Engels in the *Communist Manifesto*, who waxed lyrical on the capitalist revolutions of their day. It is well to remember, though, that if the means of production per worker doubled in the advanced capitalist economies, this also meant that effectively 'it was as though each worker was confronted by two machines where one stood before' (Armstrong et al., 1984: 168).

There was a debate in the 1970s around 'unequal exchange' between nations that also had implications for the position of Western workers in the global system. The original, if idiosyncratic, arguments for this analysis came from Arghiri Emmanuel (Emmanuel, 1972), who applied a Ricardian international trade model to derive the notion of unequal exchange: basically, unequal quantities of labour were involved in inter-national trade to the detriment of the developing countries. The model involves the international mobility of capital and the international immobility of labour power. Emmanuel saw wages as an independent variable in this model (Marx's moral-historical element) which results in capital-intensive industrialisation at the centre and labour intensive methods at the periphery. The unequal exchange of their products in the international market results in uneven development. Other writers argued to the contrary that it was the uneven source of capitalism as a mode of production which led to wage (and productivity) differen-tials and not the other way round. Emmanuel was also criticised for the divisive implications of his political consideration that Western workers benefited from unequal exchange and thus were unlikely to engage in solidarity activities with their counterparts in the develop-ing world. With hindsight, it is not so much the intricacies of the unequal exchange model which are interesting but the fact that there was a critical consensus that capital accumulation on a world scale was based on exploitation. Now the only consensus is that all must be part of the globalisation process and not suffer from exclusion.

Meanwhile, in the East workers were labouring under what has been called the 'Iron Age' (Lipietz, 1995: 355). Lenin had been a great admirer of Taylorism and he once infamously defined socialism as 'soviets plus electrification'. This was an industrial model of modern-isation which owed a lot to capitalism in spite of a commitment to centralised planning as against market allocation of resources. In the 1950s it seemed from the prodigious Soviet growth rates, that the Golden Era had its Eastern counterpart. The drive to industrialise was paying off even if the system was inefficient and the human cost huge. Janos Köllö has characterised Eastern Europe's 'dark' Golden Age thus: 'Disorder with a "human face", not the strict Taylorian rule in the factory; anomie and slyness, not the Orwellian drill; informal bargaining and individual evasion of unfavourable local conditions, not the complete submission of workers' (Köllö, 1995: 291). In the resource-constrained economies of Eastern Europe there was a rapidly growing level of employment. This was an extensive rather than an intensive pattern of capital accumulation. Unemployment rates were very low and workers had considerable rights not only to a job but also to social rights in that job. By the 1980s, this model was in crisis and the East joined the West's race into the globalisation and deregulation new order. An interesting point is whether this crisis of modernisation was more akin to the West's Golden Era crisis (see later in this chapter) or to the South's debt-driven crisis of the 1980s (see Chapter 3). We can probably surmise a third way into crisis even if the end result was, on the whole, a 'Thirdworldisation' of the East.

For Lipietz the 'Iron Age' model of Soviet labour–capital relations was a cousin to the Fordist one based on a menu of 'Taylorism plus tenure' which allowed it to compete with the West in the 1950s (Lipietz, 1995: 356). The extensive pattern of accumulation that ensued did not really require much flexibility and it was well placed to absorb a surplus of rural labourers. In the transition from a nonindustrialised to an industrialising economy this model was productive enough. Indeed, Leninism in the developing world generally took on as much the characteristics of a developmentalist ideology as those of a political philosophy. Wages grew only slowly and there was not a vast increase in mass consumption patterns, so that surpluses accumulated readily throughout this period. However, as Lipietz notes, 'the compromise of "tenure with low wage" appears then as completely stagnationist' (Lipietz, 1995: 356). There was a pressing need, even with the assumed parameters of the state socialist model, for more flexibility. With a considerable delay compared to the West, the demands of 'flexibility' nevertheless made themselves felt. So-called external flexibility – the right of managers to redeploy labour – meant the end of tenure. By the time this crisis in capital–labour relations came to the fore in the 1990s, the full-blown effects of political crisis were being felt. As state socialism collapsed, the social-democratic compromise of Fordism was no longer on offer and the workers of the East were brusquely introduced to the rigours of neo-liberal flexibility under the aegis of globalisation.

NEW INTERNATIONAL DIVISION OF LABOUR

If we take a global perspective on the long post-war boom in the West/North, perhaps the most noticeable transformation is the emergence of a new international division of labour. In the 'old' or colonial division of labour, Third World labour had been essential to the industrial revolutions in the West. Marx wrote about how Western capitalism came into the world 'dripping from head to toe from every pore with blood and dirt' (Marx, 1976: 926). This process of primitive accumulation led to plunder and forced labour across what was to become known as the Third World. The cotton industry of Britain, for example, was dependent on the slavery of the cotton-producing areas of North America. The growing mobility of capital – which began to penetrate all areas of the globe – was matched by mass migrations of labour, that unique and sometimes recalcitrant 'factor of production'. The keystone to capitalist 'development' was always labour. As Sydney Mintz writes in relation to the Caribbean, 'for most of the islands during most of their post-Columbian history, labour had to be impressed, coerced, dragged and driven to work – and most of the time, to simplify the problem of discipline labour was enslaved' (Mintz, 1974: 45). The sugar, cacao, gold, diamonds, wheat, beef and oil which fed the West's industrialisation and population created for the non-West a subordinate role in a colonial division of labour sustained for centuries by force of arms. Imperialism was an integral element in the development of capitalism and helped shape its economic, political, social and cultural characteristics.

The basic argument of the new international division of labour (NIDL) theorists is that the traditional colonial division of labour in which the Third World was relegated to the production of raw materials began to change in the 1960s. Decolonialisation, and then the 'economic imperialism' of the post-war period, began to generate pressures for change. For Fröbel, Heinrichs and Kreye three basic preconditions were required for this to happen:

1. The breakdown of traditional social economic structures in the Third World, which led to the emergence of a vast pool of cheap available labour.
2. The fragmentation of the industrial production process, which allowed unskilled sub-processes to be relocated to the Third World.
3. The development of cheap international transport and communications technology, which made this relocation possible (Fröbel et al., 1980: 13).

The NIDL is seen to have fundamentally restructured the relations of production in the Third World, with the emergence of a substantial manufacturing sector oriented towards the world market. The new 'world market factories' engaged in a process of 'super-exploitation' of their mainly female workers, recruited for their alleged submissiveness and 'nimble fingers' (see Elson and Pearson, 1981). This shift away from a purely agricultural and raw-materials-supply role, with all its limitations, was seen to create the conditions for the emergence of a classical opposition between capital and wage labour. For some of its most incisive analyists and critics the NIDL also 'contains the *possibility* of international solidarity between workers' (Fröbel et al., 1980: 406). We return later, in Chapters 6 and 7, to the issue of international labour solidarity but first we must examine the limitations of the NIDL theory.

The NIDL theory was not without its critics, even at the time (1970s) when it certainly appeared to reflect a changing global reality. Essentially it focused on the world market, the level of circulation, to the detriment of changes at the level of production. As with the dependency theory of underdevelopment, to which it related in many ways, the NIDL thesis neglected the role of the state in the Third World. It was almost as if the 'world market' had a life of its own and could impose its will across the globe. Furthermore, the NIDL thesis (at least as articulated in Fröbel et al., 1980) seriously underestimated the level of industrialisation that existed in the Third World prior to the 1960s. This led it to isolate the 'world market factories' and the famous free trade zones (FTZs) as the main, even sole, sites of capitalist development in the Third World. In fact, if we take a broader perspective on Third World social formations, their importance is relative. If we take a more historical perspective on Third World industrialisation, we also see that the 'old' division of labour was in crisis in the 1930s and had probably reached its zenith at the time of the First World War. A final weakness of the NIDL thesis is the assumption, at least premature, that labour was achieving the same level of mobility as capital. In spite of these qualifications a recast NIDL approach does direct us towards certain basic transformations in the global economy and the growing importance of Third World workers in the world system.

In reality we can point to at least two phases of the NIDL. The first was typified by the import substitution industrialisation (ISI) in the larger Latin American countries during the 1930s. For example, in Brazil the state had set up its first steel mill (Volta Redonda) and car plant in the early 1940s. This laid the basis for the expansion of capital accumulation in the 1950s, a process that acquired its own endogenous dynamic. State participation in fixed capital formation more than doubled between 1947 and 1960. It was only after this infrastructural basis had been laid by the national state that foreign capital became an important source of investment. By the 1970s, manufactured goods accounted for more than half of the total exports from Brazil. Some of these goods, like textiles and shoes, were relatively labour-intensive but there was also a major automobile industry, where the labour force was subsumed under Fordist methods of production. This pattern was typical of Argentina and Mexico too, but also, for example, in India. By the 1920s there were 4.5 million wage workers in the Indian manufacturing industry. By the 1960s, before the internationally generated NIDL was supposed to commence, these countries (and also the Philippines, for example) possessed internally generated industrial sectors based on production for the home market. To view the Third World as a whole as a simple reservoir of cheap labour (as the NIDL theories tended to do) neglects the dynamic development of capitalism in many areas.

The second wave of the NIDL saw the emergence of the East Asian newly industrialising countries (NICs) in the 1960s, such as South Korea, Taiwan, Hong Kong, Singapore and Malaysia. The export-led industrialisation of these countries since the last 1960s has often been associated with the establishment of FTZs, the modern equivalent of the nineteenth-century mining 'enclaves'. By 1975, there were some eighty FTZs across the Third World, of which fifty were located in East Asia. There were, of course, many more 'world market factories' producing for the international market. Fröbel et al. estimate that by 1975 there were 725,000 Third World workers engaged in this internationalised production sector, of which more than half were based in East Asia (Fröbel et al., 1998: 307). The NIDL led to a wave of relocation of electronics and textile plants from the West to the NICs. Thus, in the textile sector alone we saw the Third World share of total exports rise from 15 per cent in the mid-1960s to nearly 25 per cent by the mid-1970s. The restructuring of the global electronics industry was even more dramatic, with the relocation of most semi-skilled manufacturing operations to the NICs. Through the 'global assembly line' of the textile and electronics industries many more Third World workers (especially women workers) became an integral part of the world working class. By the 1990s these economies had become a leading growth area of the global economy and had also experienced their own capitalist crises.

If we take a broad retrospective view of the countries which entered the NIDL in the 1930s and then in the 1960s, there are two major characteristics of note. In the first place, this was mainly a *state*-led industrialisation and, second, was part of a *national* development strategy. As Jong-Il You writes in relation to South Korea:

> The dominance of the state in guiding economic development ... is well documented. The state dictated the direction of production and investment activities with a variety of incentives and sanctions, thereby controlling and shaping the accumulation process. The state played an hegemonic role in shaping the capital–labour relations, too. (You, 1995: 17)

This would be a general pattern, with differences of degree and format only, across the NICs and the new NICs. The role of the state is important to note because it contradicts some of the *ex-post facto* neo-liberal myths about the East Asian NICs in particular. It is also well to recall when neo-liberal globalisation rules supreme, that the big advance in industrialisation of the developing world occurred under the aegis of mainly nationalist regimes, albeit often authoritarian or openly repressive. Today, when 'reform' is associated directly with the opening of these economies to the world market, we should stress the role of a certain degree of protectionism in the past. Indeed, all development theories until the 1980s, be they conservative modernisation theories 'made in USA' or the radical alternative 'dependency' theory originating in Latin America (but which spread widely), conceived of development as *national* development.

As to the labour process which emerged under the NIDL, there are two main variants. The first is what Lipietz has called Bloody Taylorism (Lipietz, 1987). This is a Taylorism for the era of 'primitive accumulation', a labour process guaranteed by repressive political regimes which maintained the regimentation of labour as much as the classical 'time and motion' studies inside the plants. There is little attempt to construct a hegemonic type of labour process where 'acquiescence' is achieved through a 'human relations' type of approach to workers. A premium is placed, rather, on the 'adaptability' of the work-force to the demands of the Taylorist process, with fragmentation of tasks and repetitive work routines at its core. The technological revolution in the West during the Golden Age led to a breaking down of the labour process, with less skilled elements being relocated in the Third World. While relative surplus value, according to Marx's criteria, is extracted from these workers, absolute surplus value is also important given the lengthening of the working day, the employment of minors, and the constant and direct compulsion by supervisors. As Lipietz writes,

> The results are as spectacular as the means used to achieve them. The rate of surplus-value rises sharply, whereas it remains stable in the central 'Fordist' regime. The rise is due to the opening of the 'scissors' between stagnant purchasing power and rising apparent productivity. (Lipietz, 1987: 76)

This regime of accumulation proved extremely profitable to the NICs but it could not escape the basic Keynesian constraint that the home market was only slow to develop within this logic.

In some developing countries a genuine, if peripheral, Fordist system did emerge. For Lipietz, 'peripheral Fordism' is a 'true Fordism' in so far as it involves both mechanization and a growing consumer market, but it remains peripheral in that the skilled jobs and production processes remain largely outside the South (Lipietz, 1987: 78–9). This model fits countries like Brazil, South Korea and Mexico. The motor industries in these countries, for example, were only sub-Fordist in the sense that autoworkers did not reap the social benefits of Fordist factory life in the advanced capitalist countries. At the level of the factory, though, the Fordist methods of the semi-automated assembly line and the intensified division of labour were fully implemented. Perhaps more typically 'sub-Fordist' would be the average Third World textile plant of the 1970s, which adapted Taylorist principles but made no attempt to achieve the social integration of workers. This Taylorist labour process was, however, complemented by more traditional means of extracting surplus value, such as virtually unlimited working hours. Either the most 'modern' textile plants in the developing world (and, of course, not exclusively limited to this part of the world, as we shall see in Chapter 5) are liable to practise subcontracting to small workshops, with outwork – once seen as a precapitalist labour process – finding a profitable niche in the late twentieth century. Such is the story of combined and uneven development in the lead-up to globalisation.

As the Golden Age became tarnished in the North during the 1970s (see section below), the South was going through an ascendant phase. This was the period which saw the work of the famous Brandt

Commission (Report of the Independent Commission on International Development Issues, 1981); it was also, in retrospect, a high point of international trade-union influence on global development strategies. This enlightened programme for survival echoed many of the demands put forward by Third World governments in the 1970s to promote a New International Economic Order. Countries would be taxed, on a sliding scale related to national income, to provide revenues for a World Development Fund. During the 1970s the unravelling of the Golden Era in the North did not immediately impact on the South due to these moves towards a global Keynesian policy and the re-cycling of the petro-dollar. Growth was uneven, but it appeared that peripheral Fordism would have as bright a future as its central counter-part had for the glorious thirty years since the Second World War. From a political economy perspective we can recognise, with Juliet Schor and Jong-Il You, that 'the 1970s were a decade of ascendancy rather than setback as far as the South was concerned; economic growth continued, Vietnam defeated the United States, OPEC success-fully raised oil prices, and the New International Economic Order was on the agenda' (Schor and You, 1995: 5–6). It was only in the 1980s that the crisis became global as restrictive monetary policies in the North led to a massive increase in interest rates; this triggered the Third World debt crisis with its catastrophic social and economic consequences.

Towards the end of the last century, a yet 'newer' international division of labour impacted on the countries and workers of the developing world. There is no longer a unified North and South, if there ever was. We cannot even distinguish a centre, semi-periphery and periphery as world-system theory did (see Wallerstein, 1983). While the new global economy is highly integrated, it is also extremely diversified. The network of the global information-led economy has integrated various parts of the world and its workers into its web. This is not done, however, by integrating national economies which have become increasingly disintegrated. Thus, as we saw in Chapter 1, we can talk of the 'Latin Americanisation' or 'Brazilianisation' of the United States or other once unproblematically designated advanced industrial societies. Pockets of development coexist with broad swathes of 'underdevelopment' and human misery. Uneven development has always been a characteristic of capitalism, but what is striking today is the degree of development, on the one hand, and the utter disconnection of other parts of the globe, on the other. This newest division of labour certainly relegates whole regions as surplus to requirements. Globalisation has sharpened the process of social exclusion in all societies and has simply excluded some regions from even the dubious privilege of exploitation. Before we can turn to the effects of this new regime of accumulation on the workers of the world (Chapter 3) we need to unravel the precise nature of the crisis of the Golden Era.

CRISIS OF THE MODEL

We now live in a post-Fordist, post-welfare-state, post-interventionist-state, post-class-compromise era. The end of the Golden Age in the 1970s had far-reaching effects, leading to the hegemony of neo-liberalism and the birth of the era of globalisation we are now living under. A critical understanding of how and why the post-war model of accumulation came to an end is crucial to a proper understanding of the new dispensation. Most analysts are agreed that the 1970s and 1980s were different from the 1950s and 1960s, but no clear paradigm has emerged such as that of the 'Golden Age'. Many momentous events occurred in this period, such as the collapse of the Bretton Woods system of international finance in 1974, the big increase in oil prices in 1974–75, the rise of Reaganism–Thatcherism with their neo-liberal economic policies in the early 1980s, and the collapse of state socialism at the end of that decade. It was also out of this period that the basic parameters of globalisation emerged, to flourish fully in the 1990s. Where there is little agreement is on the pattern of causality in this set of events, and we will seek to clarify some of the contending explanations in this section. The importance of this crisis probably grows in significance as it become clearer that the 'great transformation' which began after the crisis of the 'Golden Age' of post-war capitalism continues to change the world around us in ways that are still uncertain.

At one level the crisis which affected the advanced capitalist economies (ACEs) at the end of the 1960s and early 1970s is clear enough. The falling rates of profit in the ACEs between 1968 and 1973 were a clear indication that something was fundamentally amiss: profit rates in the USA, Western Europe and Japan were down one-third from their previous peaks. There was a wave of strikes across Europe between 1968 and 1970 that seemed to exacerbate this capitalist crisis of confidence. The expansion of the early 1970s was based in a massive US deficit and was fuelled by a rapid rise in inflation rates. As the economists of the time put it, the economies of the West were 'overheating'. When the crisis point was reached in 1974 it coincided with a round of increases in oil prices by the OPEC countries between 1973 and 1974. 'Greedy oil sheiks' looked the likely and handy culprits. Certainly, as Eric Hobsbawm puts it, 'one of the reasons why the Golden Age was Golden was that the price of a barrel of Saudi oil averaged less than $2 throughout the entire period from 1950 to 1973, thus making energy ridiculously cheap, and getting cheaper all the time' (Hobsbawm, 1994: 262). This was undoubtedly one of the conjunctural factors triggering the crisis but it was only part of a broader configuration of structural and conjunctural factors leading to a collapse of the post-war model. The Golden Age had begun to lose its shine some seven years before the 'oil shock' hit it.

Another common explanation of the crisis, both on the right and on the left, was the profit squeeze due to the power of workers to impose wage demands on capitalists. For Stephen Marglin,

> There was ... well before the oil shock, a general 'full-employment, profit squeeze' throughout the OECD countries. This was not a phenomenon associated with business 'cycles' ... but the result of a long period of sustained growth, rising wages, high employment, and increasing security for working people. The full-employment, profit squeeze had a direct effect on accumulation. (Marglin, 1990: 19)

So the warning by Kalecki (see above) that full employment would remove fear of the sack and ultimately jeopardise accumulation seemed to be coming true. Certainly it is easy to see how a combative labour movement can in certain countries and at certain periods put a curb on profit rates. From there to deploying this argument as a full-blown explanation of the crisis is excessive, however attractive a class-struggle perspective might be from a labour standpoint. For one, the timing is wrong and it can be shown that the wave of labour militancy in the ACEs during 1969–74 was more a response to the crisis of profitability which had caused employers in the West to unleash a wages offensive on 'their' workers. Even in general theoretical terms, though, as Brenner argues, it is hard to see how the full-employment, profit-squeeze thesis 'could account for an economic crisis, meaning a long term reduction in the profit rate that produces a secular system-wide economic downturn' (Brenner, 1998: 18).

For Robert Brenner, in his commanding account of the crisis of the Golden Era, workers' action 'may certainly reduce profitability in given locales, but it cannot, as a rule, make for crisis because it cannot, as a rule, bring about a spatially generalised (system-wide) and temporally extended decline in profitability' (Brenner, 1998: 21). The crisis of the Fordist model extended into the 1980s, when the onslaught of the monetarists had successfully curbed even defensive workers' action in most of the ACEs. It is simply implausible that workers' action across the ACEs for a decade or more successfully thwarted all capitalist strategies for restructuring to escape the looming crisis. The political conclusion from that thesis argued by some, namely that trade unions had become 'too powerful' and that their rigidities were hindering techological innovation, is also lacking in credibility. An alternative explanation of the long boom and its demise would focus on inter-capitalist competition and its dynamic. The dense narrative and analysis advanced by Brenner focuses precisely on the uneven development of capitalism and the particular situation which emerged in the 1960s with the consolidation of German and Japanese exports to the USA. This was no longer as self-contained an economy as it had seemed and the 'latecomer' national blocs of capital were to become successful competitors. The outcome of declining profitability across the board would be a useful lesson for present-day gurus of 'competitiveness' at all costs, a remarkably short-sighted growth strategy.

The international financial dimension is also a crucial part of the 1968–74 story. Pax Americana and the Bretton Woods system were cornerstones of the post-war dispensation. US hegemony in political, economic and military terms (not to mention the 'cultural' dimension) was essential to global regulation. Now not only was that hegemony being contested and the once all-mighty dollar seriously weakened but the demands of the system were also changing. While Bretton Woods worked effectively in relation to monetary circulation, it was unable to control the new international credit system, which was emerging in a more 'private' and unregulated way (the 'Euro markets', for example). As Altvater puts it, 'Unregulated global credit was a factor of erosion of the (political institutional) regulation of the whole Fordist system' (Altvater, 1992: 37). The United States inexorably pulled back from full convertibility of the dollar to gold as per Bretton Woods and this whole institution was then unilaterally abandoned by the USA in 1971. What this signalled was also the abandonment by the USA of its leading international aggregate demand role. Though mild by subsequent standards, a real crisis of confidence in the international financial order ensued. The forces moving towards deregulation of the international financial markets were gathering force. This chapter, though, ended in 1974 with another oil price rise by OPEC which, as Marglin notes, 'triggered a new round of inflation which in turn catalysed doubts about the international order amid fears of a total collapse of the dollar-based financial system' (Marglin, 1990: 24).

After the immediate impact of the 1974 crisis, Fordist–Keynesian policies continued to be implemented but without solid Fordist institutions to sustain them. The 1970s were thus in some way a transition period; an interregnum in which the old had ceased to be effective but the new had not yet cohered. With the breakdown of the Bretton Woods system a two-decade-long process began in which the private financial market achieved its hegemony over state regulation. One indication of this battle is the simple fact that by 1989 international bonds and inter-bank deposits totalled $4.75 trillion, which was six times the total foreign exchange reserves of the central banks (Webber and Rigby, 1996: 29). Finance capital was beginning to cut loose from the realm of production and the 'real' economy. The other side of the coin was a concerted attack on organised labour, which also had to be disorganised to the benefit of the new capitalism. Thus the 1980s were marked by a consensus that Keynes was the 'demon of profligacy incarnate' (Marglin, 1990: 34). Supply-side economics completely obliterated any notion of demand management. Workers bore the main brunt of the monetarist onslaught but vast layers of society were affected by the rollback of the welfare state. There was even a return to an aggressive US foreign policy, with the invasion of Grenada, destabilisation in Nicaragua, the invasion of Panama, the bombings of Libya and Iraq and so on, marking the comeback of the terrorist state.

With the neo-liberal onslaught of the early 1980s, a new regime of growth began to emerge in the ACEs. The era of organised capitalism – the large organisation – gave way to a new-found faith in the operations of the free market, and a 'disorganised' (in the literal sense) capitalism ensued. The organisations of the corporations, of the government and even of civil society had mainly enabled the market in the past, while being based on rational organisational principles themselves. Now, the logic of the market was not only to dominate but to exert its logic over all sectors of society. Trade unions were not immune to this logic, and began to articulate the need to review their objectives to prioritise more the 'services' that affected their members as individuals. Deregulation and marketisation of all aspects of social and economic life could not but have a profound effect on workers. For Aglietta, author of one of the classic studies of Fordist regulation, this new growth regime leads to uncertainty and instability:

> Increasing numbers of employees cannot find their place in the division of labour ... That is a measure of the depth of the malaise which has gripped wage societies in these trying times. The very principle of the integration of labour into the corporate structure, the progressive force behind the post-war boom, is now under threat. (Aglietta, 1998: 72)

It is not a question of donning rose-tinted spectacles when looking back at the Fordist Golden Era, but some social relations do become clearer with the benefit of hindsight.

After Fordism one gets post-Fordism, it would seem, but that equation is a bit too neat. In the ACEs there were a number of alternative wage-labour/capital relations emerging after Fordism but they cannot be given a clear 'post-Fordist' label because no such dominant new paradigm has emerged. The policy of liberal flexibility in the era of global competitiveness has marked the domain of production as much as elsewhere. What seems to be emerging in many parts is a neo-Taylorism which is very much in the classical mould but without the social institutions and social compromise that went with high Fordism. At the other extreme is what Lipietz (1995) has called Kalmarism, referring to the labour relations that prevailed in the now defunct Volvo plant in Sweden, which pioneered a negotiated involvement by the workforce. However, as Lipietz writes, 'collective involvement of the workers is unlikely to emerge if there is no solidarity about goals between the forms and the workforce ...' (Lipietz, 1995: 353). Certainly there is a range of possibilities (see Chapter 4 below), and the 'Japanese model', or Toyotaism as it has become known, lies somewhere between neo-Taylorism and the Swedish model that was. The main point to make in concluding this chapter on the Golden Age of capitalism is that after Fordism this mode of production has not been able to generate a hegemonic paradigm to organise production and capital/wage-labour relations in its central or core regions.

For the developing world, work after Fordism definitely did not mean post-Fordism. This is true equally for the South and for the East, which is rapidly becoming a developing capitalist area of the world system. In many ways, the after-Fordism shock is greater here because the state-led model of industrialisation with extensive deployment of labour was so dominant. Central planning and national development plans, typical of the East and the South in the Golden Age, are now defunct strategies. For Lipietz a likely paradigm for the developing East is a form of 'Taylorism and liberal flexibility', especially given that Taylorist principles were arguably never applied to their limits there (Lipietz, 1995). Some involvement of the Kalmarian type may be possible in pockets of development in the South but are hardly likely to become prevalent. As we shall see in Chapter 5, a whole range of possibilities are opening up in the South. With de-militarisation in South Korea, for example, we saw a transition from 'bloody Taylorism' to a stunted but nevertheless real peripheral Fordism. It is hard to conceive of a democratic South Africa imposing a rigid anti-worker liberal-flexibility regime on the trade unions and their members, who were at the forefront of the anti-apartheid struggle. In short, the future is still open in the after-Fordist era of globalisation.

Back in the 1960s, a capitalist from Detroit become US government functionary once declared (in)famously that what was good for General Motors was good for the USA. If somewhat blunt, this statement had a ring of truth about it. There was a certain synergy between trans-nationalist capitalist expansion and national capitalist state development. After the Golden Era, with the era of globalisation taking shape and expanding, this position has not even got that 'truth' to it. As Tickell and Peck put it, there was a growing 'contradiction between globalising accumulation and national regulation, or, more particularly, between the emerging unregulated global credit system and the fiscal integrity of the Keynesian welfare state' (Tickell and Peck, 1995: 372). What had been a virtuous circle involving the national and the international, accumulation and welfare, capitalist and worker, production and consumption, had now turned into a series of vicious circles. Monetarism was a response to this but also a symptom of the crisis, and ultimately unsustainable. For the new accumulation regime which emerged in the 1990s, based on accelerated internationalisation, there would still be a need for a global regulatory order. This seems unlikely to emerge smoothly, at least from the evidence of the debacle of the WTO meeting at Seattle in 1999. It is this search for global regulation to meet the economic and political disorder which underlies the next chapter and which forms a key horizon for the international labour movement.

THREE

THE ERA OF GLOBALISATION

While the 'Golden Era' of capitalism was primarily national, the last twenty years of the twentieth century saw a greatly increased trans-nationalisation of economic, political, social and cultural relations. This new era of globalisation is having a decisive impact on workers world-wide, though much of the flourishing globalisation literature seems to ignore workers on the whole. This chapter seeks not only to introduce some of the major parameters of globalisation but also to explore its limits and contradictions. A fundamental thesis is that workers and the workers' movement are, and will become, increasingly central to the new globalising capitalist order. Capitalism is being reconstructed but so also is the world of work and the organisations of workers. We examine in particular the increased flexibility and so-called 'feminis-ation' of the new global labour force. This chapter sets the scene for subsequent more detailed considerations of labour in the advanced capitalist countries and in the so-called developing countries after the collapse of the Golden Era and the emergence of the era of globalis-ation and the new labour internationalism for which it is creating the conditions.

BEYOND THE BUZZWORD

It is extremely difficult to cut through the hype surrounding the term 'globalisation' but we do need to go beyond the buzzword (Scholte, 2000). Globalisation, whether viewed as a panacea for the new century or demonised as the source of all our evils, has become the new 'common sense' for our era. In a relatively short period of time the term 'globalisation' has spread across academic disciplines, spawned multiple research centres and generated a vigorous counter-movement. It is a most labile term, fluid and slippery in its meaning and its political implications. As a starting point we could do worse than Paul Drache's only slightly tongue-in-cheek conclusion that 'The simple truth is that one-third of the globalisation narrative is over-sold, one-third we do not understand because it is a process unfolding and one-third is radically new' (Drache, 1999: 7). Globalisation appears as a new grand metanarrative, just as we are told that the metanarratives of labour and socialism are dead. It is presented in much of the academic literature – not to mention its popular outlets – as a homogeneous, irreversible and all-encompassing process. It can mean everything and anything, or nothing at all it seems at times. It is seen as somehow obvious, just 'out there', as though it emerged fully fledged through some form of unknown immaculate conception. Yet to deny its existence, denounce it as ideology and refuse to enter its confused discursive terrain would be a terrible mistake. So, I propose a brief review of its economic, political and social/cultural aspects, from a labour perspective.

The main debate at the economic level is whether the increased importance of the TNCs and of international trade represent an increased internationalisation of capitalism or the birth of a new globalism. For the globalists, we are moving into a borderless world (Ohmae, 1990) where the TNC rules supreme. This is seen as part of a secular process of international integration, viewed as part of the inevitable story of human progress as in 1960s' modernisation theory. This discourse is based on a very real internationalisation of production, financial and consumption flows since the 1970s. It also rests on the very real upsurge in investment by the TNCs that now, increasingly, do have a global remit. For Ohmae, these 'stateless' corporations are the genuine movers in the interlinked economies of the Triad, comprising the USA, the EU and Japan. The decision-making process of the TNC – and the inevitably sovereign 'consumer choice' – is seen by Ohmae to be at the heart of rational resource allocation at the international level. If the TNCs are able to shake off the antiquated restraints of the nation-state and its interfering bureaucrats, they can enter the brave new world of globalisation as 'knights of the road' on its electronic highways. This open and global economy is presented as the epitome of the 'level playing field' as against the particularism and biases of corporatism. It is the international market which, for Ohmae and his co-religionists, will provide economic co-ordination not only for development on a world scale but also for effective global mechanisms given its self-interest in policing itself. Ohmae's messianic vision is, of course, but another view of the nightmare presented by the anti-globalisation gurus (see Falk, 1999).

For those concerned to demystify the programmes and the politics of the globalists, Hirst and Thompson (1996) make a considered and, to some extent, persuasive case. Their overall conclusion is that 'the globalisation of production has been exaggerated: companies remain tethered to their home economies and are likely to remain so' (Hirst and Thompson, 1996: 17). Essentially, they would prefer us to stick with the title of multinational corporations (MNCs) rather than transnational corporations (TNCs), which implies a global rather than international capitalist enterprise. The quantitative data sets used in this debate are complex and undoubtedly subject to different interpretations. Yet the basic point is that international firms still have a 'home base' and are thus also subject to political control in that nation-state. There is a historic element to this debate too, with an argument that under the gold standard (up to the First World War) the advanced capitalist countries had less autonomy than they have today. It is important to note that for the anti-globalists or demystifiers such as Hirst and Thompson the main point of the debate is a political one. For these authors '"globalisation" is a myth suitable for a world without illusions but it also robs us of hope' (Hirst and Thompson, 1996). They are keen to undermine the 'globalisation excuse' used by governments such as Britain's New Labour as an alibi for not playing a more active role in taking social control over the global economy. International firms are not 'footloose and fancy free'; they are not above the law; and nation-states can and should take steps, individually and collectively, to seek regulation of the new economic order.

While it is important from a labour perspective to counter the view that 'there is no alternative' to globalisation, a 'business as usual' outlook might not be too realistic. It is probably necessary to relativise the role of the TNC or MNC, given the hype of the globalists and the 'bogeymen' image they have on the populist left. However, there is a danger that a purely quantitative reasoning (around investment, profit rates and so on) might obscure the qualitative changes that have occurred in the last decade or two. The whole issue of financial fluidity and the new type of capitalism it creates (see Soros, 1998, for an insider account) seems strangely understated. Furthermore, as David Held points out, correctly in my view,

> there is a fundamental difference between ... the development of particular trade routes ... or even the global reach of nineteenth-century empires, and ... an international order involving ... dense networks of regional and global economic relations which stretch beyond the control of any single state (Held, 1995: 20).

It also seems that 'globalisation' is used in a very economistic and reductionist manner by Hirst and Thompson and seemingly with little awareness, for example, of the burgeoning literature on cultural globalisation (e.g. Featherstone, 1990). At times it seems that globalisation acts as a surrogate for neo-liberalism, which would make more sense as a political target. While it is important to criticise the view of globalisation as a *Deus ex machina*, it cannot be wished away, and not recognising its one-third new and one-third unknown (see above) elements leaves labour ill-prepared for the future.

At the political level, the main debate in the globalisation literature is the extent to which internationalisation of the economy has led to a decline of the nation-state and its decision-making powers. For the globalists, the day of the nation-state has gone: 'The uncomfortable truth is that, in terms of the global economy, nation-states have become little more than bit actors' (Ohmae, 1990: 12). The nation-state, for Ohmae, is simply a 'nostalgic fiction' and it makes no sense to talk of Italy or China or even the USA in an era characterised by global capital flows. Even production is multinational and no one can tell where our cars, clothes or food have been produced. Nationalism, according to these globalisers, has become the refuge of the losers: 'we don't hear much about feverish words of Hong Kong nationalism, but the people in Hong Kong seem to live rather well' (Ohmae, 1990: 13). By contrast, the nationalisms of the ex-USSR states do not seem to put food on the table. Today's borderless economy is seen to have reconfigured the nation-state out of existence, following up the job which the 'footloose and fancy free' MNCs had begun in the 1970s. So-called national interest is seen as a flag of convenience for outmoded protectionist economic policies and also a total illusion in a knowledge-driven economy that does not require a national base. This is a strongly economistic set of arguments based squarely on the illusions of traditional modernisation and convergence theories, which ignored differences in wealth and power between nation-states and the social groups within them.

Contesting the 'death of the nation-state' thesis, Linda Weiss (1998) makes a number of important points. First of all, tendencies towards economic internationalisation do not mean that globalism has been achieved. One might also ask the pertinent question of whether globalisation would have materialised without the active designs of powerful nation-states and the consent of others. Second, as Weiss puts it, 'globalists tend to exaggerate state powers in the past in order to claim feebleness in the present' (Weiss, 1998: 13). The so-called Golden Era (see Chapter 2) was not characterised by omnipotent national states. Nor is the construction of national helplessness in the face of the cold winds of globalisation an innocent political act. Globalisation is, in short, a political ideology as much as a socio-economic phenomenon. Third, the globalists 'have not only over-stated the degree of state powerlessness. They have also *over-generalised* it' (Weiss, 1998: 16). Against the illusions of the convergence theorists, even the imperatives of globalisation have not led to a 'one best way' for capitalism to develop. Instead we have national capitalisms and differential state capacities to adjust to the demands of international competitiveness (see Berger and Dore, 1997). Linda Weiss even goes so far as to see national differences increasing rather than diminishing. It does seem unlikely that the nation-state changed suddenly from being a bulwark of national capitalism in the 1970s to being a mere transmission belt for global capitalism sometime in the 1980s. We may question, however, whether in demystifying the 'myth of the power-less state' the globalisation sceptics may not be ignoring some funda-mental transformations in the world order.

It would be sensible to assume that the contemporary nation-state is neither 'powerless' nor the same mythical body that national sover-eignty theory has assumed since the seventeenth century. Globalisation, along with the ending of the Cold War, has seen the development of a certain fluidity in international relations, if not the development of a fully multicentric world. Capital would appear to be more mobile across national boundaries than, say, fifty years ago, if not twenty years ago, but that does not mean that it is disembedded totally from national territories and their social and political systems. We do, though, see some moves towards a global polity, not on the syrupy-imperialist lines of 'We are the World' but in terms of shared problems. Whether it be human rights, the environment or 'security', we tend increasingly to think transnationally now, by necessity as much as by design. Labour is, at least potentially, a transnational social movement and its prospects, policies and politics are not determined solely at the level of the nation-state. We need to go beyond the binary opposition of 'for or against' the nation-state and recognise how complex and inter-connected all levels of politics are today. The nation-state, the national level at which most politics is conducted, seems certainly to be in transformation. As Held and co-authors concluded in their analysis of political globalisation, we are witnessing 'a shift away from a purely state-centric politics to a new more complex form of multi-layered global governance. There are multiple, overlapping political processes at work in the present historical conjuncture' (Held et al., 1999: 85).

If the economic and political debates around globalisation have too often been artificially polarised between the globalists and their de-mystifiers, this is less true in the cultural domain. In some ways this area has produced some of the most original and thought-provoking analysis of the present epoch. First of all, it is important to note the perception that while 'culture, as an arena differentiated from economics and politics, has never been totally globalised it has nevertheless shown a greater tendency towards globalisation than either of the other two arenas' (Waters, 1995: 124–5). One need only think of the universalising tendencies of religions in order to see some truth in this statement. And the so-called global culture of McDonald's and Coca-Cola gives it an even more contemporary ring. In some way, globalisation seems to mean simply or mainly this emergence of a global culture. As Jameson puts it, 'here what begins to infuse our thinking of globalisation is a picture of standardisation on an unparalleled new scale' (Jameson, 1998: 57). More specifically, we operate with an image of 'the world-wide Americanisation or standardisation of culture, the destruction of local differences, the massification of all the peoples on the planet' (Jameson, 1998: 57). From a labour perspective we can actually see a lot of truth in this image. Managers fly round the world accessing the same news media, stay at the same hotels, indulge in the same pastimes. Workers across the world live under the aegis of the same neo-liberal globalisation discourses, work under similar labour regimes characterised by 'flexibilisation', and often watch the same television programmes. Managers and workers alike live in the era of globalisation and are part of the communications revolution and the network society.

Yet culture means more than television; it alludes to the way we live our lives and understand our place in the world. In this sense, homogenisation is not the obvious result of globalisation at the cultural level. It is not a unified global culture that has emerged but, rather, a proliferation of difference, intermixing and syncretism. The unity of culture and social relations typical of modernity and the nation-state era has been sundered. Featherstone points us in this regard towards the dual process 'of cultural complexity and the increasing salience of culture in social life' (Featherstone, 1995: 12). To some extent this shift is part of our greater understanding of the post-colonial, though it also reflects what some people call postmodernism. From a labour perspective, it points us towards a more complex understanding of the world about us. Our postmodern globalised world cannot be reduced to a simple opposition between labour and capital. Arjun Appadurai usefully argues that 'The new global cultural economy has to be seen as a complex, overlapping disjunctive order that cannot any longer be understood in terms of centre–periphery models' (Appadurai, 1996: 32). This proviso would apply equally to spatial development theories, economic theories of surpluses and deficits, and neo-Marxist theories of producers and consumers. Our world is characterised by flows and complexity, a disorganised (rather than organised) capitalism, even by chaos, in the scientific sense. Labour strategies of transformation need to be cognisant of these new realities if they are not to do battle on a terrain already vacated by labour's opponents.

I believe that one of the main images we need to overcome in understanding the global dimension is the notion that the global is dynamic and fluid, whereas the local is embedded, static and tradition-bound. From this powerful image Manuel Castells derives the notion that capital and labour live in different places and times. While capital is global, exists in the space of flows and lives in the instant time of computerised networks, labour inhabits the local, exists in the 'space of places' and lives by the clock time of everyday life (Castells, 1996a: 475). While this image certainly reflects a strong element of what is going on around us, it is something of a binary opposition. Ash Amin has developed what is, for me, a more satisfying interpretation of globalisation 'in *relational* terms, as the interdependence and intermingling of global, distant and local logics, resulting in greater hybridisation and perforation of social, economic and political life' (Amin, 1997: 133). This more fluid conception of globalisation as something not just 'out there' but 'in here' too seems to owe a lot to the notion of hybridity developed in cultural studies, especially post-colonial studies. Its relational emphasis is also congruent with Marx's continuous emphasis on the capital–labour *relation* as against the worlds of business and workers taken in isolation. What our unpacking of the economic, political and social-cultural dimensions of globalisation points us towards, I believe, is a more open, multi-polar and, indeed, hybrid set of solutions to the problems posed for progressive social transformation by the era of globalisation.

LIMITS AND CONTRADICTIONS

Once we 'normalise' globalisation, and set it in context, it becomes easier to explore its limits and contradictions. In fact a second gener-ation of globalisation studies focuses explicitly on its limits (see Boyer and Drache, 1995), and after the debacle of WTO Seattle 1999 no one believes the new order to be invincible. It is interesting, in this regard, to revisit a polemic of a few years ago in an influential US foreign policy journal. Ethan Kapstein addressed the economic and political masters of globalisation in the theme of workers and the world econ-omy in terms explicitly derived from Karl Polanyi (Kapstein, 1996). Neo-liberalism is seen to have undermined the social compact struck between labour and capital in the West since the Second World War (see Chapter 2). The Polanyian theme is played out on a broad canvas with a recognition that the deep restructuring of the world economy and the unleashing of unbridled competition need to be balanced by sustained and widespread counter-measures. If globalisation was created by the great powers and the dominant economic states, it can also be controlled by them. Most interesting of all, Kapstein issues an explicit political warning to the Western states (whose position he compares to those during Weimar Germany), who 'dismiss mounting worker dissatisfaction ... and the plight of the unemployed and work-ing poor as compared with the unquestioned importance of a sound currency and balanced budget' (Kapstein, 1996: 37). As a sober call to capitalist lucidity this perspective was a timely one.

Yet the gurus of neo-liberalism were not in a mood to listen to his warnings. For Paul Krugman not only did Kapstein ignore the 'consensus' around what sound economic policy had to be today, but his policy recommendations were deemed to be 'mischievous' (Krugman, 1994: 164). Other counters to Kapstein in *Foreign Affairs* argued that globalisation was not really culpable, rather more of an 'innocent bystander'. Others felt that Kapstein had no need for pessimism given the dynamism of the new global economy and the old but dubious adage that 'a rising tide lifts all boats'. The most outspoken attack was from Hilary Barnes (Nordic Correspondent for *The Economist* and Copenhagen Correspondent for the *Financial Times*), for whom globalisation might be doing some harm to workers in the developed countries but for billions of workers in the developing world it was good news all round (Barnes, 1996). She went on to say that while full employment may be gone, social welfare was still around and so comprehensive 'that it is no longer a solution; it is the problem' (Barnes, 1996: 173). In case we did not get the message, we are told that reform 'requires more flexible labour markets and fewer privileges for trade unions.... Workers are not disaffected. They are mollycoddled' (Barnes, 1996: 174). Kapstein, in a response to his critics, reiterated the lessons in political economy which the generation of the 1930s had learnt from Keynes. While economics has become more sophisticated since then, it does not seem to have got wiser. Most European leaders (even conservative ones), however, know that 'beggar-thy-neighbour' economic policies can only lead to disaster.

An increasing number of writers from within the citadels of financial and political power are beginning to warn the architects of globalisation of what might politely be termed its side-effects. None is better qualified than George Soros to tell about the foibles of the financial system, speculating in which has made him not only very rich but someone who can cause governments to fall. Soros starts from the premiss that 'I want to prevent the global capitalist system from destroying itself' (Soros, 1998: xxvii). For Soros, the current state of affairs is not only unsound but unsustainable:

> Financial markets are inherently unstable and there are social needs that cannot be met by giving market forces free rein.... There is a widespread belief that markets are self-correcting and a global economy can flourish without any need for a global society. (Soros, 1998: xx)

Market fundamentalism is simply not an adequate vehicle to take global capitalism forward if it ignores these contradictions. The key issue for Soros is not market discipline but rather the social instability it causes. Practically echoing Polanyi, he calls for a reassertion of social control through collective decision-making and a foregrounding of the public interest. Of course, we can question whether Soros's utopia of an 'open society' is politically viable or even adequate to the task. But the point is that an influential insider from the world of global finance can so clearly articulate its failings.

From the heartlands of social democracy there are also new cries of warning. Thus Tyll Necker, head of the Association of German Industry, declares that 'globalisation leads to a pace of structural change that more and more people are unable to cope with. How can we steer this process in such a way that markets open up but change remains under control?' (cited in Martin and Schumann, 1998: 231). Thus even the beneficiaries of globalisation are beginning to wonder if things are beginning to spin out of control. The question asked is the one Polanyi dealt with, namely how can social control over market forces be ensured? From a broader, more 'global', perspective, Klaus Schwab, founder and president of the influential World Economic Forum at Davos, believes present trends are 'multiplying the human and social costs of the globalisation process to a level that tests the social fabric of the democracies in an unprecedented way' (cited in Martin and Schmann, 1998: 231). The social costs of globalisation simply cannot be withstood by the social fabric. Schwab, somewhat apocalyptically, sees a disruptive backlash emerging in what he perceives as a critical phase of the new world order. What is ultimately utopian in his vision is his call for the economic and political leaders of globalisation to demonstrate 'how the new global capitalism can function to the benefit of the majority and not only for corporate managers and investers' (cited in Martin and Schuman, 1998: 231). As with ex-President Clinton's concern at Seattle with the 'little guy', this seems a somewhat forlorn hope, naïve at best, cynical at worst.

What the above rather impressionistic perspectives point towards is a more balanced understanding of how contemporary capitalism works. Above all they lead us to contest the view of a rootless system beyond the control of society. It is now increasingly recognised that markets are not the ideal co-ordinating mechanism for high-tech industries in our societies. It is no coincidence that Francis Fukuyama, author of the apocalyptic immediate post-Cold War hit *The End of History* (1992), has more recently written a popular and influential treatise on *Trust* (1998). Complex production systems cannot be based exclusively on impersonal market mechanisms; they require individual and social trust. Roger Hollingsworth and Robert Boyer point out that 'Trust is an important lubricant in a capitalist economy.... As consumer demand becomes more diversified, technology more complex, and the economy more centralised, there is potentially more uncertainty among actors and therefore trust may evade' (Hollingsworth and Boyer, 1996: 24). Yet only high degrees of trust can sustain the complex systems of production which the new capitalism is creating. Flexible specialisation requires co-ordination and co-operation between economic actors. The politics of sustainable economic growth also increasingly calls for co-operation or 'concertation' between the various social 'partners' in the development enterprise. These partners may even include the unemployed, women's organisations and consumer groups representing interests usually ignored in the traditional pre-globalisation corporatist structures.

One of the main themes in critical analysis of contemporary capitalism is the necessary social 'embeddedness' of its institutions. There has now been a swing against the conception of TNCs as 'footloose and fancy free' which stresses precisely how they are embedded in social and political relations. The governance of large firms is now understood to include 'traditional' family ties as well as regional and even feudal links. As Boyer and Hollingsworth argue, 'the social embeddedness of relationships in capitalist societies permits actors to circumvent the limits of pure rationality and the interaction of anonymous markets' (Boyer and Hollingsworth, 1996: 451). Even a good economic performance, if it is to be sustainable, requires a favourable social setting and an enabling political environment. National economic institutions must, however, also be part of a more complex regional and international mode of regulation of capitalism. In that vein, Boyer and Hollingsworth argue for a shift from the post-Second World War pattern of embeddedness of national institutions, 'with the present *nestedness* of major institutions which is a complex intertwining at all levels of the world, from the global arena to the regional level, also including such continental entities such as NAFTA and the European Union' (Boyer and Hollingsworth, 1996: 470). Its main characteristic is its multi-polar nature with no single level self-sufficient. These variable configurations are typical of the more fluid patterns that globalisation is creating in terms of economic development and governance.

A perspective based on social embeddedness, in many ways following the tradition of Polanyi, also allows us to see the variations in governance systems possible in the global era. In the international arena it is not just capital units which confront one another but whole social systems of production. Convergence has not occurred under globalisation any more than it did in the 1950s in the era of modernisation. There are national capitalist paths and forms of governance where the role of labour varies markedly. Hollingsworth and Boyer note perceptively that 'economic competition is increasingly becoming competition over different forms of social systems of production, and competitive pressures for better economic performance are more and more often translated into pressures for broad societal change' (Hollingsworth and Boyer, 1996: 38). So what is competing is not capital but capitalist social systems. This throws new light on the role of labour that can now be seen as more central to the concerns of capital. There is certainly scope for arguments to situate global competition in this way. In these terms, a 'race to the bottom' in relation to labour conditions is not the only or even the most rational response, and gearing up the social system of production to take the 'high road' of high productivity and good wages in a co-operative environment is perfectly plausible.

It is important, finally, to recognise that globalisation may not be uniformly negative for democratic political and social forces. Agnew and Corbridge argue that 'Globalisation is not only a synonym for disempowerment: it creates conditions for democratisation, decentralisation and empowerment as well as for centralisation and standardisation. Globalisation opens as many doors as it shuts' (Agnew and Corbridge, 1995: 219). Globalisation has led to, or at least accompanied, a certain degree of decentralisation of production and work methods. Politically it has tended to 'hollow out' the national state and, perhaps, made it more porous regarding social initiatives. At the cultural level it is now accepted that globalisation has not led to standardisation (or Americanisation) but, rather, has created multi-faceted, polydirectional and hybrid flows and cultural formations. It can thus plausibly be said that globalisation may 'open doors' or create the conditions for a new wave of social advance. For a long time now the responses to globalisation have opposed total acceptance with total rejection. However, it is now recognised, as Linda Weiss points out, that 'neither resignation nor resistance define the real range of options' (Weiss, 1999: 127), which include a whole series of institutional reforms and policy actions. Globalisation can be 'managed', as Weiss points out, but it can also be controlled socially, as an analysis building on that of Karl Polanyi would show. Globalisation is still subject to the demands of governance, for its own survival apart from anything else, as we have seen above.

In the world of labour, the positive potential of globalisation has not been missed. Thus SID, in a bold new trade-union manifesto, declare that 'The time has come for trade unions to use the positive sides of globalisation to the advantage of workers and poor people all over the world' (SID, 1997: 23). The question of will or agency is usually ignored in analyses of globalisation, but here a major trade union says simply that 'It is time to change our own defensive attitude' and go on the offensive both nationally and internationally. Some of the positive aspects of globalisation detailed include the effects of the ICT revolution in terms of providing workers and unions with instant information from around the world. It is not just that information has become more accessible; it is also that 'There is more transparency, monitoring and control of what is happening around the globe than ever before' (SID, 1997: 29). The ICT revolution can be seen to create, to some extent and not of course always, a new democratic equivalent allowing for better international communications, technically, socially and politically. Thus, for example, we have the emergence of the political or ethical consumer keen to support moves to make MNCs respect basic human rights and environmental norms.

This section has forced us to reconsider the way we view globalisation as a context for work and workers in the twenty-first century. We need to reject totalising and messianic views of its implications. For too long radical political economy has tended to reify what we call globalisation and ascribe to it a logic and coherence it simply does not have. This way of thinking of globalisation makes it very difficult to 'think' an alternative to it or imagine another future and work towards it. Its perpetrators remain anonymous – as though some blind or mystical force just created globalisation one day – and the whole world becomes its passive victims. In a telling parallel reading of the globalisation and rape 'scripts', Gibson-Graham explains how we might 'read' globalisation:

> as a scripted series of steps and signals ... attempting to place regions, workforces and governments in positions of passivity and victimisations and being met by a range of responses – some of which play into the standard script and others that don't. (Gibson-Graham, 1996: 132–3)

Workers who 'buy into' the globalisation message and 'progressive' national governments which automatically accept its hegemony are thus part of the standard script. The protestors who, from a whole range of social and political standpoints, contested the nostrums of free trade at Seattle in 1999 were definitely not part of this script. Workers who do not prioritise an alliance with business in their nation, region or city, and instead carve out social and political alliances with other workers, community groups and consumer organisations, are equally not part of the plot as written by the powerful but contestable agents of globalisation.

LABOUR CENTRE STAGE

As Marx once said,

> Let us ... in company with the owner of money and the owner of labour-power, leave this noisy sphere, where everything takes place on the surface and in full view of everyone, and follow them into the hidden abode of production on whose threshold hangs the notice 'No admittance except on business'. (Marx, 1976: 279–80)

In the market the sphere of circulation, the free-trade ethos and formal equality rule supreme: 'It is the exclusive realm of Freedom, Equality, Property and Bentham' (Marx, 1976: 280). But the secret of profit-making lies in that hidden abode of production where the capital/wage-labour relation works itself out. Today, in the era of globalisation, as much as in Marx's time, production is at the heart of social and economic development. Financial fluidity and e-commerce notwithstanding, down-to-earth people still work. The death of the working class, the end of work, and so on, are slogans that have come and gone. The transformations wrought by globalisation may have reconfigured the world of production but they have not done away with it. So, labour is centre stage in terms of the dynamic of contemporary society, and the labour movement has also gone through a reconfiguration which at least leaves it with the possibility of impacting on the future trajectories of globalisation.

With regard to the effect of globalisation on labour we could do worse than begin with the World Bank's authoritative 1995 report *Workers in an Integrating World* (World Bank, 1995). The World Bank notes, with undisguised glee, that by the end of the century less than 10 per cent of the world's workers would not be fully integrated into the global capitalist economy, compared to the one-third of the global workforce which twenty years ago was told it was building socialism. The driving forces of global integration are seen as unstoppable by the World Bank, and the world's workers have no option but to submit. Or, in the World Bank's own words, 'Globalisation is unavoidable – the welfare of Joe, Maria and Xiao Zhin is now more closely linked than ever before' (World Bank, 1995: 54). These 'representative' workers are seen to face risks, but deeper international integration (i.e. globalisation) is seen to hold positive prospects 'for those countries and groups of workers with the capacity to respond' (World Bank, 1995: 188). Of course, the Bank acknowledges that increasing international competition and 'freewheeling' capital will not only cut jobs and wages but will, effectively, wipe whole nations and regions off the economic map. It understands that the scenario of workers' fortunes worldwide converging is less likely than growing divergence. In brief, according to the World Bank, 'Globalisation offers opportunities but also exacerbates risks' (World Bank, 1995: 124). This may well serve as a watchword (and possibly the epitaph) for a new era of global capitalist expansion. The World Bank makes optimistic noises about workers' fortunes but, at the end of the day, holds out few prospects.

Perhaps one of the more interesting asides in the World Bank report is the argument that 'the lives of urban workers in different parts of the world are increasingly intertwined' (World Bank, 1995: 1). There is rapid change underway in the global political economy: 'revolutionary times' says the World Bank. For workers it means many things; not all of it is positive, but it has created an objective community of fate, in so far as workers' futures in different parts of the world are becoming more integrated. There are also, against dire predictions of the 'end of work' in the era of computers, more workers entering the labour market. As Castells points out, 'Workers do not disappear in the space of flows and down to earth, work is plentiful' (Castells, 1996a: 474). Indeed, it is calculated that the world's workforce doubled in the last three decades of the twentieth century. So work is expanding and so are the working classes. This labour force, increasingly integrated by the internationalising tendencies of globalisation, is also changing its centre of gravity. It is calculated that fully 99 per cent of the workers projected to join the workforce in the next three decades will be in the low- and middle-income countries (World Bank, 1995: 7). It is the maelstrom of development of the capital/wage-labour relation that is generating what truly might be called a second 'Great Transformation'.

The World Bank paints a largely realistic picture of the transformations that are occurring in the world of work worldwide. However, it clearly and expectedly takes for granted that things will continue as they are. While concerned with the 'downside' of globalisation and arguing for a stronger role for the state than desired by market fundamentalists, the projection of globalising trends is seen as inevitable. After Seattle 1999 we cannot be so sure that this will, indeed, be the case. As Diane Elson (1996) notes, the World Bank view of globalisation suffers from technological fetishism (technology as the driver of globalisation), the invisibility of capital (not seeing how capital drives this process), and the 'fallacy of composition' (the belief that all countries would have benefited had they decided early on to take advantage of the opportunity). What are then seen as 'transitional costs' for workers adjusting to the new global order may well become permanent costs because the World Bank simply assumes that it will all work out for the best in the end. The negative effects of globalisation, actually built into the process and not just potential risks, are largely ignored by the World Bank. We see in fact that globalisation is creating an increasing level of social exclusion. The World Bank report is even behind the times in not recognising the need for better international co-ordination and regulation of market mechanisms. The series of international capitalist crises since this report was issued is ample testimony to the continued validity of Polanyi's perspective regarding social regulation of the market.

A logical question to ask following the World Bank report on workers worldwide is whether a global labour market is now emerging. For some commentators the world has become a huge labour bazaar where states offer 'their' labour forces at ever lower rates. The increasing demands of international competitiveness have made workers prime cost-cutting candidates. Workforces are offered up to the international capitalist as educated, pliable and compliant 'social capital'. Labour is thus now truly a global resource; however, as Castells notes, 'labour markets are not truly global, except for a small but growing segment of professionals and scientists' (Castells, 1998: 93). The increased mobility of labour through migration has definite limits. The computer communications specialist is not as mobile as the Indian homeworker or the African rural labourer. Our conclusion has to be two-sided, I believe. On the one hand, capital now has a global perspective and its dominant fractions are integrated internationally. Their view of labour is as a global resource. On the other hand, we must reject sensationalist accounts of a global labour market/bazaar. In the developing countries it is only something like 15 per cent of the workforce which is engaged in the production of tradable 'modern sector' goods. For most workers the national, even the local, labour market is more important still.

The globalisation debates, if they have done nothing else, have forced the social sciences to take on board the spatial dimension. If space is where capital is constructing its brave new world, it is in place that labour lives and constructs its social relations. As Jamie Peck argues, there is a growing move towards reducing place to space: 'Places to live seem increasingly to be reduced to spaces in which to earn, or strive to earn a wage' (Peck, 1996: 233). Global competition, neo-liberalism and structural adjustment programmes are constantly eroding labour's bargaining strength. Deregulation, in all its multiple facets, is exposing labour to this new capitalist onslaught. The point, however, as Peck stresses, is that 'This does not mean that place – as a theoretical category or as a political site – somehow matters less, but is rather to insist on an appreciation of the local in the context of (and in relation to) the global' (Peck, 1996: 233). Workers still live in Buenos Aires, Bombay and Birmingham; they work in these places and their aspirations are in relation to these places. Globalisation is not just 'out there' in cyberspace but exists, operates and is contested in these local places. Globalisation has prompted new identities, and new interests within local, political processes. Local politics in the global era has not been shut down; rather, it has been transformed and in many ways reinvigorated by the multiple identities and fluid processes of the current era.

The problem with most of the literature on labour and globalisation is that it tends to conceive of labour as passive victim of the new trends, the malleable material from which globalisation will construct its new world order. Capital is seen as an active, mobile, forward-looking player in the globalisation game while labour is seen as static, passive and basically reactive. The game has changed and labour is seen to have few cards. Only rarely will someone point out, as Andrew Herod does, that 'workers and unions have been actively involved in shaping the processes of globalisation ... both by modifying the impacts of capital's activities and by shaping internationally the very possibilities for these activities' (Herod, 1998: 40). The reality is that labour has been back centre stage since the mid-1990s at least. General strikes have occurred in many parts of Europe, in Latin America, in Canada, in South Africa and, most crucially, in South Korea. The disorienting changes suffered by the labour movement in the first decade of globalisation seem, at least in part, to have been overcome. Change was a slow but organic process, often initiated by the middle ranks. As Kim Moody recounts, 'The unions took on new roles: as champions of the interests of the working class as a whole, not just as representatives of their members, and as political surrogates for failed parties of the left' (Moody, 1997: 14). I am not suggesting that this process is universal – it is clearly uneven; nor that it is irreversible. However, we need to view the new-found interest of the ICFTU in international labour solidarity in this light and not just assume that it is a cynical exercise in political correctness (see Chapter 7).

We increasingly find trade unions worldwide moving beyond the factory gates and breaking with a narrow, economistic conception of trade unionism. As DeMartino argues, in relation to the USA, there was once a powerful left workerist orthodoxy which 'grants privileged status to workers in an enterprise, they alone are empowered to determine when and how to struggle, and for what' (DeMartino, 1991: 116). The broader community could express its 'solidarity' when called upon, but could not interfere with union 'autonomy'. Today it is widely recognised in labour circles that unions are not simply about defending workers' rights at the place of work, and the artificial barriers between workplace and community are not so impregnable. After all, workers are gendered, they are citizens and they are consumers too. Often unions become 'populist' campaigning organisations, from South Africa to Poland to the USA, with a fluid view of how to pursue their struggle under contemporary capitalism. The emerging social-movement unionism is an active, community-oriented strategy which works with a broad conception of who the working people are. It breaks down the binary oppositions between workplace and community, economic and political struggles, and between formal-sector workers and the working poor. When workers adopt this orientation they often find allies among the 'new' social movements and, in particular, in NGOs. The ICFTU campaign against child labour with its broad alliance strategy, including active collaboration with the relevant NGOs, is in its own way a reflection of the growing power of social-movement unionism in the trade-union imaginary. The clearly perceived diminishing returns of 'business as usual' strategies lead even sectarian and bureaucratic trade-union leaderships in the direction of social-movement unionism.

It is always wise to take a long-term perspective on labour, especially in its conflicted relation with capital. Arrighi makes the useful point that there has always historically been a considerable time lag in terms of labour's response to capital's restructuring (Arrighi, 1996). Looking back to the previous period of global financial expansion in the late nineteenth century, Arrighi finds that there were twenty-five years of organisational instability with more defeats than victories, and then it took another twenty-five years 'before the ideological and organisational contours of the world labour movement became powerful enough to impose some of its objectives on world capitalism' (Arrighi, 1996: 348). We can now expect that due to the current condition of 'time–space compression' the labour revival this time will not take fifty years to materialise. Indeed, the signs of this revival are already there to be seen; it is more a question of when and how, not whether, it will take place. What is also clear is that this new labour movement will be much influenced by the example of the 'new' social movements that have come to the fore over the last twenty years. In that sense labour will be increasingly a social movement once again. Current labour activity worldwide is no longer confined to desperate rearguard actions against neo-liberalism, as was the case in the 1980s and early 1990s. While still weakened by the ravages of the last twenty years, the international labour movement has begun a process of recomposition. The first reactions of fear and insecurity in the face of the forces unleashed by globalisation have given way to a more settled and confident mood.

MATTERS ARISING

Many issues are opened up by the analysis above, but I prefer here to concentrate on three 'global' issues, leaving more particular matters for the next chapters on workers North (Chapter 5) and workers South (Chapter 6). The first of these overarching issues is that of labour standards and the social clause; the other two are the 'feminisation' and the 'flexibilisation' of labour under globalisation. The practical link between international trade and core labour standards predates even the foundation of the ILO in 1919. The ILO constitution, however, made it explicit and referred to how 'the failure of any nation to adapt humane conditions of labour is an obstacle in the way of the nations which desire to improve the conditions in their own countries'. Motives of social justice were probably 'overdetermined' by a wish to put war and unrest behind and to reduce 'social dumping' in the new post-war international order. The core labour standards the ILO was to promote included the freedom of association, the right to collective bargaining, nondiscrimination in employment and the prohibition of forced labour. For many decades lip service was paid to these basic human rights, but, as the era of national capitalism gave way to the new global capitalism, relationships between trade and labour standards were to come to the fore again. Political alliances were to be formed for and against this linkage; labour movements were sometimes split, with their relationships with the social movements becoming fraught at times.

It is sometimes forgotten that the International Trade Organisation (ITO) developed the Havana Charter in 1948 with quite ambitious social and labour clauses. It successor, the General Agreement on Tariffs and Trade (GATT) charter, also contains labour standards clauses with sanctions provisions, at least in theory. It was, however, at the Uruguay Round of GATT that the notion of a social clause came to the fore. The International Trade Secretariats (ITSs), in particular in the International Metalworkers' Federation, had been calling for a social clause since the mid-1970s. Some governments, such as that of the USA, supported the move, but the mood was on the whole against it in capitalist circles. So, as Denis McShane noted, 'The Uruguay Round of GATT was signed without a social clause, and progress in that direction has been put on hold for the moment' (McShane, 1996: 9). Not for long, though: in the lead-up to the 1999 gathering of the WTO, the GATT's successor, the 'social clause', as it became known, was a key issue. The US government and most Western European social-democratic governments supported moves towards a 'social clause', which was strongly promoted by the ICFTU and most international trade unions. However, there was a coalition of interests against the 'social clause', including neo-liberal states in Australia, authoritarian states like Indonesia and Malaysia, and more traditionally anti-imperialist states such as India. The argument against the social clause, supported by quite a few developing-country trade unions, was that it represented a hidden form of protectionism to the benefit of the industrialised countries and against developing economies.

The arguments in favour of the 'social clause' are quite straightforward. At one level it is simply the case that workers' rights are human rights and thus universal. There is also an efficiency argument to add to the equity one: 'When companies in the developing world need to develop high productivity, flexible production systems, they are unlikely to do so with oppressive labour relations and no worker representation' (McShane, 1996: 17). In a general sense we can argue that development and democracy go hand in hand. It is partnerships between employers and trade unions that have led to increases in productivity and the introduction of high technology. Yet this case does not answer the charge that the 'social clause' is a protectionist measure by Northern governments and their trade-union protégés, keen to stem the 'flow of jobs' to the South. There is a conservative case against the 'social clause', made by those such as Malaysia's prime minister, Mahathir Mohammed, who denounce it as 'imperialist' and defend an 'Asian exceptionalism' which does not require trade unions. There is, however, a progressive argument against the 'social clause' as it stands, for example from the Third World Network (TWN), a coalition of NGOs, and from many trade unions in India. They raise the quite persuasive objection that the WTO (not to mention the IMF and the World Bank) is not the body to defend the poor of the developing world. These bodies are so tied to Northern imperialist interests that they should not be encouraged to spread their powers to other areas, even if they are labour standards everyone is in favour of. When we saw President Clinton at the Seattle WTO meeting in 1999 waxing lyrical about the evils of child labour this angle became clearer.

While, ultimately, the arguments for and against the 'social clause' will be resolved in practice, we can still seek to clarify what is at stake. Too often the debate is posed in stark oppositional terms. But it would, for example, make a world of difference if the 'social clause' were to be applied to companies rather than to countries, as current debates assume. An underlying point here is that some developing countries already have considerable labour rights in theory. The campaign to have MNCs adopt 'codes of conduct' has taken up this strategy of targeting the real agents of exploitation with a view to 'punishing' locally any transgressions of global codes of conduct. In the debates within the labour movement of India there are a whole range of positions taken and interests being represented. These cannot for one moment be equated with the interests of a Third World government to maintain low wages and poor working conditions. With multiple social interests at stake it is inevitable that there will be multiple strategies, but there is no reason why these cannot be reconciled within the broad parameters of the labour/social movement milieu. North–South divides are as important as those between employers and workers, equity arguments are as valid as the rights discourse underlying the 'social clause' campaign. From a social-movement perspective informed by the transformation wrought by globalisation, it is also clear that links between local communities across the globe are equally as much a part of internationalism (to say the least) as is the ICFTU. On specific issues, such as the campaign against child labour, some of those links were made in practice.

If the 'social clause' is the main political issue at stake for labour in the era of globalisation, for capital the main issue over the last decade has undoubtedly been the so-called 'flexibilisation' of labour. The dominant theme is that labour flexibility leads to economic growth, which in turn creates more jobs. According to the OECD the flexibility of labour takes five main forms:

1. External numerical flexibility – number of employees adjusted in accordance with employers' needs.
2. Externalisation – part of the firm's work is put out through subcontracting.
3. Internal numerical flexibility – working hours and their 'delivery' adjusted according to employers' needs.
4. Functional flexibility – workers' jobs modified according to employers' needs.
5. Wages flexibility – labour's reward according to productivity and market conditions (cited in Van Dijk, 1995: 223–4).

If we added spatial or geographical flexibility we would have a fairly comprehensive picture of the model worker at the end of the twentieth century. Flexibility, in its multiple but interrelated guises, is probably the defining characteristic of labour in the era of international competitiveness. The drive towards labour flexibility – which is a global one, albeit taking different forms given the particular national forms of embeddedness of the labour market – is spelling smaller workforces, fewer rules in the workplace, weaker unions and wages being tied to the business cycle (see Lagos, 1994, and Pollert, 1998, for Southern and Northern perspectives, respectively).

There are, of course, alternative routes to labour flexibility and it can take different characteristics. For example, Robert Boyer (1988) has distinguished between offensive and defensive flexibility:

> the latter is introduced as a means of coping with the unpredictability of economic crisis but is not, necessarily, a means to overcome the crisis itself. On the other hand, offensive flexibility is a more concerted long-term perspective (for example, that launched by the EU to cope with the perceived rigidities described by the term 'Eurosclerosis') which would combine technological modernisation with social progress both within firms and globally. (Boyer, 1988: 25)

We can also distinguish between a subordinated and a co-operative source of labour flexibility (e.g. Standing, 1992). The first route implies a unilateral move usually explicitly directed against labour, typical of many developing countries (and in the developed capitalist economies). It is also possible, however, for there to exist a co-operative route to flexibility where certain labour gains may occur. Labour flexibility, if agreed consensually with workers and their unions, can lead to more flexible working traits. The rhetoric of flexibility is dominated by the ethos of deregulation, but if we take a broader view, conscious of the fact that the Fordist model is exhausted (see Chapter 2), we can see to what extent flexibility also calls for a process of re-regulation of the labour market if it is to be sustainable.

Labour flexibility is a social process but it is also a discourse, a contested political terrain. As such it exemplifies the importance in the 'era of globalisation' of critically examining, deconstructing perhaps, the dominant discourses of work. If flexibility is read simply as deregulation then its negative effects will inevitably prevail. But it is possible to see the drawbacks of this implementation not only in equity terms but also in terms of efficiency. What may be good for the firm (at least in the short term) may not be good for the national economy. Then, in terms of global economic growth – the mantra of the competitiveness advocates – there could also be a contraction of world demand if this policy is followed unilaterally. As Boyer puts it, 'In a nutshell, the pursuit of flexibility, a rational response to the crisis, may actually exacerbate it, by undermining international trade' (Boyer, 1988: 251). The increase in more precarious forms of employment is an obstacle to increased productivity as well, of course. A consensual or 'concertation' approach to labour flexibility would not be based on the assumption of labour market rigidities. Instead, it would focus on growth, but also on better levels of education and training for workers. Above all, it would develop new forms of regulation as required by the new internationalised production systems and the more flexible labour markets that have developed. Effective production restructuring and innovative forms of competitive advantage have usually emerged in situations where trade unions are strong and labour is treated as a human resource and not just another cost to be cut.

Related to the 'flexibilisation' debate is that around the 'feminisation' of labour, which could potentially have the most far-reaching social consequences. Throughout the 1970s and 1980s there was a marked increase in the number of women entering paid formal employment in many regions. Most noticeable was the upsurge in female employment in the electronics industries of South Asia, Mexico and other regions, entering the 'new international division of labour' (see Chapter 5). In the 1990s we saw the development of a theme encapsulated by Guy Standing as 'global feminisation through flexible labour' (Standing, 1989, 1999a). With deregulation, the retreat of the state from economic affairs, and 'flexibility' as the new watchword in labour relations, we could expect a shift in gender patterns of employment. Standing found that overall, 'With many more women continuously in the labour force or finding it easier to move in and out of it, or combining labour force and other work, more women are remaining in the labour force until a later age' (Standing, 1999a: 588). What was noticeable was that these tendencies increased in the 1990s as export-led industrialisation gave way to a more profound internationalisation. To some extent the apparent increase in female participation in the paid workforce reflects a decrease in male rates of employment, especially in the formal sector due to the process of 'informalisation (see Chapter 5). This tendency towards 'feminisation' cannot be seen as irreversible but it does appear to be a major aspect of globalisation.

Yet the 'feminisation' of global labour thesis is by no means unproblematic. In the first place, the term seems to conflate increased participation by women in the paid labour force with informalisation and other forms of destructuring of labour under late capitalism. In Standing's own use of the term he refers to how 'the type of work, labour relations, income and insecurity associated with 'women's work' have been spreading, resulting ... [in] a transformation – or feminisation – of many jobs traditionally held by men' (Standing, 1989: 1077). Yet what constitutes 'women's work' is socially constructed and varies across societies. Nor is it clear on the evidence that women's share of employment in traditionally 'female' sectors such as textiles has actually been increasing; to the contrary. In that much-vaunted female employer, the electronics industry, trends in the 1970s have since been reversed, with women losing jobs faster than men on the whole. Diane Elson's persuasive conclusion is that 'The gender division of labour, which tends to confine women to relatively subordinate and inferior positions in the organisation of monetised production, is not overridden by "flexibilisation"' (Elson, 1996: 40). Indeed, it tends to set the parameters of how 'flexibility' operates in a gendered fashion. What is also gendered is the 'take' on 'flexible' modes of production, where women have been able to carve out some advantages while men tend to view them as uniformly deleterious.

We must always remember that women make up approximately 80 per cent of homeworkers worldwide, according the ILO. In this sense flexibilisation and feminisation are nothing new. This 'hidden' workforce also highlights the problems with traditional trade-union notions centred around the male worker in a factory and the 'family wage'. The linkages which have occurred in many developing countries between factory workers, homeworking campaigning groups and women's organisations are now occurring at the international level. This has even moved beyond networking and information exchange to organise concerted activities – for example, in the Women Working Worldwide campaign (see www.poptel.org.uk/women-ww). The processes of global restructuring of labour that are occurring have created the need (but also the opportunity) for what Chhachhi and Pittin refer to as strategies and policies which are 'multi-faceted, utilising interlocking industrial, economic and political structures and processes' (Chhachhi and Pittin, 1996: 21). One could also add the cultural dimensions to get the full picture of multivalency which now characterises labour responses to globalisation at their most progressive or transformative. The link between workplace, household and community has become most clear in relation to research and action around women's work worldwide. The creative forms of organisation, the refusal of binary oppositions (e.g. reform or revolution) and the links with other social movements may well be characteristics that will spread.

FOUR

WORKERS NORTH

The workers of the economic North had already begun to suffer under neo-liberalism, but the new era of globalisation reduced Fordism to an almost mythical Golden Era. Under the guise of 'flexible specialisation', new work practices almost completely transformed the world of work. This chapter begins by examining the new model of flexible finance-oriented capitalist development. We also survey the newly important dimension of regionalisation, both in North America and in Western Europe, that seems to go hand in hand with globalisation. The key issue this chapter then addresses is whether in the North we now have a stable post-Fordist social regime of accumulation. Is there a new virtuous circle of capitalist growth and worker prosperity emerging in the capitalist heartlands? What are the implications of bringing the workers of the once-socialist East into the capitalist orbit? Finally, what has been the trade-union reaction to the new capitalism? We hypothesise that, after an era of disorientation, disorganisation and demoralisation during the 1980s, some new patterns of worker resistance emerged towards the end of the last century.

FLEXIBLE FINANCIAL CAPITALISM

The new growth regime that followed the collapse of the Fordist Golden Era was to be characterised, above all, by the dominance of finance capital. Whereas under the Fordist regulation model (see Chapter 2) national governments to a large extent determined financial matters, now this latter domain seemed to acquire a life of its own. The opening of financial markets across the West in the 1980s set up a contradiction between an unregulated global financial system and the fiscal role of the Keynesian welfare state. The booming of the stock markets and the credit systems in the 1990s created a widespread mood of optimism about the future of capitalism. The 'new economy', as it became known, would sweep away all that, and that included trade unions, and generate a new knowledge-based society. That trade unions might be seen to be part of the 'old economy' is testified to by the fact that in Britain in 2000, while the average age of all workers was 34 years, the average age of trade-union members was 46 years. It was only slowly that the trade unions would realise that the new economy and the 'imperialism of finance' (Tabb, 1999) would necessitate new strategies, tactics and, indeed, mind-sets.

If finance ruled in the 'new economy', the term 'flexibility' came to dominate the labour market and the labour process. The discourse of labour 'flexibility' dominated throughout the 1980s and into the 1990s. Poor economic performance in the West, particularly in Western Europe, was blamed on labour 'rigidity' in terms of wages, labour conditions and constraints on capital imposed by trade unions. Flexibility became synonymous with dynamic change, and an ability to adapt to pressures and incentives. It did not appear to be either socially or economically desirable to argue for the opposite of 'flexibility'. What the much-vaunted strategy actually entailed was a reduction in wages ('labour costs flexibility'), a reduction in the number of workers ('numerical flexibility'), and an increase in the number of tasks the remaining workers had to perform ('functional flexibility'). Overall, across the North the 'flexibility' offensive had created by the end of the 1990s a workforce which was much more insecure and had seen many of the welfare rights gained under Fordism wiped away.

The transition to the 'new economy' cannot, however, be seen as a panacea for capitalism. After all, economists and capitalists also thought that the Golden Age (Chapter 2) would last indefinitely. Yet the virtuous circle of Fordism turned vicious as internationalisation of production put pressure on wages, which in turn impacted on consumption. To some extent, the 'new economy' of flexible-financial capital can be seen as a response to this crisis; it may well not be a stable new regime of accumulation. Tickell and Peck argue that the restoration of sustainable economic growth had not occurred by the late 1990s and that 'the search for a new institutional fix continues' (Tickell and Peck, 1995: 373). From this perspective, neo-liberal globalisation can be seen as 'a symptom of continuing political-economic disorder' (Tickell and Peck, 1995: 375) rather than a harbinger of a new order. In particular, there is nothing to suggest, especially after the debacle of the 1999 Seattle WTO ministerial meeting, that stability of the capitalist order can be achieved without setting up an acceptable global regulatory order.

An assumption running through most of the debates and polemics around globalisation and the new financial capitalism is that national economic policy-making is now ruled out. If that was to be the case, national governments would be simply pawns in the big game of globalisation, and workers organisations would be bereft of strategies at the national level. The TNCs are seen to be 'footloose and fancy-free', roaming the world for the best locations. Increasingly globalised markets are seen to lead to the logical corollary of open world labour markets. Thus an influential article on 'Global Work Force 2000' in the *Harvard Business Review* (Johnston, 1991) argued that 'The global-isation of labor is inevitable.... As labor gradually becomes inter-national, some national differences will fade' (Johnston, 1991: 126). With capital globally mobile and labour rapidly becoming so, the role of the nation-state in regulating capital, labour or the capital/wage-labour relation obviously fades away. That there are tendencies in this direction seems clear enough, but it is also the case that they can (and do) simply serve as an alibi for national governments that want to 'go with the flow' of globalisation.

Now that the first wave of globalisation has passed it is less plausible to see the irreversible decline of the nation-state as due to exogenous technological changes. To a large extent the portrayal of the nation-state as anachronistic has been part of the disempowering rhetoric of globalisation. From this perspective, as Bienefeld puts it, 'Globalisation is treated as beneficial and inevitable, [while] demands for national sovereignty are dismissed as misguided and foolish' (Bienefeld, 1994: 415). The optimism, arrogance and ahistorical blindness of the globalis-ers have given rise to a counter-movement of progressives calling for a return to nation-state hegemony and a reaffirmation of sovereignty (and even of protectionism). Apart from Bienefeld himself, the most articulate case comes from Paul Hirst and Grahame Thompson, who not only argue, with considerable statistical support, that the globalis-ation of production has been exaggerated but also suggest that 'far from being undermined by the processes of internationalisation, these processes strengthen the importance of the nation-state in many ways' (Hirst and Thompson, 1996: 17).

It is not a question of steering a middle course between the 'globalisers' and the 'nation-staters', I believe. As with development theory more generally, there is always an interplay – or 'dialectic', if you will – between internal and external factors in explaining employment patterns and inequality trends. The answer is never simple, as Andrew Glyn shows in a careful statistical analysis of 'internal and external constraints on egalitarian policies' (Glyn, 1999). Certainly no one should ignore national histories, modalities of class struggle, and responsibilities of national governments. The regulation school analysis of the Fordist era always stressed national trajectories, and in development theory this led to a healthy 'internal causation' reaction against dependency theory. However, under the regime of flexible financial capitalism the space for different 'models' has diminished. As Chesnais puts it, in a recent restatement of the regulation approach,

> The modalities of integration into the international system of the globalised regime of accumulation with financial predominance [our flexible financial capitalism] are both infinitely more constraining and more homogenising that they were in the Fordist accumulation mode. (Chesnais, 1997: 297)

Another underlying assumption of, for example, the 1999 Seattle protests against the WTO is that globalisation will lead to a 'race to the bottom' in terms of labour standards. While the globalisation optimists were predicting an equalisation upwards of wages across the world (as predicted by the Heckscher–Ohlin model of international trade), the sceptics were predicting a 'bargaining down' by national governments and the spread of 'social dumping'. With competitiveness the watchword across the world, cost-minimisation strategies by businesses are bound to have an effect on labour. However, as we shall see below, there is no clear, universal and irreversible tendency for wages to decrease and inequality to increase. Only a small proportion of the world's workers are part of what might be conceived of as a global labour market where such tendencies might prevail, and, anyway, the analysis is not sufficiently disaggregated.

Nor should we accept the simplistic thesis that the 'new economy' spells the 'end of work', as articulated in the work of Rifkin (Rifkin, 1995), Stanley Aronowitz (Aronowitz and Di Fazio, 1994) and others in the ostensibly progressive camp. It is argued that manufacturing jobs will disappear in the face of the new information technology as agricultural jobs were decimated by Fordism and urbanisation before. A shift of occupation to the services sector is also ruled out due to the increasing impact of automation in that sector. Society will divide up into workers and non-workers, with 'social exclusion' becoming more important than economic inequality. However, as Manuel Castells notes, the forecasters of a jobless society 'do not provide any consistent, rigorous evidence of their claims, relying on isolated press clippings, random examples of firms in some countries and sectors, and "commonsense" arguments on the "obvious" impact of computers in jobs' (Castells, 1999a: 255). What is ironic, over and beyond the lack of any clear link between computerisation and joblessness, is that these predictions were issued in the USA in the mid-1990s, a period in which 8 million jobs were created over a four-year period.

The new economy – flexible financial capitalism, as we have called it here – is characterised by combined and uneven development as much as the old one was. There are tendencies towards financial autonomy, flexibility and a reduction in labour standards. Yet there are also elements pulling in the opposite direction. The need for social and political embeddedness of economic standards still remains. The need for some social regulation of market processes increasingly makes itself felt. Robert Boyer, for one, is extremely sceptical of the suggestion that current transformations will lead to the emergence of a totally novel regulation mode based on a finance-led accumulation regime (Boyer, 2000). As in the past, with Fordism, institutional configurations and institutionalised class compromises will vary across countries and regions, and a universal 'new economy' is not likely to materialise. For Boyer, in a similar way to the combined and uneven development option, the result is likely to be a form of 'hybridity', with different forms in different countries according to their diverse social and political legacies.

What is not in question throughout these debates is that the era of globalisation is having profound effects in the world of work. In Chapter 3 we saw to what extent 'marketisation' is bringing more and more workers across the globe directly under the sway of capitalist relations. While in the 1970s around one-third of the world's workers lived under central planning regimes (the 'socialist' camp), by the 1990s they were under fully (if 'primitive') capital accumulation regimes. Such giants as Russia, India and China have entered or are entering the domain of fully marketised societies. The cutting edge of the new economy is, of course, the information technology sector and here international mobility and flexibility have reached a peak. This technological revolution and associated drops in the cost of communication and transport have been the drivers of the increased economic integration that is at the heart of the globalisation process. Workers in this sector have, to an increasing extent, become part of a global labour market. But what about the two-thirds of the world's workers still on the land and the industrial workers of the old North?

It would seem that it is the industrial workers of the old smoke-stack industries who are one of the main losers in the globalisation race. Economic theory (in the shape of the Heckscher–Ohlin model) would tell us that increased North–South trade should lead to a fall of wages in the North and an increase in the South as markets integrate. But both sets of workers are said to gain in terms of efficiency. Leaving aside the picture in the South (see Chapter 5), we should consider here the impact of globalisation on Northern workers. The main losers are undoubtedly the 'unskilled' workers of the North, hit by the practical disappearance of the labour-intensive section of the North's manufacturing sector. The optimistic reading of current trends is that the increased efficiency referred to above due to market integration will eventually pay off and a new Golden Era will emerge for labour too. For the pessimists there is a large global labour surplus, and increased trade with the South exposes vulnerable sectors of the North's economy and workforce to competition it cannot deal with. Inevitably wages and conditions will go down and unemployment will go up. Any gains from increased economic integration will go to capital and not to labour, especially the traditional working class outside of the high-tech sectors.

Adrian Wood considers the effect of increased North–South trade on employment and inequality and concludes that, at the very least, the 'optimists' above 'greatly underestimate the adverse side effects of this trade on income inequality in the North' (Wood, 1994: 4). But at the same time he berates the 'pessimists' for advocating a retrograde protectionism in which all workers across the globe will lose. It is thus not a matter of labour losses generally in the North, but that while skilled workers have gained from the 'new economy', the traditional unskilled workforce has invariably lost. Less costly than protectionism would be government intervention to assist those sectors affected by this process. The European Union discourse of 'social inclusion' has precisely that function, while in North America the rhetoric of 'flexibility' rules supreme. The much-vaunted increase in employment in the USA during the 1990s (referred to above) was extremely precarious, and badly paid jobs were typical of this process. Perhaps more important than North–South comparisons for workers of the industrialised countries is the competition between the USA and European social regimes of accumulation, which are the real elements in competition rather than largely fictional 'national' economies.

REGIONALISM

If we take a balanced look at the new internationalised, informationalised, flexible capitalism we would see that it is not so much global as regional in its impact. Regionalisation is not a counter-tendency to globalisation but, probably, an integral element in its operationalisation. Nor should we ever underestimate national variations in the development of capitalism, often obscured by terminology such as 'Western capitalism'. While regionalism in the South tends to create nodes for the globalisation network as it extends its tentacles – such as Mexico and Malaysia – in the economic North it denotes the turn-of-century 'Triad' of political-economic powers which have come to dominate the world, namely North America, the European Union and the Japan-dominated Asia–Pacific region. As Barbara Stallings puts it, 'trade and investment are increasing *both* within the so-called Triad area (the United States, Japan and Europe) *and* within the three blocs. Other areas are being marginalised in the process' (Stallings, 1993: 21). This results in both conflict and co-operation under a regime of non-hegemonic interdependence at the global level.

We begin our analysis of the different regional models of capitalism inevitably with the United States, given that Fordism was also the 'American Epoch'. During the long post-war boom American capitalism shaped the global economy in many ways. However, after the reconstruction of Europe and the re-emergence of Japan as an economic power its hegemony was no longer uncontested. After the collapse of the Golden Era (see Chapter 3), US capital sought to restructure itself on a profitable basis mainly through an attack on the workers. A startling statistic is that while US employers had between 1950 and the mid-1960s accepted nearly half of all petitions for trade-union elections, this proportion fell to 26 per cent in 1970 and 16 per cent in 1973 (Brenner, 1998: 109). Following the 1974–75 oil-crisis-driven recession the employers' offensive deepened. Work practices were shaken up, austerity drives were mounted and the safety net of social services virtually disintegrated. The weaker traditional sectors of industry, established in the 'Keynesian' era, were also ruthlessly undercut. So, was a new prosperous 'American model' the result of this drastic surgery?

According to many commentators, the USA has now entered a period of sustained economic growth which will pull the world economy along in its wake. Certainly, by the mid-1990s US manufacturing had recovered to the profitability levels of 1973, but still far short of the 1950s and 1960s levels (Brenner, 1998: 187). Yet there is little to justify faith in a 'new era' other than the Wall Street stock market's sustained boom. To a large extent the claims for a new turbocharged capitalism come from the new economy sectors where productivity is notoriously difficult to measure. The rise, and subsequent dramatic decline, of the e-commerce sector is testimony to how difficult it is to make confident predictions for the new capitalism. Robert Brenner argues that even 'the low rates of inflation and unemployment of the late 1990s are "unremarkable" based as they are on an "extraordinarily slow growth of both demand and wage costs"' (Brenner, 1998: 249). Neither gross domestic product (GDP) growth rates nor those of aggregate demand point towards a dynamic US model of capitalism capable of launching a new 'Golden Era' matching the post-war boom.

US regionalism in North America, as concretised in NAFTA and aspired to in the broader Free Trade Association, is entirely consonant with the advance of free-market liberalism since the 1980s. While regionalism in the Americas had effectively collapsed in the 1970s due to the debt crisis and an absence of an agreed development paradigm, that has all now changed. Erstwhile economic nationalists in Latin America have turned their backs on national development to fully embrace economic integration, albeit subordinate, with the North. While no one believes that textbook economics will prevail and working conditions and reward will equalise across the continent, there is a belief that integration is not a zero-sum game and that less powerful economies may also benefit to some extent. From the perspective of the North, the NAFTA process points towards the limits of an inde-

pendent economic policy for a country such as Canada. It also indicates that the USA does retain the option of applying 'open regionalism' in its own sphere in such a way that it discriminates against
non-members, for example in Europe or Japan.

The European 'model' of capitalism and industrial relations is often contrasted favourably with its US counterpart as being somehow
more 'social'. There is an implicit contrast between a US-model 'low
road' to capitalism and a European 'high road' based on high skill
levels, productivity and wages. Once human resources are recognised
as a crucial economic input it makes sense to increase expenditure on
education and training and to ensure minimal health and social security
provisions as a 'safety net' for those who fall out of the labour market.
While deregulation and flexibility were the watchwords in Western
Europe throughout the 1980s, this did not necessarily conflict with
corporatist arrangements where those successfully regulated capital–
labour relations. Whether it was neo-liberalism, neo-corporatism or
even some notion of social consensus or partnership, the overriding
objective was to 'modernise' European capitalisms to make them more
'competitive' in the era of globalisation. It is important always to
realise that behind the European 'model' lay a diversity of national
configurations and distinct pathways.

Certainly Europe provides interesting material for the debate on
whether globalisation will promote convergence or diversity between
national societies (see Berger and Dore, 1996; Crouch and Streeck,
1997). Overall, the pattern of change in the social systems of production and industrial relations in Western Europe since the 1970s points
towards a prevalence of diversity, albeit a renewed or revised diversity.
Thus, for example, Robert Boyer finds that in the race for flexibility
in the 1980s specific national factors re-emerged to the extent that 'one
of the main lessons to be learnt from this international comparison is
that each country [in Europe] has its own way of adapting to a lower,
less stable, rate of growth' (Boyer, 1988: 212). The uniformity of the
Fordist era, underwritten by steady rates of growth, is giving way to
greater instability and diversity. The specific history, structure, even
'custom and practice', of each country's capital/wage-labour relations
sets the context of how an overriding imperative such as 'flexibility' is
dealt with, modulated, possibly even subverted, in practice.

As to the European Union, it has been inherently contradictory in
its policies in the last decades. The drive towards the single currency

and deregulation is a major element in the neo-liberal revolution, but concern with 'Social Europe' (albeit resisted in the UK) points towards a more socially integrationist model. The EU, while no worker's paradise, has seen a concern to balance 'flexibility' with security and to ensure that the drive towards competitiveness does not lead to wholesale social exclusion. A crucial question (see the next section on Eastern capitalism) is to what extent an expanding European Union will maintain the tendency and not create a two-tier Europe as divisive as was the North–South split in Europe during the 1970s and early 1980s. There is a clear tendency for the continuation of the welfare state to be sacrificed at the altar of competitiveness. However, as Castells notes, 'the political debate and the social conflicts around the ways to control, and guide, the transformation of European societies throughout their gradual integration into an increasingly globalised economy' (Castells, 1996: 325) has now opened, and it cannot be reduced to brave new informatised globalisers versus the old bureaucratic public sector.

The last leg of the 'Triad' is of course Japan, home of 'Toyotaism', and sometime model and sometime culprit for the other capitalisms. The post-war transformation of Japan is one of the success stories of contemporary capitalism. The social and cultural embeddedness of Japanese economic institutions has been a key to this success. Nor can Japan's economic crises in the 1990s justify the apostles of neo-liberalism who use it to proclaim the superiority of noninstitutionalised, free-market capitalism. Not only did the state play a key role in promoting economic development, but firms continued to act as 'institutional companies' exercising a degree of regulation. Against the fashions of current development theory, Japan has always been characterised by a national development strategy and a strong developmental state. High rates of investment have been associated with rising living standards for the working population. As Castells outlines, this remarkable economic performance 'relied on social stability and high labour productivity through management–labour co-operation, made possible by stable employment and by seniority-based promotion, for the core labour force' (Castells, 1998: 219). The 'Japanese miracle', however, entered into crisis in the mid-1990s and no longer seems such an attractive option.

The regional dimension of Japan within the Pacific-Asia region is extremely significant, pointing towards what Castells has called 'a powerful, semi-integrated Asian Pacific economy that has become a major centre of capital accumulation in the world' (Castells, 1998: 169). Indeed, up until the 1990s this appeared to be the only dynamic growth area in a generally stagnant capitalist world economy. Japan, with the NICs of East Asia, is already the largest industrial area of the world, and the looming giant of China is just over the horizon. Whether this will lead to a new 'Pacific Era' for global capitalism to match the 'Atlantic Era' of the twentieth century is, however, open to question. Castells, while optimistic that this new economic network will be the harbinger of a new multicultural global economy, somewhat contradictarily says that there can be no Pacific Era because 'there is no Pacific region as a separate or integrated reality' and its process of development 'has been, and is, enacted by parallel nationalisms' (Castells, 1998: 308).

To sum up this section, we have passed from the sometimes abstract concept of globalisation to its unfolding through regionalisation, a process which picked up steam in the 1990s. While this process may well complement liberalisation, it may also undermine liberalisation, and lead to reconstituted forms of (inter)national pooled sovereignty. Regional development policies, for example, in Europe are well able to deal with and constrain the allegedly all-powerful transnational corporations. What European integration also points towards is the advantages to capitalism of social stability. The 'other side' of globalisation as driven, dynamic and despotic process is what Thelen and Kume, writing on Germany and Japan, refer to as 'employers' heightened dependence on stable and predictable relations at the plant level' (Thelen and Kume, 1999: 478). Not only are production networks much more tightly integrated today but the demands of just-in-time labour processes (see section on after-Fordism below) also point towards the limits of deregulation. The destabilising effects of the neo-liberal-driven process of globalisation impact on capitalists as much as workers and can drive them back towards more co-operative relations with the workforce.

What this leads us to, finally, is the issue of the social embeddedness of economic relations, a theme derived from the early work of Karl Polanyi. Contrary to the nostrums of neo-liberalism, markets exist within society and firms are embedded in social relations. The different national and regional models of capitalism examined above are all distinct social systems of production. The high tide of neo-liberalism has passed and the once unlikely terms of trust and co-operation are returning to rational long-sighted capitalist discourse (see, for example, Soros, 1998). What is particularly important to note, again with Hollingsworth and Boyer (1996: 46), is that in the era of global competitiveness it is not 'economies' that are competing, but rather social systems of production. The very nature of a country's social and political fabric is being tested in the era of globalisation, and while this may well have destructive effects it also presents an opportunity for progressive social and political transformations.

EASTERN CAPITALISM

What has made capitalist globalisation a plausible prospect is, above all, the collapse of the alternative socialist, state capitalist or bureaucratic collectivist mode of production which prevailed in the East. The reintegration of Russia's, Eastern Europe's and eventually China's workers into the capitalist world economy will represent a fundamental social transformation. These so-called 'transition' economies have moved from Marx to the market without mediation in a dramatically short time span. The World Bank in its influential 1996 report entitled *From Plan to Market* (World Bank, 1996) pushes the line of a 'short, sharp shock' to build capitalism in the East but admits that 'More Russians are dying during transition. Male life expectancy fell by six years between 1990 and 1994 (from 64 to 58) and that of women by three years (from 74 to 71)' (World Bank, 1996: 120). The box text, cheerfully entitled 'Is transition a killer?', looks around for contributory causes such as an increasing consumption of vodka, but, while stressing that it is still 'the subject of continuing investigation', one might, in all fairness, conclude that 'the transition itself is a direct cause' (World Bank, 1996: 128).

It is important to understand why the socialist model collapsed because that has serious implications for the future of workers in these countries, and elsewhere for that matter. Basically, I would argue that it collapsed under its own contradictions, primarily the failure of the statist industrialisation model to adapt to the new capitalism emerging in the 1970s and 1980s. As Castells puts it, the crisis of the Soviet economy and society from the mid-1970s onwards 'was the expression of the structural inability of statism and of the Soviet variant of industrialism to ensure the transition towards the information society' (Castells, 1998: 7). While the Soviet model of industrialisation was able to some extent to compete with industrial capitalism, it lacked the dynamism and flexibility to make the leap into post-industrial information capitalism. There was a need to shift from an extensive to an intensive model of development and the system simply collapsed under the pressure. It was a similar transition to that which many developing economies, particularly in Latin America, had to make in the 1970s, namely from the collapse of the import substitution model of industrialisation to the export-led, more intensive model which prevailed from then onwards.

Once the old statist model had collapsed, and with it the welfare state which it represented to workers, capitalism had to be constructed. As with the original emergence of capitalism in the West, its Eastern variant had to engage in a process of what Marx called 'primitive accumulation' to create a capitalist class. Workers were 'freed' from welfarism to create a pool of proletarians and the nomenklatura was given free rein to loot the state so as to acquire capital. The free-market advisors brought in from the USA to oversee this process were ostensibly shocked to see the development of a 'gangster capitalism' quite unlike the serene model of capitalist development their textbooks suggested would occur. The World Bank found that liberalisation had led to 'rampant corruption and rent seeking' (World Bank, 1996: 23) but still stressed the need to ensure private property rights:

> Property rights are at the heart of the incentive structure of market economies.... They determine who bears risk and who gains or loses ... they spur worthwhile investment ... promote work effort ... reward effort and good judgement. (World Bank, 1996: 48–9)

It is now debated openly in Western financial centres whether 'good judgement' was displayed by those who encouraged the development of 'gangster capitalism' in the East, which even in its own terms is proving unviable.

It was an integral part of the logic of this transition that Russia's workers would suffer. In just a few years industrial employment was cut by one-third and wages fell by almost two-thirds. The ILO notes the emergence in all the 'transition' economies of high and long-term unemployment and that 'The worst aspect of economic restructuring is the appalling growth in the number of people living in poverty' (ILO, 1995: 111). Women workers are being particularly hard hit as they are driven by the new capitalism back into the home. The general picture is that in the USSR there were 100 million people living below the official poverty line by 1991, and in 1992, after a bout of hyper-inflation, it was officially reckoned that 80 per cent of the population had incomes which put them below the poverty line (ILO, 1995: 112). Many workers, if they were lucky enough not to lose their jobs, were pushed into precarious, low-income jobs with the concept of a minimum wage being seen as a quaint relic of the past. The welfarism which actually existing socialism represented in practice for workers is also an increasingly patchy or simply rhetorical affair.

We need to grasp the extremely fluid and uncertain situation of the East's workers as they come into capitalism. Castells is surely right when he argues that 'the most enduring legacy of Soviet statism will be the destruction of civil society after decades of systematic negation of its existence' (Castells, 1998: 68). There are no dense networks of activated civil society to call on, no 'social capital' to build on, in reconstructing the world of workers after the collapse of real socialism. Individual survival strategies will simply be no match for a globalised capitalism in full flow seeking to incorporate the uncolonised lands of the East. In these fast-moving economic flows of 'globalisation' the reconstruction of a Soviet cultural and political identity is proving very hard. The social and economic devastation, impacting particularly hard on women, youth, elders and the disabled, is creating a social wasteland. The ILO is understating when it declares that these growing socio-economic disparities 'threaten the political stability of the new nations, bring the risk of social discord much closer and undoubtedly contribute to a substantial worsening of socio-economic inequality' (ILO, 1995: 111). This is the context in which Russian and other post-socialist countries' workers are struggling.

As Mikhail Gorbachev began his fateful policy of perestroika in the second half of the 1980s the Russian labour movement became re-activated. In 1989 the powerful miners' union began an all-Russia strike, which, according to Kiril Buketov, 'awoke the country from its lethargic slumber. For the first time in many years hundreds of thousands of workers gave notice of their dissatisfaction with their wretched position and of their unwillingness to remain mute slaves' (Buketov, 1999: 100). Perestroika then began to operate within the trade unions as the old statist apparatuses – 'transmission belts' of the Party line, according to official doctrine – came under pressure from below and from the broader economic and political transformations under way. New independent trade unions, outside Party control, were formed in many sectors. The 1989 miners' strike thus prompted a massive re-organisation of the trade unions and brought the workers' movement to the fore in the process of political change. However, while the strikes of 1989, and a reprise in 1991, were instrumental in bringing down the old regime, Simon Clarke is right to note that 'the workers had neither the time nor the space in which to constitute their own organisations, and consequently have had a very small part to play in the unfolding of the crisis' (Clarke, 1992: 26).

The Soviet trade unions had conceived of their role from 1917 onwards as 'transmission belts' between the Communist Party and the working masses. They came to play a crucial role in maintaining the stability of the Soviet system, oiling the relations between workers and the state. Now, with the collapse of the Soviet model and the rapid process of economic transformation, the very *raison d'être* of the trade unions was called into question. The drive towards marketisation imposed the logic of a capital/wage-labour conflict on the situation very abruptly, albeit mediated by the specific features of the Soviet transition. The trade-union leadership sought, naturally enough from its point of view, to carve out a role for itself under the new dispensation, under the banner of 'social partnership'. Thus keying into a dominant Western paradigm, the accumulated economic, political and social weight of the trade unions under communism could be re-configured in the nascent capitalist order. To what extent that mission has been successful is debatable, but the point is that the trade unions did not just shut up shop and go home.

It is not a 'normal' capital/wage-labour relationship that is emerging in Russia in so far as the trade unions tend to ally with their direct employers against the government and the new 'raw' capitalist meas-ures. Notwithstanding the lingering concept of a 'labour collective' and the nostalgia for a productivist capitalist model, the new capitalism is becoming a reality. Significantly, in mid-2000 a Moscow court ruled that McDonald's had improperly disciplined one of its employees who was seeking to establish a trade union. Yevgeny Druzhimin, a forklift operator on the ruling body of the huge multinational's small union, had been disciplined six times in as many months in an attempt to cow the union. Russia's official labour code was still worker-friendly enough to prevent the company from disciplining an employee without the union's permission. Significantly a broad survey of popular opinion conducted by VTSIOM (All-Russian Centre for the Study of Public Opinion) found that 58 per cent of employees were owed back wages, 60 per cent said they had lived better under socialism, and 82 per cent blamed the new 'economic system', rather than 'drunkenness or laziness', for poverty under the new regime.

Worker organisations did not just dissolve when faced by the new capitalising logic of the market. Whether in the shape of the Polish Solidarity, workers' councils or bureaucratic statist trade unions, workers' organisations played a role albeit sometimes a negative or passive one. Very few just fell into line with the wishes of the mainly Western neo-liberal economic gurus advising the proto-capitalist class of the East. One Polish commentator refers to 'the persistence of *homo Sovieticus* – the attitudes and habits of passivity, welfare dependency, poor labour discipline, disrespect for the law, etc.' (Mokrzyaki, paraphrased by Bryant, 1994: 66). Over and above the unduly negative perspective this list betrays, there is the undoubted truth that the social conditioning of fifty years will not dissolve in five years, however frantic the pace of economic developments. A study of workers in Hungary during the transformation phase (Burawoy and Lukács, 1992) also shows how flexible and resourceful workers have been in the East when faced with the whirlwind of capitalist neo-liberal globalisation.

If we stand back from the fast-moving pace of economic, political and social transformation in the East, we can see how Karl Polanyi's notion of a great transformation might help us understand the underlying dynamic. For Polanyi (himself Hungarian), 'Socialism is, essentially, the tendency inherent in an industrial civilisation to transcend the self-regulating market by consciously subordinating it to a democratic society' (Polanyi, 1957: 234). In the East, going through a second Great Transformation as dramatic as the first nineteenth-century version described by Polanyi, this is not happening. Instead, democracy is being curtailed and deformed to allow the so-called 'free market' (which is not spontaneous but created) free rein over an atomised society. The destruction of society in a very real sense is a precondition for the creation of a market society. The question to ask now is whether Polanyi's counter-movement, a conscious social regulation of market mechanisms, will emerge in the East. I tend to agree with Glasman's verdict that 'Polanyi underestimates the moral attractiveness of the market as a foundation for freedom and prosperity – a crucial part of its appeal in Eastern Europe at present' (Glasman, 1994: 200).

The choice facing the East is posed starkly as state or market, as in the World Bank's 1996 report *From Plan to Market* (World Bank, 1996), where the transition was seen as simple and unequivocal. Yet when democracy is denied and stable social associations are derided, even the much-vaunted market reforms become vulnerable. Polanyi, at one point in his analysis of a market unmediated by the social, declared that greed was 'elevated to a moral principle' (Polanyi, 1957: 84). In theory, an unrestricted global market would provide the optimum match between security and freedom. As the World Bank puts it: 'The freeing of markets is the basic enabling reform from which all the potential benefits of transition flow' (World Bank, 1996: 7). Though they call for 'stabilisation' as a vital component of liberalisation, so as to prevent hyperinflation and promote productivity, they have not grasped Polanyi's nettle and understood that a social 'counter-movement' is necessary even to ensure the sustainability of the market reforms.

AFTER-FORDISM?

After the collapse of Fordism comes post-Fordism, or maybe not. The debate on the nature of the labour process in the advanced capitalist countries is a crucial one, both there and in the developing countries where it will inevitably impact (see Chapter 5). Having examined the main contours of the social system of production in the West and in the East we must now turn to what Marx termed the 'hidden abode of production', namely the labour process that generates production and wealth. We begin with the broad-brush debate on the transition from Fordism (see Chapter 2) to post-Fordism, then go on to the specifics of 'lean production', the 'feminisation' of labour and the prospects for a new form of social regulation. It is important to note at the outset that these debates are about more than just the technical organisation of work; they go to the core of how we live in contemporary society. The workplace is embedded in social, cultural and political institutions, discourses and visions of how we should lead our

TABLE 4.1 FORDISM AND AFTER

	Fordism	After
Economic regulation	Keynesian	Monetarist
Markets	Mass	Niche
Lifestyle	Conformist	Pluralistic
Systems	Centralised	Decentralised
Organisation	Bureaucratic	Dehierarchised
Regulation	National	Global
Lead sector	Consumption	Finance
Skills	De-skilling	Multi-skilling
Workers	Mass	Polyvalent
Characteristics	Rigidity	Flexibility
Production	Assembly line	Flexible
Society	Welfarism	Privatisation
Driver	Resources	Demand

lives. At the moment the undisputed hegemony of the market in regulating these processes has been challenged but the future is uncertain. Thus we genuinely refer to 'after-Fordism' (*l'après Fordisme*) as an open question.

If we take a wide-angle view of the transition from Fordism to post-Fordism as paradigms of social systems of production it would look something like Table 4.1. It is important to bear in mind, though, that these are ideal types probably not existing in reality in such a neat form. The list in the table could be extended but the general picture is clear. Fordism, as described by Gramsci in the 1930s, was a new industrial lifestyle based on the 'American way' but it came into its own during the post-war boom. Its methods, its philosophy and its prescriptions for the 'one best way' to organise work spread across the world. Post-Fordism emerged in the 1980s partly as a way to think through a coherent alternative to the dying Fordism which would be more progressive socially than the then dominant free-market liberalism of Thatcher and Reagan.

To flesh out the broad paradigmatic shift beyond Fordism we need to examine the specific delineation of the new workplace and the social system of production. The new post-Fordist configurations would have serious effects at the level of industry, production and the division of labour. Industries move towards a horizontal de-concentration, production processes deal with uncertainty and unpredictability through flexibility, and the division of labour moves from a focus on the individual worker to flexible work teams. There is also a shift from economies of scale to economies of scope. Production norms also move from standardised products to specialised ones, hence the term 'flexible specialisation'. The productive process shifts from an emphasis on quantity to a focus on quality. It is ironic that Benjamin Coriat, after drawing up this model and arguing that 'Flexible specialisation practices or strategies of dynamic flexibility [as he prefers to term it] open certain opportunities to create profitable niches or segments of markets', can only conclude realistically that on current trends 'there is only a very slight probability that this model will become a reality' (Coriat, 1992: 155).

If we now look at what happened in practice in the North we will find that outside of the odd experiment in Sweden and elsewhere it was in fact a form of neo- (as against post-) Fordism which prevailed. Certainly increased automation of the workplace and some of the new 'flexible' work practices offered some resolution to the crisis of Fordism. Flexibility of production could only be an improvement on the rigidity of Fordist and Stalinist mass-production methods. Yet in a sense this only gave a new lease of life to Fordism, so at most it can be termed a neo-Fordism. For Aglietta, who in many ways launched the contemporary analysis of Fordism, neo-Fordism involved 'the transformation of the totality of the conditions of existence of the wage-earning classes' (Aglietta, 1979: 168). The attempted renewal of US capitalism in the 1970s to cope with its loss of undisputed hegemony led directly to a shift from a regime of extensive accumulation to one of intensive accumulation in which work was intensified through an application of the new information technology and automation. This regime also spread from industry to schools, hospitals and the leisure industry.

If neo-Fordism prevailed in the 1970s, a post-Fordism was detected in the 1980s. As already mentioned above, the main drive of the after-Fordist work practices was 'flexibility', and a major model was the Japanese one, sometimes known as Toyotaism. The Toyota experience was codified and generalised by an MIT study entitled *The Machine That Changed the World* (Womack et al., 1990). This study extolled the virtues of 'just-in-time' (JIT) – to reduce stocks and work in progress – and the dramatic productivity increases of Japanese car plants during the 1980s. They dubbed this approach 'lean production' (which for workers also meant mean) and sought to generalise it across industries, arguing that its requirement of skilled and committed workers made it equally attractive to labour and to capital. Subsequent studies (e.g. Williams et al., 1992) show this picture to be oversimplified even for the car industry, in so far as it overrates the difference between 'Japanese', 'European' and 'American' work practices. Nor is it plausible to establish such a binary opposition between bad old mass production and good new lean production in this way, as real workplaces are more complex and conflictual places.

The 'Japanese' model has now, of course, lost much of its shine since Japanese capitalism has shown itself vulnerable to the contradictions of the species. Nevertheless, as Elger and Smith note, many commentators in the West 'remain mesmerised by idealised contrasts between production paradigms or broad-brush conceptions of Japanisation' (Elger and Smith, 1994: 12). As with 'Fordism', Japanisation or the more specific Toyotaism has tended to suffer from conceptual inflation. It has also become a contested discursive terrain with different commentators stressing more the technical elements (JIT) while others emphasise the more autonomous worker supposedly required. Certainly the concept of Japanisation acquired a life of its own, especially the claim by the MIT study that a Japanese car was produced with half the amount of labour and material than its US counterpart required. Whether this was a myth or not, lean production spread across the globe in the 1990s, although in different versions and with more or less compliance from the workers concerned.

We can only conclude that the path after-Fordism has many forks. For some analysts mass production is set to decay steadily and progressively and fall away (see Hirst and Zeitlin, 1989), whereas for others a major element of mass production will remain central in the economies of the North (Coriat, 1992). A new virtuous circle of productivity growth based on flexible production in its benign form seems at least unlikely. A reversion to Fordism may also be entirely logical in situations of stagnant economies with a large labour surplus. In terms of the broad social system of production it thus seems unwise to predict that any one work regime, such as flexible specialisation, will become the 'one best way' as Fordism was in its heyday.

While the new principles are generalisable – no one can argue against 'flexibility' in principle – older systems of production may be too well embedded to change. A pattern of uneven and combined development of the old and the new seems thus most likely, the main criteria always being the same, namely productivity and profitability.

The flexibilisation of work in the North in the 1980s and 1990s also meant its 'feminisation'. Indeed, one of the proclaimed benefits of 'flexibility' is that it would attract more women into the paid labour force. What we do know is that of the extra 29 million people that entered the recorded labour market of the EU between 1960 and 1990, 20 million were women (Rubery and Fagan, 1994: 146). We also know that the steady growth of the service sector in most countries of the North since 1970 is associated with the growth of female employment. However, the conclusion of Rubery and Fagan in relation to these trends is that 'There is no mechanical relationship between the growth of atypical employment [part-time, temporary or other 'flexible' forms] and the increasing participation of women in the economy. Likewise there can be no simple equation between feminisation and employment flexibility' (Rubery and Fagan, 1994: 159). As with other issues, we need to set employment relations within the broader societal context, in this case the particular national configuration of gender relations which shape the contours of employment.

What is clear is that 'Labor market flexibility is both a racialised and gendered concept' (Peck, 1996: 136). Flexibility is as much a political as an economic concept and is set in the context of segregated or segmented labour markets. Thus 'flexibility' can spell 'responsible autonomy' and 'multi-skilling' to the white male core worker of the new capitalism and, at the same time, create insecurity and even harder work for the woman or black worker. Women do not come into the labour market simply as workers but within the parameters of societies that discriminate against women in different ways. And, of course, behind the new male 'flexiworker' giving his all to his high-powered City job lies someone (usually female) who in a very 'flexible' way is caring for his household needs. In the social construction of work at the turn of the century it is thus necessary to bear in mind that 'New forms of labor flexibility are associated with new forms of labor control, new forms of labor exploitation and, by implication, new forms of gender and racial oppression' (Peck, 1996: 136).

Flexibility, as we have seen, has come mainly to mean deregulation;

it is part and parcel of the drive to remove the state and society from any role in regulating the capital/wage-labour relation. Yet we are beginning to see moves to re-regulate and reconstitute the institutions which once governed training, for example. In particular, it is now widely accepted, even by the OECD, that eliminating state interference in employer–employee relations will not in itself generate more jobs, as textbook economics had predicted. The so-called rigidities of the labour market – strong unions, labour protection legislation, high wages – are no longer seen as credible culprits of unemployment. If deregulation is not the answer then it follows that one may regulate the working day, holidays, leave entitlements, temporary employment, and explore the possible positive implications of 'flexibility' at work. It is noticeable that the critique of deregulation is coming not only from those concerned with equity but also from those motivated by efficiency. The instability in employment which results from deregulation conspires directly against productivity, after all, and precludes a long-term training programme as well.

It would be interesting to explore a possible positive scenario for the after-Fordism work scene. Manuel Castells calls the new information-economy-led workers 'networkers' and goes on to argue that, despite the real problem posed by authoritarian management, 'information technologies call for better-informed workers to deliver the full promise of its productivity potential' (Castells, 1996: 242). Not just better-informed but more self-reliant, less supervised and more motivated workers are needed in the new economy. Most routine, repetitive tasks have been automated and the remaining decision-making requires a worker with initiative, skill and experience, not the unthinking automaton considered ideal fodder for the Fordist assembly line. Of course, the term 'networker' may cover different types of jobs, from Silicon Valley whiz-kids to the sorely oppressed workers in the call centres who work under conditions which make the old car assembly line seem almost worker-friendly. So, while there is a 'high road' for the new capitalism, one that requires workers with at least a 'responsible autonomy', there is also a 'low road' where direct control of the workforce still prevails. At any rate, this new sector is currently being targeted by the trade unions, and initial indications are that some inroads to capital's prerogatives are being made.

Finally, we need to mention the regional level because, in Jamie Peck's words, it 'is not just that *regulation matters* (i.e. that it has important, material effects on accumulation), but that *regional regulation matters*' (Peck, 1996: 146). Social regulation mechanisms are inevitably developed unevenly across regions and operate within distinct institutional matrixes. This means that social regulation is also local regulation, and it is in the great cities and regions of the North where some of the more creative experiments in social regulation are happening. Notwithstanding more recent setbacks, the bottom-up system of flexible production pioneered in Emilia-Romagna (Italy) still repays attention. In many city regions the 1990s saw a move beyond the beggar-thy-neighbour boosterism of the 1980s, where they competed to 'sell' their workforce on the global labour market. As Boyer and Hollingsworth remind us, 'The most competitive firms, regions, or nations are not mimicking the market but on the contrary, they are struggling to manufacture consensus, trust, collective forms of governance, and long-term vision' (Hollingsworth and Boyer, 1996: 477).

TRADE-UNION RECONFIGURATION

Trade unions, and labour movements more generally, are not just passive mirrors of capital's transformations: they are constantly renewed and reconfigured in their identity and strategies. As social movements, they can be reflexive, learn from mistakes and setbacks, rethink accepted nostrums and develop a more productive approach to the problems they face. One way of entering this complex and developing terrain of debate would be through a review of some of the political and organisational changes undergone within the US labour movement, once considered the epitome of conservatism, if not of corruption, within progressive labour circles. The victory of the 'New Voice' slate in the 1995 AFL–CIO elections marked a significant turn in US labour politics. A once large and vibrant labour movement (particularly in the 1930s and 1940s) had slipped into decline and was virtually moribund by the 1980s. Its numbers had been reduced by nearly half and its strategic vision was almost non-existent. A whole range of factors, from capital's offensive (alluded to above) to the weaknesses of the labour leadership, were responsible for this, but what was to be done?

   The post-1995 union leadership set in motion a process of change, which is still continuing. Much of the change was straightforward enough, such as a massive recruitment drive and a much greater, and overdue, focus on gender and 'ethnic' issues. What was probably most significant, though, was a major emphasis on unions as organisers of a social movement. Breaking with the language of corporatism the US unions began to speak the language of democracy. Above all, in a perhaps unknowing borrowing from the experience of Southern unions (see Chapter 5), the AFL–CIO began to promote a new 'community unionism':

> The definition of community unionism is union organising that takes place across territorial and industrial communities much larger than a single workplace. Community unionism recognises that a worker's identities and interests are much broader than just who they work for or what they do. Workers have different identities, some that are connected to occupation or employer, some that are not – but most of which are relevant to organising. (Fine, 1999: 128)

So, not only did the AFL–CIO rediscover the language of class which had been so prominent in the 1930s but it also moved into a 'post-modern' conception of the worker with multiple identities and the union as a social movement.

If there was always one area where US unions were a byword for reaction across the world, it was in relation to their international policy of acting as the labour arm of the State Department and US corporations. Now, the AFL–CIO has not only turned decidedly in-ternationalist, recognising the overwhelming reality of globalisation, but it has acknowledged its murky past and sought to build a progres-sive future. Barbara Shailor, new director of the AFL–CIO Inter-national Affairs Department, acknowledges that 'too often in the past the international stage was dominated by the arguments and differ-ences of the past' (Shailor and Kourpias, 1998: 281) and goes on to declare that

> No worker in the world should be exploited by any multinational within the reach of a US-based union.... We need to strategically organise companies, industries and entire sectors of the global economy. For this, we must be clear that our unions are operating independently of the foreign policy considerations that so dominated the Cold War period across the world. (Shailor and Kourpias, 1998: 282)

At last, there is a recognition that what is good for General Motors may not necessarily be good for US workers.

We cannot pretend that the changes outlined above are without limitations and contradictions. For example, when the AFL–CIO calls for a return to the expansionary economy where 'a rising tide lifts all boats', we should point out that 'those days, to whatever extent they ever existed, may well be gone' (Mantsios, 1998: 56). By romanticising Fordism, one is incapacitated to deal with after-Fordism. Also, leaderships come and go and the lure of the Democratic Party can always be renewed. However, we can only but agree with Denis McShane when he says that it is premature to bid 'Adieu to the trade unions' (McShane, 1997). They have shown themselves capable of regeneration and have even sought to catch up with the 'information age'. The rise of the union website and of the 'cyber-picket' signals a new era in labour organising. British TUC (Trades Union Congress) leader John Monks, in launching a new electronic database for trade unionists in Liverpool, recently declared that 'we have been slow to pick up on information technology but it is where the unions in the future need to be'. New communication methods are aiding inter-union dialogue and the ongoing struggle to organise against capital.

Across the North the trade unions began to revive after the mid-1990s. There were, for example, general strikes in France, Belgium, Greece, Italy, Spain and Canada in the second half of the 1990s, not quite but nearly matching those across the South. The trade unions were to some extent taking up the mantle of the working-class leadership abandoned by the social-democratic parties now busy administering neo-liberalism. Kim Moody rightly points out that this return to working-class action 'had deep roots in the previous period and was shaped by it. The changes within the working class had been disorienting, but had also made new developments possible' (Moody, 1997: 14). Social recomposition can take a decade or more after an intense period of economic restructuring such as that experienced by the working classes of the North in the 1980s. The political disorientation caused by the collapse of communism and the definitive defection of social democracy to the cause of capitalist modernisation took even longer to recover from. And, of course, this recovery is quite uneven, hesitant and faltering, but nevertheless seems real.

The brief answer to the state of the unions worldwide at the turn of the century is, according to the ILO, 'battered but rising to the challenge' (ILO, 1997). Basically,

> The proportion of union members in the labour force has declined, sometimes sharply, almost everywhere over the past decade. But numbers alone

tell only part of the story. Considerable variations exist between regions and within each one. (ILO, 1997: 2)

So, for example, against the general trend Spain and the Netherlands saw a significant rise in union membership from the mid-1980s into the 1990s. The decline was most precipitate in the East (see below). The South saw considerable advances (see Chapter 5). Furthermore, the influence of trade unions in national politics has increased in many countries. And, as we saw above, there has been a new repertoire of actions and strategies developed. As in the past, periods of numerical decline have also been periods of political renewal. For the ILO, 'What is involved here is militant unionism rather than weight of numbers' (ILO, 1998: 2). Most workers do not have the luxury of abandoning their main means of representation. The trade unions will often fight to make themselves relevant again after a period of retreat, as the 1980s undoubtedly were.

As to the issues facing the labour movement, we could well start with a list developed by an ILO- and ICFTU-sponsored electronic conference in 1999–2000. The background document for this conference on organised labour in the twenty-first century listed the following:

1. Changing patterns of employment and union membership – decline of the manual working class and the public sector.
2. Changes in labour-management relations – decline of the historic capital–labour social compromise.
3. Public status of trade unions – legal restrictions on unions and decline of the state's role in industrial relations.
4. Challenges of a hostile economic environment – end of the Golden Era, supremacy of flexible financial capitalism.
5. The international economy – globalisation challenges the hitherto national regulation of the employment relations (ILO, 1999: 1).

Most significant were the range and depth of responses from various trade unions to this agenda. Locating the right questions is always half the battle and here the unions were beginning (perhaps rather late, certainly patchily) to address the major issues facing working people across the North.

Two examples of labour's responses can be given from different ends of the technological spectrum: the airline industry and the garment industry. Since the 1990s, the civil aviation industry has been engaged in a paradigmatic exercise in liberalisation and deregulation that has had profound effects on the industry's workforce, which has also been paramount in the companies' considerations. The intensification of labour and the decline in job security have prompted a serious reaction from this 'structurally' globalised workforce. The new management strategies have forced the unions into a more internationalist approach (see Blyton et al., 1998). For their part, the superexploited garment workers (often immigrants) in the North's ghettos have also responded in novel ways to conditions imposed by neoliberal globalisation. Traditional trade-union strategies were often beaten back by ruthless employers in the non-union sweatshops. Hence, as Andrew Ross puts it, 'the leading edge of activism has shifted towards the high-end publicity stakes of targeting the image of large, well-known companies' (Ross, 1997: 26). Not only have these campaigns against household names, particularly in the USA, been successful but they have helped bridge the gap (in theory and practice) between production and consumption, and between workers of the North and of the South.

Lest we be carried away by an 'optimism of the will' regarding a labour revival it is well to review the very serious challenges facing labour in an exercise of 'pessimism of the intellect'. From outside the trade unions but from a broadly progressive stance, Manuel Castells tells the trade unions that, 'If unions carry on negotiating within the framework of the enterprise, globalisation or the informationalisation of the enterprise will overwhelm them' (Castells, 1998: 2). From a strong trade-union but now independent perspective, Denis McShane advises that 'Unless trade unions reinvent themselves their role in the twenty-first century political economy will get smaller and smaller' (McShane, 1997: 165). The past may be a source of inspiration and historical experience but it cannot provide the answers. Society is today more complex and is changing at an ever faster speed. Capital is dynamic and setting the pace of change. Labour is still marked by the economic structures, political reflexes and aspirations of the past, when not totally browbeaten by the new capitalism. Reinventing oneself is not easy, whatever postmodernism tells us!

If we briefly examine two sectors – the state and the high-tech – we can see some of the major practical challenges facing unions today. The restructuring and recomposition of the state in most Northern countries have fundamentally altered the position of public-sector workers. The public/private, profit-making/public service divide has largely evaporated. Even at an international level now public services are becoming completely subordinated to market logic. The outcome, as Peter Fairbrother explains, is that 'in the state sector broadly defined ... industrial relations are no longer as predictable as once was the case' (Fairbrother, 1999: 1). While this may lead to novel tactics it also, predominantly in the short term, disrupts what was once a traditional trade-union bastion in many countries of the North. Likewise, the 'flexiworkers' or 'networkers' of the information and communication sectors may one day be the new trade-union vanguard, as dockers and miners were in their day. Today, however, these workers, many on short-term contracts, find it very difficult to unionise. At the 'up-market' end, the young high-fliers of the 'Internet revolution' see little point in trade unions, which they see as male/manual/modernist relics. To build up their membership, relevance and capacity for action in the 'new economy' is the key task for the North's trade unions.

It is a truism but still worth pointing out that the main challenges facing trade unions today are ideological and political. The major international trade-union body, the ICFTU, which sponsored the electronic conference on the future of trade unionism mentioned above, is indicative of that crisis. Its ideological identity for the whole post-war period up until the 1990s was shaped by the 'struggle' against communism, but now with its demise there is a curious vacuum. With no one to fight against, its ideological bearings are unclear. Certainly, the 'challenge' of globalisation is recognised, and its main promoters, the US state and capitalism, are now regularly criticised. Yet, one of the main documents for the electronic conference argued that

> Trade unions ... need to demonstrate their approach is not incompatible with the creation of successful market economies.... Few trade unions have managed so far to come to terms with the new world of increasing globalisation but if they hope to survive and grow again they will have to make radical accommodations. (Taylor, 1999)

It is all very well being cynical about wishful thinking but the accommodation with the dominant paradigm seems too enthusiastic and appears to leave little room for reinvention let alone subversive thinking.

Finally, if I were to identify the principal challenge facing workers' organisations today, it would be the development of national policies in a globalised world. The ILO in fact dedicated its whole 1996–97

World Employment Report to precisely this issue (ILO, 1997). The problem is that the organisations promoting these debates, such as the ILO and the ICFTU, are part and parcel of the national era, the national way of perceiving the globe. They encapsulate the post-war social compact between labour, capital and the state within the envelope of the nation-state. To break out of this historical framework and mind-set is difficult if not impossible. Yet today it is widely recognised that only a global social answer will suffice to deal with economic globalisation (see Chapter 8). In the meantime, workers and their organisations operate on the national terrain and require answers and strategies for national electorates. They are thus within the nation-state and needing to be without. In some sense strategies need to be transitional, then, providing some provisional answers to national dilemmas while pointing beyond to the global framework. We cannot simply see the global as hostile, to be kept at arms length, or, conversely, the national as irredeemably passé and to be surpassed by internationalism (see Chapter 7).

FIVE

WORKERS SOUTH

The workers of the developing world, now becoming known as the global South, were also to be severely impacted by globalisation. This would happen when it brought previously closed (or semi-closed) economies into its orbit, but also, by omission, when it excluded parts of the world (such as broad swathes of Africa) from the new order. This chapter traces the transition from the NIDL to the era of globalisation, with particular attention to transformations in countries such as Brazil, South Africa and South Korea where considerable levels of industrialisation were achieved. We also examine what was once particular to the South (but now also increasingly a Northern phenomenon), namely the high level of informal working relations and practices. Trade-union responses to this new order are also analysed with a view to the future patterns which may emerge. Finally, this chapter looks at some aspects of the so-called 'social clause' debate from a broad perspective. This final section shows the extent to which we cannot really any more study workers in the North and South separately.

FROM NIDL TO GLOBALISATION

It is sometimes forgotten, or denied, by the critics of development that 'The period of 1950 to 1980 was also – and in an important sense – the Golden Age of development for the poor countries of the world' (Singh, 1994: 171). This is not the wishful thinking of a modernisation theorist or the preachings of a World Bank apologist. This was the sober verdict of the ILO. It is indeed vital to recognise the unprecedented economic development of the South in the post-Second

World War period, in spite of all its unevenness and its glaring in-equalities. In fact, the industrial revolution in the South actually bettered the record of the global North in the first 'great transformation', which occurred in the second half of the nineteenth century. As Singh summarises this startling historical reality: 'The South did this in half the time, at twice the growth rates, and with five times the North's population in the nineteenth century' (Singh, 1994: 171–2). This dynamic transformation of the South was to lead to a new international division of labour, with profound effects on workers across the world.

The 'old' international division of labour was centred around the overwhelming social, economic and political reality of colonialism. The imperialist or colonial powers began to produce manufactured goods, and the colonial world (later to become the South) was exploited for its raw materials, especially minerals. Even as industrialisation proceeded in some parts of the South in the early and mid-twentieth century, this was, arguably, a 'dependent' form of industrialisation with the colonial (or ex-colonial) powers retaining control over the leading sector. However, from around the 1970s onwards a 'new' international division of labour was diagnosed, most categorically by a group of German researchers, Folker Fröbel, Jürgen Heinrichs and Otto Kreye (1980). Their basic thesis was that the transformations which accumulated in the post-war period 'generated a world market for production sites and for labour which embraces both the traditional industrialised and the underdeveloped countries' (Fröbel et al., 1980: 44). This was seen to have undermined the traditional division of labour whereby there were only two global sectors, the industrialised countries and the producers of raw materials.

On this basis, the NIDL fundamentally restructured the relations of production in the South with the emergence of a substantial manufacturing sector oriented towards the world market. These 'world market factories' often employed women workers and thus had an impact on the gendering of work in the South as well. We must bear in mind the limits of this pre-globalisation internationalisation of production: in 1975, according to the German study cited above, there were 725,000 workers in the South engaged in the internationalised production sector, of which 420,000 were based in Asia, 265,000 in Latin America and 40,000 in Africa (Fröbel et al., 1980: 307). The next wave of internationalisation would impact on far more workers of the South.

While the NIDL theorists did point towards some fundamental transformations, there are serious flaws in the overall paradigm. Essentially, it focuses on the world market to the detriment of changes in the production process and neglects the role of the state in the South, assuming that the world market could simply impose its policies across the globe. It also seriously underestimates the level of industrialisation which existed in the South (particularly in Latin America and India, for example) prior to the 1960s. This leads the NIDL theorists to isolate the 'world market factories' and the so-called free trade zones (FTZs) as the main sites of capitalist development in the South, when in fact their importance was relative. At a general level we can also concur with Robin Cohen, for whom 'The NIDL theorists use as their predominant data, aggregate trade and investment figures – i.e. they use measures of the migration of *capital* to measure changes in the division of *labour*' (Cohen, 1991: 130). A labour-oriented study would have to focus on the shifting contours and flows of labour rather than capital. Nor should a focus on manufacturing (as per NIDL theorists) allow us to neglect the big shifts between and within agriculture, industry as a whole and the services sector.

The NIDL did not occur only at the level of international trade but also impacted on the relations of production in the South. A form of what has been called 'bloody' Taylorisation was created in the super-exploitative FTZs in Sri Lanka (and elsewhere) and in the textile *maquila* plants of the Mexican border. A form of 'peripheral' Fordism also emerged in the big new car plants and manufacturing factories which emerged in Brazil, Mexico, South Korea, Indonesia and South Africa in the 1960s and 1970s. Lipietz provides the classic definition of this new labour process as

> an authentic Fordism based on intensive accumulation combined with market expansion but [which] remains peripheral to the extent that, in the world circuits of productive branches, jobs and production corresponding to skilled work processes and above all engineering remained outside these countries as a whole. (Lipietz, 1987: 78–9)

Today, probably many of these processes do exist in the South but these economies will still remain peripheral to whatever is the 'hightech' technology of the day, be it information technology, biotechnology or some other new technology.

If the 1970s were dominated by the NIDL, so the 1990s were overwhelmed by the process of 'globalisation' (see Chapter 3) which had been maturing in the 1980s. While the development process of the post-war period was centred around nationally oriented industrialisation, the new dominant process of 'globalisation' breaks with national economic development models. By the 1980s development had been redefined in the dominant discourse to mean liberalisation in all domains – that is, opening up the economy to the world market – doing away with the role of the state wherever possible, and making private profit the *sine qua non*. McMichael detects an explicit 'globalisation project', which encapsulates well that this is something driven and does not just occur naturally (as the weather!). For McMichael,

> the globalisation project combines several strands: (1) an emerging consensus among policy makers favoring market-based rather than state-managed development strategies; (2) centralised management of global market rules by the G7 states; (3) implementation of these rules by the multilateral agencies: the World Bank, the IMF, the WTO; (4) concentration of market power in the hands of transnational corporations and financial power in the hands of transnational banks; (5) subordination of former Second and Third World states to these global institutional forces. (McMichael, 2000: 177)

What globalisation means to the majority of the world's workers living in the global South is, above all, a closer integration with the world economy. Compared to the situation of the 1950s,

> The world economy [today] is more closely integrated than ever before: the market is rapidly superseding government controls and planning as a mechanism for allocating resources ... Thus the context in which employment, income inequality and poverty are discussed has changed beyond recognition. (ILO, 1995: 68–9)

By 1995 there were 2.5 billion workers in the global labour force, which is almost twice as many as in 1965; and, most significantly, 99 per cent of the projected 1 billion increase in the world's labour force between 1995 and 2015 will occur in what are known as the low- and middle-income economies or the South (World Bank, 1995: 9). What is particularly significant in comparing the NIDL era of the 1970s to the globalisation era of the 1990s is that, while in the earlier period fully two-thirds of the world's workers were living in either planned economies (East) or under nationalist-statist regimes (South), by the mid-1990s less than 10 per cent were 'cut off from the economic mainstream', as the World Bank put it (World Bank, 1995: 50).

It would be wrong to assume that if the NIDL brought Fordism to the South, so globalisation would bring post-Fordism. Certainly, some aspects of JIT ('just-in-time') associated with post-Fordism or Toyota-ism were introduced but not a 'social model', which was in a way more 'advanced' than peripheral Fordism. One of the most interesting aspects of the labour process in the advanced technological sectors of the South is their combination with 'traditional' forms of exploitation. Thus in India the consumer electronics industry is characterised by an unbroken chain, from the large 'modern' firm employing thousands of workers in reasonable conditions through to the smallest of workshops employing 'technology ranging from automatic processes in controlled conditions to hand-operated presses of monotonous hand assembly by rooms of girls' (Hölmstrom, 1984: 127). The cosy Northern image of the 'electronic cottage' where autonomous 'teleworkers' enjoy the benefits of post-Fordism is matched in the South by a high-tech cottage industry where computers are put together or used in dilapidated workshops under alternative future labour regimes. Development is always a combined process, but it is also uneven.

That globalisation is an uneven process, as was the NIDL, should go without saying, given the generally uneven and combined development of capitalism since its origins. Only certain regions of the South, and then certain countries and then certain social sectors of them, are being drawn into the accelerated pace of capitalist development in the era of globalisation. While the social inclusion of millions of workers in the capitalist world economy is occurring (as we saw above), there is also an increase in social exclusion both within and between nations and regions. Thus Castells refers, with very little exaggeration, to 'the rise of the Fourth World' (Castells, 1998: 70). The social regression in the former Soviet Union, the so-called 'lost decade' of the 1980s in Latin America, and, above all, the marginalisation of most of sub-Saharan Africa (with the exception of South Africa) from the world economy, are part and parcel of the globalisation process. Economic development in some parts has economic underdevelopment in other parts of the world as its necessary counterpart; social inclusion is matched by social exclusion.

What is important to note at the general level is that globalisation does not have necessary, inevitable or automatic consequences for labour in a given situation. There is no better example to demonstrate this than a comparison of Chile under Pinochet and democratic Chile in the 1990s. Much radical ink has been spent trying to show that the Christian Democrat and Socialist governments which followed the dictator Pinochet carried on with basically the 'same' economic policy. The export-driven growth model under Pinochet (1973–89) was an early neo-liberal experiment based on extreme labour repression. The subsequent Chilean 'model' has, indeed, maintained the outward orientation of its predecessor (an alternative under globalisation is hard to imagine for one country) but with a social and economic growth policy aimed at sustainability and diminishing inequalities. Political democracy, social stability and the broadening of the domestic market mark off the 1990s from the dictatorial period. For the rest of Latin America and, indeed, for the South as a whole the two Chilean models contradict the mantra 'There is no alternative' reiterated by the gurus of globalisation. The complexity and nuances of the Chilean 'models' also contest simplistic left models that act on the basis that in the dark all cats are black.

Finally in this section I would like to emphasise that the NIDL and the 'newest' international division of labour called 'globalisation' hinge around workers above all. As Castells puts it,

> the position in the international division of labour does not depend, fundamentally, on the characteristic of the country but in the characteristics of its labor (including embodied knowledge) and of its insertion in the global economy. (Castells, 1996a: 147).

The famous issue of 'competitiveness' that dominates contemporary economic policy debates is, in fact, not something that occurs between nations (which cannot 'compete' in any meaningful sense) but between workforces or, to be precise, labour regimes. It is an apparent paradox of the era of globalisation that while the labour movement has never been weaker, workers have never been more important to capitalism. The implementation of the new ICT and the development of a new(er) international division of labour depend on workers to implement them, in the South as much as (if not more than) in the already industrialised North. Workers are not pawns in the game of globalisation but, rather, an integral element in its successful 'take' in a given region or sector of the economy.

INFORMALISATION

If we were to cast around for just one distinguishing characteristic of working life in the South compared to the North it would have to be what is called 'informalisation'. Informal work is usually defined as any which takes place outside the formal wage-labour market, such as clandestine work and illegal work, but also including various forms of self-employment. It is a global phenomenon and not just pertaining to the South, although its level there is considerably higher. It is estimated that informal work in the industrialised economies involves between 2 and 15 per cent of the working population (Standing, 1999a: 112), while in the South it is considered to fluctuate between 30 and 80 per cent of the working population (ILO, 1997: 175). Such a wide variation in estimates indicates that no one really knows the extent of the informal sector. What we shall stress in the pages that follow is less the informal sector (which gives it a unity and coherence it does not possess) than the *process* of informalisation, a tendency accentuated by globalisation for work and workers to become informalised.

The informal-sector model was developed in the 1970s as a theoretical device to account for the reality of 'underemployment', a category derived from the formal labour markets of the industrialised economies of the North. It assumed exclusion of workers from the formal economy and their absorption in the informal economy of small enterprises, often employing family members. It was assumed that 'barriers to entry', in terms of capital skills or technology, were less than in the formal capitalist economy. There was an implicit expectation in the model that this sector would help 'absorb' the growing mass of people thrown off the land or out of urban jobs through capitalist development. However, as Alison Scott writes, 'informal sector theory has been extensively criticised on empirical, methodological and theoretical grounds' (Scott, 1994: 181). Barriers to entry were not so low, and the implicit dualism of the model (the formal/informal divide) was dubious given the movement of workers between the 'sectors'. The optimism of these theorists was also seen to be misplaced; the informal sector was no panacea for the labouring poor of the South.

The problem of dualism was probably the most fundamental one in the informal-sector theorising. Like all dichotomies or binary oppositions, the notion that formal/informal employment were rigid categories was flawed. It assumed a distinction between the two sectors that did not exist, given that the two were completely interrelated. It ignored intermediate or mixed forms of employment. It failed to recognise the diversity of class interests within the overall category of the informal sector. The sector was said to embrace a whole range of occupations, including the small manufacturing workshop, small-scale retailing and transport units, casual building labour, domestic service and various illegal activities. The only unifying factors across the range of work and workers are a certain general instability of employment, an avoidance of most labour laws, and a tendency to remain outside normal capitalist rules of contract, licensing and taxation. If the first attempt to theorise the sector was flawed, we might seek to examine this kind of work and workers from within a class perspective.

From a world systems perspective, Alejandro Portes sought to integrate the notion of informality within a class analysis of peripheral societies (Portes, 1985). The urban informal sector (the petty-bourgeois self-employed and the informal proletariat) is seen as a subsidy to capitalist accumulation given its high levels of self-exploitation. In a later landmark analysis with Manuel Castells, Portes pointed to how the informal economy 'simultaneously encompasses flexibility and exploitation, productivity and abuse, aggressive entrepreneurs and defenceless workers, libertarianism and greediness' (Castells and Portes, 1989: 1). These dichotomies capture well the essentially contradictory nature of informalisation, even more significant perhaps than its universal character. Its social boundaries are fluid and its politics are indeterminate. As a specific production relationship, the informal should not be read as a simple euphemism for poverty or social exclusion. This unregulated relationship of production and income-generation activity is not 'marginal' to capitalist development in the South today but an integral element of its dynamic.

It is important to realise that the informal sector is not some unfortunate carry-over from an earlier era. What is most noticeable in Latin America is precisely the continuity in regard to the informal sector that accounted for 30 per cent of all employment in 1980, exactly the same proportion employed in informal activities in 1950. Nor is informalisation a process which governments resist on behalf of the rule of law; on the contrary, it is a rich source of patronage and a potential means to defuse social conflict. As to the dynamic of informalisation, Castells and Portes are surely right to argue that 'Undermining organised labor's control over the work process seems to be a common objective of informalisation, although it is not its sole cause' (Castells and Portes, 1990: 281). Certainly, a major incentive for the managers of informalisation is a weakening of the social role of labour and an atomisation of the workforce. Yet, informalisation can also be seen as an early precursor of the 1980s' wave of liberalisation as 'entrepreneurs' sought to escape state regulation of the economy in terms of taxation, labour legislation or general rules on the conduct of capitalist business.

A major issue to emerge in the reconstituted-informal-sector analysis of the 1980s was that of its gendered nature. Alison Scott summarises the findings of this research in terms of 'a) a disproportionate concentration of women in the informal sector, compared to men, b) excessive gender segregation within both formal and informal sectors, and c) significant male–female earning differentials' (Scott, 1994: 28–9). Informalisation can thus be seen to proceed hand-in-hand with the feminisation of the labour force *and* of poverty. According to the ILO, women make up 80 per cent of the world's homeworkers (ILO, 1997). It is the economic restructuring on a world scale which preceded and accompanied globalisation (see Chapter 3) that has, according to Val Moghadam, 'entailed increasing utilisation of female labour in formal and non-regular employment' (Moghadam, 1995: 118). While women increasingly entered the paid labour market in the 1980s, they did so largely in a subordinate role. Women in the process of informalisation also provided, however, a crucial link with the domestic economy and the community in a process which would have far-reaching effects.

Turning to the present situation, we need to examine the thesis that globalisation is leading to an increase in informalisation along with all forms of social exclusion. The World Bank advances an optimistic view that 'The informal sector shrinks with development' (World Bank, 1995: 35), but provides little evidence beyond aggregate statistics for a few countries. There are considerably more indications that informalisation is on the increase. Consider, for example, that nine out of ten jobs created in Latin America in 1997 were in the service sector, and out of those nine out of ten were in the informal services (ILO, 1997: 173). So, only one in ten of these new jobs is in the 'new economy', in the communications or financial markets sector for example. The rest are in domestic service, non-professional self-employment or in micro-enterprises – all poorly paid, unstable and precarious forms of employment, on the fringes of legality in many cases. Yet again we see the combined and uneven development of the labour market as globalisation brings high-tech sectors to the South, but also reproduces the 'traditional' informal activities of domestic services and other such occupations.

Informalisation has distinct connotations in different regions of the South. According to the ILO it is estimated that in Africa the urban informal sector today 'employs about 61 per cent of the urban labour force and will generate some 93 per cent of all additional jobs in the region in the 1990s' (ILO, 1997: 179). The ILO estimates that in Asia the informal sector accounts for between 40 and 50 per cent of the urban labour force, but this figure masks a wide variation between the NICs or Asian Tigers at around 10 per cent and Bangladesh with a figure as high as 65 per cent. In Latin America, as already mentioned, nearly nine out of ten jobs generated in the first half of the 1990s were in the informal sector. This growth of informalisation can be accounted for generally by a lack of dynamism in the formal economy, the severe contraction of public-sector employment due to the structural adjustment programmes (SAPs) of the 1970s, and the overall trend towards flexibilisation of the labour market (see Chapter 3). Indeed, for the workers of the South the much-vaunted 'flexibilisation' of work actually spells informalisation.

We can conclude, with Guy Standing, that the 1980s saw 'the romanticising of the *informal sector*, as a vehicle for labour absorption and means of redistribution' (Standing, 1999b: 581). As late as the mid-1990s a major United Nations University study of 'global employment' still felt compelled to warn that 'the informal sector should not be idealised or considered a permanent panacea for unemployment and underemployment' (Simai, 1995b: 20). Even this framing of the issue seems to concede too much: is it even a 'temporary' panacea? The whole notion of 'upgrading' the informal sector, which permeates most of the literature, seems misconceived. Capitalism would not be capitalism if it was willing and able to 'upgrade' the informal sector with 'more stable and sustainable and skill-intensive production' (Simai, 1995b: 20) as the informal sector's reformers argue for. Instead we need to recognise that informalisation is a critical component of capitalist globalisation today, particularly but not exclusively in the global South. Its main effect is to undermine organised labour and facilitate the development of disorganised capitalism.

Our final theme in relation to informalisation is organisation, the question of whether the trade unions can mobilise workers in this sector. As the ILO puts it, 'It would be unrealistic to expect trade unions and/or employers' organisations to cover entirely the needs and demands of such an expanding and heterogeneous sector' (ILO,

1997: 193). However, as with the high-tech and information sector *worker* – employees of the North – a breakthrough in this sector is probably the litmus test of the continued relevance of trade unions to the world's workers of today. What we do detect is a serious willingness on behalf of the trade unions, including the international leadership, to engage with the issue. Thus Luis Anderson, a leading ICFTU unionist, argues that the trade unions in Latin America have become involved with the informal sector, 'assuming responsibilities that should be borne by governments, the political parties and the more powerful classes. They assume that role due to solidarity' (Anderson and Trentin, 1996: 52). They engage with the informal workers, perhaps assisting them in creating a co-operative or a 'third sector' firm which, if successful, may in time lead them to distance themselves from the union.

It is in relation to women workers that some of the most significant organisational advances in the informal sector have occurred. As the ILO noted in the mid-1990s, 'The past decade has witnessed a proliferation of women's groups in the informal sector' (ILO, 1997: 197). Ties of solidarity based on gender interests have been significant. Perhaps the paradigmatic case is that of SEWA (Self-Employed Women's Association) in India, which evolved out of the women's wing of the Textile Labour Association. This case shows most clearly that while informal workers may resist, for good reasons and bad, incorporation into traditional trade-union structures, they can readily find common ground with trade unions that allow space for their particular characteristics and needs. As an ILO report notes, specifically referring to SEWA, 'informal workers would normally welcome any association with mainstream trade unions if this allowed them to deal with issues concerning their precarious situation and economic and social disadvantage' (ILO, 1997: 204). When dealing with women-only or gender-oriented organisations we also find a much greater role being played by NGOs and other non-labour-movement bodies.

Confronting the issue of informalisation has also made trade unions more aware of the community beyond the workplace, and issues beyond wages and conditions. Informal workers' organisations are often neighbourhood-based, thus breaking with one of the essential characteristics of trade unions. Less bound by the traditions of labour, if at all, and often individualist and then communalist in orientation, they are still recognisably labour organisations. A traditional industrial relations structure and a 'free collective bargaining' orientation by the trade unions would hardly be relevant in these situations. Workers in the informal sector may well not organise around traditional 'worker' issues as, necessarily, they will need to deal with the threat of eviction, access to credit, and low prices for their goods, for example. However, it is also important to realise that many of those working under conditions of informalisation may have been industrial workers before structural adjustment, back in the 1980s. While informalisation, in essence, conspires against the strength and interests of organised labour, the informal workers themselves have played an important role in helping revive labour strategies in the 1990s.

WOMEN WORKING WORLDWIDE

There is a general perception that the number and the proportion of women working (i.e. in paid as against unpaid work) worldwide has increased significantly in the era of globalisation. Indeed, one of the main features of the NIDL diagnosed in the 1970s was, precisely, the increased employment of women workers in the 'world market factories'. This shift in the composition of gendered labour in the 1970s and 1980s was consolidated in the 1990s as globalisation got into full swing. In the East (ex-Soviet Union and Eastern Europe) half the paid labour force was female still in 1990; in Southeast Asia that proportion was around 40 per cent; and, as Val Moghadam puts it, 'even regions where cultural restrictions and economic structures inhibited female employment – the Middle East, North Africa and South Asia – saw increases in female labour force participation and in the female share of the formal sector labour force' (Moghadam, 1995: 111). It was these changes, just sketched in here, which led to the development of the 'global feminisation' thesis in the 1990s.

In 1989 Guy Standing (of the ILO) systematised this perspective, arguing that the 1980s were the decade of labour deregulation but 'also marked a renewed surge of feminisation of labor activity' (Standing, 1989: 1077). This entailed not only an increase in the proportion of women in the paid labour force but also the transformation/feminisation of what had hitherto been considered 'male' occupations. Export-led industrialisation and the SAPs severely impacted on the economics of the South and in the political economy of labour. In particular they led to the deregulation of labour standards, a 'flexibilisation' of work, and a decomposition of jobs. What the 'global feminisation' argument

then does is link these transformations with the growing incorporation of women into the paid labour force, which, argues Standing, has
'almost certainly more to do with the feminisation of labor, a desire to
have a more disposable (or 'flexible') labor force with lower fixed costs,
and so on' (Standing, 1989: 1086) than with changes in legislation or
women's educational levels or other factors. This thesis was not without its critics, however suggestive it might seem.

First of all, there can be too quick a leap from detecting increasing
participation by women in the paid labour force to conclusions about
a changing gender division of labour. Diane Elson rightly concludes
that 'the restructuring of labour contracts and the altering of job
boundaries in the name of "flexibility" is in fact much more likely to
take place in a gender differentiated way than to be a force for over-
coming the sexual division of labour' (Elson, 1996: 38). Gender segregation and subordination within the world of work is not 'overridden'
in some way by flexibilisation. In both the formal and the informal
labour sectors, a gender division of labour pre-exists which structures
how 'flexibilisation' will occur and even how it will be interpreted (e.g.
its positive or negative connotations will be gendered). The second
main issue is the implicitly negative connotation Standing and others
put on 'flexibility'. It has been argued on the basis of case studies –
for example, Martha Roldan's study of women in the light engineering
industry in Argentina – that 'it should be possible to adapt JIT systems
to women workers' co-operatives and other units of the social sector'
(Roldan, 1996: 85).

At an empirical level we need to take note of what changes the
global feminisation argument draws attention to. In a follow-up analysis in 1999, Guy Standing examined trends in male and female activity
rates between 1975 and 1995 in a sample of developing countries and
found that in 74 per cent of cases women's participation increased,
compared to 17 per cent where men's did (9 per cent showed no
change) (Standing, 1999a: 587). The change in the gender composition is seen to be even greater when we add that in most of the
countries where male participation rates fell, the total labour force
participation actually increased. While it would be wrong simply to
equate flexibilisation and feminisation, Standing is surely right to draw
attention to the possible linkages between the two processes. The
point for Standing is that while women's participation in the labour
force is leading (at least potentially) to greater gender equality, the

conditions under which they are working have not improved. Indeed 'the trend is towards greater insecurity and inequality' (Standing, 1999a: 600). While some positive potential for 'flexibility' may exist, from a labour point of view its negative connotations, in this sense, should not be ignored.

The global 'feminisation' of work thesis is intimately related to the issue of 'flexibilisation' supposedly characteristic of the new information economy. There is an optimistic rendering of 'flexible specialisation' which imagines it as a panacea for workers today. Yet this benign view is imbued with a deep-rooted Northern perspective inimical to the interests of the majority of the world's workers. Thus Piore and Sabel, leading proponents of the flexible specialisation school, argue that 'It is conceivable that flexible specialisation and mass production could be combined in a unified *international economy*. In this system, the old mass production industries might migrate to the underdeveloped world, leaving behind in the industrialised world the high-tech industries' (Piore and Sabel, 1984: 279). Here we find a continuity between the implicit dualism of the core/periphery model of segmented work in the North and the uncritically accepted dualism between North and South in the international division of labour. While the 'new technology' cannot be seen as progressive or even neutral, it has had a significant impact in the South.

From the Fordist assembly line of the 'world market factories' in the 1970s to the JIT methods of the 1990s, technology has been upgrading in the South. Though not linear or necessarily cumulative – because development is always uneven and combined – technological change is having a profound impact on the social and sexual division of labour. In the 1970s, as never before, female labour power became a marketable commodity in the South. A Malaysian investment brochure illustrates well how capitalism and patriarchy have a synergy in this regard, telling the potential Northern investor, 'The manual dexterity of the oriental female is famous the world over. Her hands are small and she works fast with extreme care. Who, therefore, could be better qualified by nature and inheritance to contribute to the efficiency of a bench-assembly production line than the Oriental girl?' (cited in Elson and Pearson, 1981: 149). It was not surprising to see capital, the state and patriarchal interests in society working together towards the efficient exploitation of women in these factories created by the new international division of labour.

Yet, it is well to remember that the one thing worse than exploitation is not being exploited at all, as Joan Robinson is supposed to have said. Thus Kumudhini Rosa, in a broad overview of women workers in the FTZs, points out how 'some recent [research] contributions have stressed the gains for women in terms of greater freedom and status from earning a wage' (Rosa, 1994: 74). So, in spite of the precarious, exploitative and patriarchal nature of this employment, it could be empowering for women workers. Co-operation and different forms of solidarity – of gender, of class, of community or others – could be generated in their workplaces. Sites of exploitation can also be sites of contestation. Coincidentally, or probably not, many women workers in 'world market factories' began to lose their jobs in the late 1980s in a reverse process of 're-masculinisation', we might say. What continued in these workplaces, and in their new 'post-Fordist' successors, was a totally gendered struggle between capital accumulation strategies and strategies of labour defence and renewal.

There are two general points to be made usefully at this stage, I believe. The first is that in much of the 'feminisation' debate there is an implicit male norm against which transformations are measured. Yet the notion of a full-time, permanent, skilled male job is basically a myth. To measure the 'flexible' job of today against a mythical norm can only lead to a debilitating binary opposition. Second, neither 'flexibilisation' nor 'feminisation' can be seen as unidirectional or permanent trends. Rather, they reflect specific capital accumulation strategies at different times in different places. They reflect also differentiated state strategies in specific conjunctures and regions. The third problem is in relation to the 'visibility' of the high-tech sectors (as the world market factories before them) compared to the more 'irregular' (though the term is problematic when it describes what is actually the regular) forms of employment in the informal sector and in homeworking, where the majority of women, especially in the South, actually work.

If some women have been sucked into the maelstrom of the globalised, informationalised economy, many more are working in the informal sector and are the mainstay of the homeworkers' labour economy. As Alison Scott notes, in much of the informal sector research 'the focus has been on the way women's activities complemented and replicated their domestic roles: much of women's informal work was carried out in the home (e.g. outwork, front-room shops, laundry work)' (Scott, 1995: 29). Work and home intersected here in a way that was extremely profitable for capital. The role of women in terms of basic 'household survival strategies' across the South was harnessed in the interests of capital accumulation. In the reproduction of that particular commodity known as labour-power (people's capacity to work) women's work both in the home and in the labour market thus acts as a substantive subsidy. In terms of women working world-wide, this sector is probably where most research needs to be done to understand better the relationships between class and gender, produc-tion and reproduction, domestic economy and labour markets.

What work in the informal sector mainly means for women workers is 'casualisation'. That is to say, 'For women, flexible working often means greater insecurity, reduction in working hours and pay, changes in shifts, loss of national insurance benefit, loss of overtime bonuses, and loss of holidays, maternity leave, sick pay and pension' (cited in Mitter, 1994: 13). This type of worker is as much part of 'flexible specialisation' worldwide as is the graduate computer expert in Silicon Valley. It is an integral part of the way the big MNCs operate on a worldwide basis. International subcontracting out into the informal sector has become normal practice even (especially?) for the big brand names. The advantage, as Swasti Mitter explains, is that 'the workers employed by the local sub-contractors remain flexible and invisible' (Mitter, 1994: 21). Of course, as we shall see later, this growing con-nectivity between capital and labour, in all its myriad forms world-wide, also exposes it to various new forms of campaigning, for example from the consumption end.

Homeworking, as a specific form of waged employment, has since the mid-1980s been recognised by the international trade-union move-ment as a priority for organising. Previously there would have been an attitude that this was not 'proper' work or that it 'undercut' work done by established trade-union members in the formal sector. In 1990 the ICFTU issued a quite comprehensive report entitled *On Organising Workers in the Informal Sector* (ICFTU, 1990), which was helpful in pushing the ILO towards new legislation for homeworkers across the globe. Though subsumed under the slightly anomalous label of 'atypical' work, homeworking was now placed firmly on the labour movement agenda. It is significant that the issue of homeworking also broadened out the way trade unions operated. Inevitably women's organisations internationally played a major role in the networking, researching and organising involved and thus, to some extent, influenced the way trade unions operated. In many ways these activities were precursory and exemplary of what later became known as social-movement unionism.

In conclusion, while in the era of globalisation (and the period leading up to it) women entered the labour market in greater numbers than ever before, they did so in a situation dominated by the watchwords of liberalisation, privatisation and flexibilisation. In short, women working worldwide entered what can only be called a 'casualised' labour market. Even the World Bank acknowledges that

> women [workers] are often more vulnerable than men, disproportionately concentrated in low-wage sectors or occupations and often segregated into the informal sector. Not surprisingly, their relative position has often deteriorated during structural adjustment. (World Bank, 1995: 1071)

Women are often among the last to be drawn into the labour market when an economic upturn occurs, and among the first to be expelled from it during cyclical downturn. However, from a long-term perspective it can be said that women workers are no longer a 'reserve army' of labour, having been fully integrated into the capitalist labour market on a worldwide scale.

TRADE-UNION RESPONSES

If in the Golden Era it seemed that the workers of the North were the undisputed pioneers of organisational methods and ideological innovation, in the era of globalisation the lead has in many ways passed to the workers of the South. It is symptomatic that US labour analyst Kim Moody heads one of his chapters on labour's response to globalisation 'Looking South' (Moody, 1997: 201). The labour leaders of Europe and North America have been forced to leave behind their paternalism towards the labour movements of the South. Globalisation integrated production on an unprecedented scale and (as seen in Chapter 2) brought together the fates of workers across the globe to a much greater extent. If US labour leaders were 'looking South' with other than a 'trade-union imperialist' perspective, it was because the workers of the South now counted in the global political economy of labour. One area in particular where a breakthrough had occurred was in the semi-industrialised or semi-periphery countries such as Brazil,

South Africa and, more recently, South Korea where vibrant labour movements had crystallised in the 1980s.

As part of the NIDL (see above), countries such as Brazil and South Africa went through a process of forced industrialisation from the 1970s onwards. This was a state-led industrialisation under conditions of severe political repression – in short, what at the time was dubbed a 'savage capitalism'. As Gay Seidman explains in a powerful analysis,

> From the perspective of both states, economic growth required high profits to attract foreign and domestic investors to new industrial sectors; and it required closure of political space to protect the stable business climate required to compete with other potential investment sites. (Seidman, 1994: 259)

In these pressurised hothouse conditions capital accumulation flourished, but so did a new industrial working class. In practically 'classical' capitalist growth conditions a proletariat was generated which began to take consciousness of its situation, to organise and to act on behalf of its social needs. We need only note that in South Africa there were 30,000 black trade unionists in 1973 and 550,000 by 1983. In Brazil the 'new unionism' shot to prominence after strikes at the end of the 1970s and played a key role in the later transition to democracy.

In South Africa, the best organised of the first independent labour federations, FOSATU (Federation of South African Trade Unions), was by 1983 operating in over 500 factories, committed to:

- democratic factory floor organisation;
- a united labour force irrespective of race, gender or creed;
- social justice, a decent standard of living and fair working conditions for the whole working class (cited in McShane et al., 1984: 38).

FOSATU and its affiliates were key players in a number of successful consumer boycotts against recalcitrant employers, campaigns around housing issues, and for cheaper transport. Though FOSATU was dubbed 'workerist' in the inter-trade-union debates, it was increasingly drawn into community-based as well as factory-floor struggles and began to take positions on the key political issues of the day. By 1985, a united labour federation, COSATU (Congress of South African Trade Unions), had been formed, which went on to play a crucial organisational, mobilising and political role in the struggle against apartheid rule and in the new democratic South Africa.

In Brazil, strikes in the metallurgical plants in São Paulo's industrial belt in 1978–79 spread to other professions and to the remotest
provinces of the country. An important feature of these strikes was the
advanced level of organisation in the form of a general strike committee, with struggles frequently cutting across occupational lines and
massive street demonstrations. Struggles in the working-class districts
occurred around a whole series of day-to-day issues such as health
care, running water and, above all, housing. When the strike wave
began, the dense social networks built up in these communities played
a crucial role in generating solidarity for the factory workers. Churches
often provided shelter and cover for the organising of the then clandestine trade unions. In the words of Zé Pedro, one of the São Paulo
metalworkers' leaders, workers started 'by demanding a share of what
they produce, they want better wages, better living conditions, and
then start viewing political parties in a different light' (cited in
Antunes, 1980: 33). After the formation of the united CUT (Unified
Worker Central) in 1983 unions and others effectively went on to form
the Workers Party in 1989, which was to play a key role in the struggle for democratisation and beyond.

Practically a decade later a new unionism was generated in South
Korea, one of the much-vaunted Asian Tigers, under fierce authoritarian rule. An even more intensely forced capitalist growth – by the
mid-1990s, 80 per cent of the population of this once rural economy
lived in the cities – created the conditions for a veritable explosion of
labour activism from the late 1980s onwards. Women workers accounted for 40 per cent of the workforce and, as one Korean study
puts it, it is they who 'have really been the driving force not only to
bestow on the nascent labor movement a dynamic character but also
to actually lead it at the grassroots level' (cited in Moody, 1997: 214).
With the formation of the Korean Confederation of Trade Unions
(KCTU) in 1995 this labour movement had come of age. The 1996
general strike, an unprecedented confrontation by labour with capital
and the state, established that labour movement on the political scene
and within civil society. In the future these trends may repeat themselves in Indonesia (see Lambert, 1999), in Mexico or in the countries
of the East.

Over and beyond the particular cases cited above and their specific
national histories, there seem to be certain general conclusions to be
drawn. The particular conditions of late industrialisation generated

not only a new working class but also a new form of trade unionism, which we can call social-movement unionism as against the economism of 'free collective bargaining' and the tradition of 'political bargaining'. These workers turned increasingly to those beyond the factory gate, including the informal sector, and took up issues other than production ones, such as consumption or transport concerns of the broader working population. Their trade unions also turned to organisations and movements beyond the traditional confines of the labour movement, including community groups, women's organisations, human rights movements and radical church groups and networks. The social-movement unionism that emerged also turned naturally to the political arena, articulating a clear workers' voice in the struggle to impose democracy on the repressive political order that had prevailed as it took shape.

Another area already mentioned, where workers in the South pioneered labour strategies of renewal and resistance, was in relation to the informal sector. Though we must be wary of elevating the case study into a trend, SEWA in India remains exemplary. Renana Jhabvala, analyst and member of SEWA, describes how this movement cut across occupational categories in its organisation and combined trade-union and co-operative methodologies: 'When the co-operatives become part of the trade union it changes the image of the union and helps it win allies, sometimes even with the "enemy"' (Jhabvala, 1994: 133). Thus SEWA could combine aggressive trade-union demands with 'softer' action in health and childcare co-operatives for workers in conjunction with the district administration: 'even the employers were shamed into supporting the childcare centres' (Jhabvala, 1994: 133–4). What SEWA has created in its imaginative and forceful discourse and activity is a vision of a new society. It has shown how an organisation of the labouring poor can be grounded in the day-to-day reality of its 'non-pure-proletarian' members and articulate a general alternative to dependent capitalist development.

What SEWA and other similar organisations across the South have actually done is to break with the formal/informal labour-sector dichotomy. SEWA members include many sectors of the self-employed ('casualised labour' being rejected as derogatory), from small-scale vendors and traders, home-based producers such as weavers and *bidi* (cigarette) makers, as well as agricultural and other labourers. This array of occupations is unified (if at all) only by gender. In the same

way that SEWA cuts across work categories, it conflates political categories, combining distinct forms of organisation and synthesising
different oppositional ideologies. Unsurprisingly from the perspective
of 'contradictory class locations' (Wright, 1985), or fluid identities, it
organises and defends the interests of labourers and the co-operative
self-employed in a given industry at the same time. The context in
which SEWA and similar organisations operate is, of course, always
that of underdevelopment and the overarching need for social and
economic development. In this sense, finally, they represent not just
the 'particular' interests of their members but the general interests of
society as well.

The ILO concludes a broad review of industrial relations worldwide at the turn of the century with the verdict that 'Almost everywhere … including in the informal sector of developing countries,
successes have been achieved in defending and promoting the interests
of the weakest section of the population' (ILO, 1997: 228). Though
this is far from being an established trend, a totally negative view
would probably be incorrect. There are many problems for a labour
response, including the 'crisis of representation' of what a trade union
actually is. Certainly a view looking towards (or from) the South would
stress the heterogeneity of the labour condition and the breadth of
coverage and vision needed by workers' organisations today. Strategic,
and not just tactical, alliances are being forged by these organisations
– generically described as social-movement unionism – with consumers, organisations, campaigning NGOs, SME (small and medium enterprise networks), women's groups and mutual aid organisations, for
example.

While much of the impetus for change came from workers at the
base, trade-union leadership had undergone major shifts by the 1980s.
Certainly the resolutions of the ICFTU became more 'progressive' in
the 1990s and even the archetypal 'business unionism' of the AFL–
CIO took on a more 'social' flavour. Rather than review these statements, a more revealing, and probably more genuine, understanding
arguably comes from a 'conversation' between Luis Anderson (a leading ICFTU Latin America trade unionist) and Bruno Trentin (a leading Italian trade unionist) recorded in the mid-1990s. The exchange
seemed to be a real engagement with some of the issues raised in this
chapter as challenges for the trade-union movement today, and a serious attempt to develop more than rhetorical alternatives to 'really

existing' trade unionism. I record some of Anderson's and Trentin's comments here.

On the informal sector:

> The objective of representing informal work in our countries implies a true cultural revolution and, yes, it would be a bit like going back and confronting situations, conditions and strategies similar to those the trade-union movement confronted when it was born. (Anderson and Trentin, 1996: 66)

On 'representativity':

> We need to broaden the base of representativity, widen it to include new categories or workers, to include and offer representation to those not enrolled. This would reinforce the representativity and democratic nature of the union. (Anderson and Trentin, 1996: 110)

> The union suffers a crisis of representativity and of identity, in all its forms and in all countries. (Anderson and Trentin, 1996: 15)

On the ICFTU:

> It has huge potential. However, it resists abandoning the old way of governing economies, inherited from the Cold War. It should be proposing new instruments to control the process of globalisation ... to counter the exclusion and impoverishment of whole areas of the world which has reached intolerable levels. (Anderson and Trentin, 1996: 97)

On trade-union renewal:

> We speak of a cultural revolution, because it means changing completely the horizon of trade-union strategy and to change, at the same time, the forms of representation which the trade union had adopted for a whole century (Anderson and Trentin, 1996: 93).

Trade unions, labour movements, social movements and the labouring poor in the South were severely affected by so-called 'structural adjustments' to meet the requirements of liberalising globalisation. Trade union 'density' (i.e. union membership as a percentage of all wage and salary earners) declined on the whole between 1985 and 1995 but not everywhere, as we see in Table 5.1.

Even this complex and uneven picture is only part of the story and masks the qualitative picture on the ground in developing countries. It tells us very little about development in the broader social movement of labouring people or of political transformations. Our conclusion

TABLE 5.1 TRADE-UNION DENSITY

Country	1985–95 change (%)
Egypt	−9
South Africa	+130
Argentina	−42
Cuba	−30
Mexico	−28
Venezuela	−42
South Korea	+3
Philippines	+85
Hong Kong	+34
Singapore	−18

Source: ILO, 1997: 45.

can only be a cautious one. Some notable 'success stories' have been mentioned where trade unions responded imaginatively to the forces unleashed by globalisation. This picture must, though, be tempered with an acknowledgement of the fundamental social weakening of labour during this period.

THE 'SOCIAL CLAUSE' DEBATE

The 'social clause' debate is at once the most divisive issue separating workers in the South from their counterparts in the North and the strategy best placed to unify the world's workers. We examine here what it is all about: arguments for, arguments against and a credible way forward for a global labour rights strategy. The current round of interest in a 'social' or 'workers' rights' clause in international trade agreements became marked during the Uruguay Round of the GATT negotiations in the early 1990s. However, the concept goes back at least to the period after the Second World War. Though in the heyday of the neo-liberal drive in the early to mid-1990s this initiative was presented as some form of protectionist nightmare, the issue of 'labour standards' was taken up by the WTO, which succeeded GATT in

1995. What was at one time a fairly marginal (even token) concern of the international trade-union movement (the ICFTU to be precise) was now to become a key debated point in the world's powerful multi-lateral trade regulator.

The basic argument in the 'social clause' is that trade liberalisation promoted by GATT and the WTO would undermine workers' rights without such a clause, as investment would inevitably move to where workers' rights were weakest. This would create pressure on all countries to weaken labour regulation to make their products competitive and their territory an attractive investment location. What the 'social clause' to be incorporated into multilateral trade agreements would include are basically the main ILO 'core conventions', as they are known. This included No. 87 (1948) on freedom of association, No. 98 (1949) on the right to organise and engage in collective bargaining, Nos 29 (1930) and 105 (1957) on the abolition of forced labour, No. 138 (1957) on the abolition of child labour, and Nos 100 (1951) and 111 (1918) on discrimination in employment. These were deemed 'core' conventions because governments, employers and trade unions (part of the ILO's tripartite structure) across the globe freely subscribed to them as applying to *all* who work, including in the informal sector and in the FTZs. In 1998 the International Labour Conference adopted the ILO declaration that obliged all member states to implement the 'core' conventions, even if they had not ratified them previously.

At first glance there is little here that any worker anywhere could object to. It is also fairly easy to dispose of the arguments against core labour rights from a neo-liberal perspective that sees them conspiring against the hegemony of market principles. First, 'it is neither conceptually nor empirically clear that higher labour standards mean higher labour costs' (Freeman, 1994: 108). Thus, in terms of international competitiveness there would be no undue burden on particular nations or companies if basic labour rights were to be respected worldwide (starting with the USA, where ILO core conventions still remain unratified). To harmonise labour standards worldwide would prevent a 'race to the bottom', which would not be beneficial to capital. There is also a view that adhering to international labour standards would be detrimental to the prospects of developing countries. The OECD, in a lengthy study of this issue, concluded, however, that 'any fear on the part of developing countries that better core standards would negatively affect either their economic performance or their competitive position in world markets has no economic rationale' (OECD, 1996: 105). So, labour standards are not necessarily bad for business.

One of the issues where a 'social clause' has most plausibility and potential consensus is in relation to child labour and its abolition. However, it can be, and has been, argued that proscribing child labour in the South without compensation would lower the living standards of those who are already desperately poor. Those underage who would be 'saved' from child labour – for example, working on carpets or footballs – could be driven into prostitution or destitution. While the child-labour debate is a complex one, and not immune to various forms of paternalism or racism, we cannot just conclude that a policy initiative is vitiated by its unintended negative side effects. I find myself in agreement fundamentally with Rohini Hensman, for whom

> there is surely an element of class racism in any justification for allowing the children of the Third World poor to be subjected to deprivation and abuse which would be unthinkable for 'our' children. Nor is there any basis for arguments that eradicating it is somehow very complicated. It merely requires some very clear public policy choices. Child labour should be banned, and those employing children punished. (Hensman, 2001: 439)

The argument 'for' the social clause is perhaps best summarised through the ICFTU's ten campaigning ideas on the issue, which are, in summary:

1. The standards in a workers' rights clause as proposed are among the most highly ratified of the ILO.
2. A workers' rights clause would be protective and not protectionist, seeking not to undermine economic competition but to enhance it by removing unfair advantages.
3. It would restore policy against the enormous MNCs, aiming to limit the abuse of power.
4. It would ensure discriminations would be penalised in the world trading system.
5. It would eliminate export competitiveness through the exploitation of child labour (although the informal sector is excluded).
6. Free rider countries who do not respect labour standards would be penalised in the interests of the majority.
7. Improvement of workers' rights should accompany promotion of free trade, and the ILO should work with the WTO.

8. If periodic reviews show non-compliance, the ILO should assist in achieving compliance before the WTO exercises sanctions.
9. The violation of core labour standards calls into question the legitimacy of a trading system which allows unscrupulous governments or companies to gain short-term advantage by abusing workers' rights.
10. A multilateral framework for core labour standards would prevent a populist call for protectionism by workers afraid to lose their jobs (from Anner, 2001: 30–31).

The ICFTU campaign can be summarised thus: 'By guaranteeing fair trade, a workers' rights clause would protect free trade.' As trade unions always have, this approach seeks to protect workers' rights without challenging the capitalist system they work under.

It is easy to advocate a 'social clause' as a universal good and counterpose it to nationalist or chauvinist responses. An anti-WTO position can easily be equated with the views of a Pat Buchanan (in the USA) or a Jörg Haider (in Europe), who take on globalisation and the WTO but also extend this to immigrant workers, Jews and others who threaten their Aryan 'way of life'. So in India there is a vigorous campaign against the WTO (and the social clause) by the Hindu nationalist right from the perspective of local capital, cultural nationalism and upper-caste values. As Rohini Hensman writes, 'Economic and cultural nationalism, hatred of multinationals on one side and minorities and communists on the other, are closely linked' (Hensman, 2001: 430) in this ideology. Xenophobia, or even localism, is not an adequate, and certainly not a progressive, alternative to globalisation. Compared to the anti-WTO discourse from the nationalist (right or left) perspective, the discourse of WTO director Mick Moore sounds eminently reasonable. There is certainly a sound case for inclusion of basic labour rights (and a 'fair deal' for the South) within the parameters of the WTO, which will govern international trade in the years to come.

Yet the case against the 'social clause', particularly as articulated within the WTO debates, is a powerful one. It is slightly confusing, as some of the arguments would appear to be inconsistent. On the one hand, some of the Seattle protestors and others believe that given a choice between 'fix it or nix it' in relation to the WTO the choice is a simple one. This position, opposed in principle to transnational regulatory bodies as simple arms of global capitalism, merges into the cultural and economic resistance stances. On the other hand, many in the South oppose the social clause element in particular, on the grounds that it is effectively protectionist. Thus Vandana Shiva on the social clause states that 'It is a one-sided protectionist measure favouring developed countries without giving developing countries the right to protect their economies in specific areas which need protection' (cited in John and Chenoy, 1996: 152). Though an unintentional consequence for activists who argue this position, it is effectively saying that protectionism hinders free trade. Yet, over and above a certain degree of confusion, there is a case to be made against social clauses from a South-based perspective.

The governments of the South have good reason to see the US government's new-found enthusiasm for social and environmental clauses in trade agreements as somewhat suspect. They would almost certainly operate in a protectionist way in denying market access in the North to developing country exports. For Vandana Shiva the social clause does not empower civil society in the South but, rather, business and governments in the North (Shiva, 1996: 108). Furthermore, she argues that the social clause 'does not challenge the logic of free trade and the globalisation of every aspect of local and national economies'; nor does it 'stop the processes that cause Third World poverty' (Shiva, 1996: 108). On the level at which it is posed, this argument is incontestable. Certainly, as in the ICFTU campaign for the social clause, there are huge concessions to the logic of globalising neo-liberalism. However, it is akin to telling trade unions not to pursue higher wages for their members as this does not tackle the roots of oppression in the capital/wage-labour relation. Indeed, there is now an argument being made that all the anti-globalisation protests need to be unified under an anti-capitalist banner to tackle the 'real' roots of all their specific complaints.

There are more specific and grounded criticisms of the 'social clause' campaign made by organisations such as Women Working Worldwide. Thus we can critically unpack what a social clause would mean for women workers in the South. We have already seen above how the ICFTU campaign explicitly excludes from the child-labour campaign the informal sector but also most children working in the countryside. In relation to women workers, Angela Hale makes the apparently simple but far-reaching point that the social clause 'is mainly raised in high-level international forums where there are few women, and workers are referred to without reference to gender. Yet women's work situations are not the same as men's' (Hale, 1999: 28). Much of women's work is in the informal and domestic economies far from local let alone international regulation. Women workers may also have other demands arising from their strategic gender interests. From this perspective the social clause campaign as it exists appears somewhat over-general, rather top-down, and not thought through as to how it might benefit the workers, who are also gendered, who are also citizens in the various regions of the South.

The overarching criticism of the social clause (within the WTO domain) comes from the likes of Third World Network (TWN), a coalition of NGOs that has specifically addressed the issue in international fora. Their main concern is with the extension of the WTO mandate to deal with more issues, such as core labour standards. They view the whole campaign, including the participation of the international trade-union movement, as irredeemably Northern-centred. In essence, the argument is that 'countervailing measures imposed unilaterally by powerful countries on weaker nations (and hardly conceivable the other way round) would lack legality, moral authority and effectiveness to lead to any effective improvement in workers' conditions or human rights situations in poor or rich countries' (cited in O'Brien et al., 2000: 87). While the ICFTU would find it hard to contest the huge North–South gap at the heart of the TWN critique, it is on surer ground in seeking to ensure the global capitalist strategy has a global labour strategy rather than retreating to national strategies. Furthermore, groups like TWN would need to address the question of their representativity even more than the trade unions before their critique could carry more than moral weight.

It is probably not fruitful to continue debating the 'social clause' as a for-or-against issue. To pose a North/South, male/female, formal/informal, industrialist/environmentalist, globaliser/localist set of binary oppositions will simply not advance the debate. This chapter 'looks South', and we return to the 'social clause' from a global perspective in Chapter 7. However, it is worth posing now briefly an alternative perspective to the binary oppositions. I would begin with Amartya Sen's politico-philosophical statement that 'The increasingly globalised world economy calls for a similarly globalised approach to basic ethics and political and social procedures' (Sen, 2000: 127). Not only does this approach mean going beyond an international approach to a truly global one; it also entails viewing labour in a holistic manner. Work is situated within its broad social, economic, political and cultural context. In specific terms, for Sen this means that 'The universality and comprehensive conception of goals is a well-chosen alternative to acting only in the interests of *some* groups of workers, such as those of the organised sector; or those already in employment or those already covered by explicit rules and regulations' (Sen, 2000: 120).

The social clause debate is permeated with vague formulations and undeclared political stances. It demonstrates often an almost complete absence of even a common discursive terrain. Yet a broad holistic approach does allow us to move forward. There is no reason why a campaign for international labour rights should rely on an organisation such as the WTO. It could lobby there certainly but also campaign independently. There is no reason why development priorities should conflict with basic workers' rights. There is no reason why the debate within the WTO, or within the ILO if that is more appropriate, should not be more transparent. There is no reason why it could not formally incorporate the voice of civil society through international trade unions and NGOs. There is no reason why the specific ICFTU campaign should not become less Northern-centred and dovetail more openly with the various campaigning NGOs. To develop a holistic campaign for global labour rights along these lines, however, requires the development of a new understanding of international solidarity, which we now turn to in Chapters 6 and 7.

SIX

THE 'OLD' INTERNATIONALISM

At its inception the labour movement was almost instinctively internationalist in its outlook. However, in the twentieth century there was a steady drift towards a more 'nation-statist' perspective by most Northern unions and labour movements. Conventionally the First World War is seen as the point at which international labour history died. Following the Second World War, the international labour movement was split by the Cold War between the West and 'Communism'. This gave rise to the nefarious practice of 'trade-union imperialism', through which Western unions sought to influence their counterparts in the South. However, the international trade unions also began to counter the MNCs in the 1970s by trying to build countervailing power on the labour side of the capital/wage-labour relation. Finally, this period, before the onset of globalisation in the late 1980s, also saw a number of important internationalist labour campaigns, most notably against the apartheid regime in South Africa, which we can refer to as development solidarity.

NATIONALISM AND INTERNATIONALISM

It is remarkable how relevant the early debates in internationalism are for us now in the era of globalisation. The second half of the nineteenth century also saw a move towards globalisation, with world trade increasing sixfold between 1850 and 1890. Marcel van der Linden, writing about the period of Western state formation, could be referring to the present: 'an improved transport and communication network led to a heightened mobility of labour power and capital, and in its wake a weakening of unions organised solely at a local level' (Van der Linden, 1988: 324). In a very real sense these local unions were forced to become international before they became national. It is as well to remember that in this era, especially after the European revolutionary year of 1848, internationalism was the ideology of the rising liberal bourgeoisie. The *Communist Manifesto* made the ringing declaration of 'Workers of the World Unite' in 1848 and from then on internationalism became the banner of the ascendant labour movement, too, in a way which transformed the term utterly.

In the relatively open borders of Western Europe in the second half of the nineteenth century craft workers could, and did, travel in search of work across countries quite readily and naturally. International contracts between workers happened regularly and solidarity across frontiers followed inevitably. As Eric Hobsbawm puts it,

> the class struggle, in its most elementary but also spontaneous and rooted form of the trade union struggle, *was* internationalist insofar as any division along national, racial or religious or other lines *inevitably* weakens the collective of workers in dispute with an employer. (Hobsbawm, 1988: 91)

There were common experiences, common problems and certain community interests shared by British, French, German and Dutch artisans. Mutual help across borders was a logical extension to mutual help within a particular country. The use of overseas 'scab' labour was being used by employers in the 1850s and this, in particular, needed to be countered by links between workers in different countries. As British workers put it in a famous address to their French counterparts in 1863: 'A fraternity of peoples is highly necessary for the cause of labour ... not to allow our employers to play us off one against the other and so drag us down to the lowest possible condition' (cited in Van der Linden, 1988: 331).

If internationalism was an active and crucial ingredient of the nascent labour movement, it also had its limits. It was essentially limited to Western Europe and the lands that those countries had colonised, such as North America and Australasia. There was concern with the inhabitants of the colonies but this was largely pacifist and humanitarian in tone. There was no specific labour or socialist discourse on the colonial questions which might distinguish the labour movement from bourgeois liberalism. As Tichelman concludes (in relation to the Second International but applicable earlier too):

The dominant aim [of the labour movement] was to prevent war as a possible outcome of international rivalries around colonial expansion. Somewhat lower on the priority scale was the need to protect the natives and the duty to educate and 'civilise' them. (Tichelman, 1988: 91)

In short, the labour movement shared the notion of 'White man's burden' of the time in relation to the colonies and semi-colonies. Even Marx shared in the general evolutionary conception of human progress and the inevitable advance of Western 'civilisation'.

The landmark in the early history of internationalism was clearly the foundation of the International Working Men's Association, or First International, in 1864. This first labour international was formed on the crest of a strike wave and in a mood of revolutionary democracy. As Knudsen puts it, 'The International represented the future, the emancipation of the labouring poor, the entire liberation of the working class from all forms of social, political and religious oppression' (Knudsen, 1988: 307). Karl Marx was personally responsible for much of the internationalist ethos of the First International. In the late 1860s another wave of strikes in continental Europe put the International firmly on the map and reinforced its transnational ethos and practice. By now 'proletarian internationalism' was coming into its own with a distinctive and oppositional profile. Employers now began to counter workers with an aggressive nationalism, their liberal free-trade internationalism being confined more to theory. Workers and the labour movement were becoming firmly identified discursively and in practice with internationalism.

The First International brought together diverse social categories of labour and different political ideologies. It was not a particularly strong organisation and was riven by personal and political conflicts. It had to fight hard just to keep in existence; it was eventually dissolved acrimoniously in 1876. Nevertheless, it established and consolidated a tradition of labour internationalism that echoes through to the present. It was a revolutionary democratic organisation with labour at its core. However, from the 1870s through to the end of the nineteenth century, labour was to become steadily 'nationalised' as the European nation-states consolidated and rudimentary welfare states began to wean workers away from an internationalist perspective. From the Franco-Prussian War of 1870–71 the labour movements of Europe began to enter a close relationship with their respective nation-states. The phrase *la nation des prolétaires* (the nation of proletarians) springs from this era . ... the growing symbiosis between nation-building and the so... ...ce of labour. Internationalism from now on would have a dis' ...national' flavour, as we can see.

The Eur... labour movement reacted with a certain maturity with the for... ...on of the Second International in 1889. Engels provided continu... with the era of Marx until his death in 1895, but essentially a n w labour and socialist ideology, 'social democracy', was now being forged. International networking and activity certainly continued in this era from 1890 to 1914. As Visser puts it, 'a considerable volume of international exchange, through migration, travel propaganda or money did occur and helped to propagate ideas or set example' (Visser, 1998: 180). There was international support for striking workers and 'best practice' was generalised across national frontiers. The 1890s also saw the creation of the main International Trade Secretariats (ITSs), bringing together national unions in a given sector, organisations that have continued to the present day. The struggle for trade-union rights and the eight-hour working day was an international one, although significantly the struggle to improve social regulation was reserved for the national sections of the Second International.

There is a popular myth that labour internationalism died in 1914 as the European powers lined up for the First World War, a conflict generated by the scramble for colonies. Certainly the collapse of internationalist rhetoric was dramatic as labour and socialist leaders across Europe scurried to stand behind 'their' respective nation-states and armies. If the outbreak of war and the subsequent collapse of the International was a shock for its leaders, the workers of Europe saw less of a contradiction. As Hobsbawm puts it, 'in 1914 class-conscious workers in belligerent countries rushed to the colours in a spontaneous *levée en masse....* Having won the right to be full members of their nation through their movement, they now behaved as full citizens were supposed to' (Hobsbawm, 1988: 11). So, while 1914 brought out the contradiction between the rhetoric and the reality of workers' internationalism, it was more a confirmation of trends towards a 'nationalising' of the working classes than a dramatic bolt out of the blue.

With the Second International sinking into 'national chauvinism', the communist or Third International emerged in 1919, firmly committed to holding high the banner of 'proletarian internationalism', but understood in its own particular way. Born during the inter-imperialist carnage of the First World War and the irruption of the

Bolshevik revolution in Russia in 1917, the Third International was strongly internationalist in orientation. Lenin's principle of 'proletarian internationalism', as accepted by the Second Congress of the International, established national sections as explicitly subordinated to the international centre. However, the international centre was also defined as 'the most advanced country' – that is, the USSR. Certainly Lenin would have preferred to move the headquarters out of Russia to Germany if the revolution in the latter had been successful. However, after Lenin's death in 1924, Stalin effectively began to run the Third International as a branch of the foreign affairs policy of the USSR.

The labour arm of the Third International was the Red International of Labour Unions (RILU), which claimed a membership of over 10 million workers in the mid-1920s. The RILU operated in thirty-eight countries and was an effective radical minority force in a number of trade unions. This led to a major realignment of labour politics across the globe, with the communist tradition a key organising and radicalising influence in many countries. The communist attack on parliamentarianism and the 'class collaboration' of the social democrats inevitably led to a split in the international labour movement. The strong political line and centralised discipline of the communist labour movement gave it influence beyond its numbers. It was certainly internationalist and believed in the concept of 'world revolution', but this was ultimately subordinated to the national interests of the USSR. What is also significant in terms of internationalism is the Third International's decisive turn towards support for the national and democratic revolutions in the colonial world. Mao summed up this orientation and shift in the meaning of internationalism with his proclamation that 'in wars of national liberation patriotism is applied internationalism'. The 'colonial question' now firmly joined the labour question at the core of the socialist project for liberation.

One collection of writings has characterised the century from 1840 to 1940 as 'the main period of working-class internationalism' (Van Holthom and Van der Linden, 1988: i). There were indeed, as we have seen, great waves of internationalism, but also fierce national revivals. In fact, internationalism can hardly be seen as the opposite of nationalism; the two discourses can easily coexist. We have noted also a fundamental shift in the meaning of internationalism, from a type of European cosmopolitanism at the start of this period, to an identification with the defence of the USSR as beacon of the international proletariat, to support for national liberation struggles in what we now know as the South. In terms of strictly trade-union internationalism, as against the broader labour and socialist movements, it has probably always been ambiguous. Visser writes about the 1950s, though it could equally apply to the 1850s, that 'Help your friends abroad to help yourself' is an old game in international trade unionism, and the suspicion of protectionism is never far away' (Visser, 1998: 245). It is as well to understand the material basis of trade-union internationalism as mutual self-interest, and not be disappointed when it is seen to be not all altruism and solidarity.

TRADE-UNION IMPERIALISM

Following the Second World War, the development of the international trade-union movement was dominated by the Cold War between the West and the 'communist' East. Pragmatic and isolationist tendencies now came to the fore and there was not even the pretence of 'labour internationalism' that even the bad patches of the previous period still saw on paper. While in the earlier period the labour movements of the West had become largely 'nationalised', now the state/union nexus became truly consolidated. During the Second World War itself many exiled trade-union activists found themselves in London, where most of the ITSs now based their headquarters. Many of these trade unionists joined the British undercover military operations on the Continent, including socialist and communist activists seeking to pursue the struggle against fascism. After the war the struggle of many in the Western unions focused on the 'communist threat' and they continued to work with their national governments to this end. This is when 'trade-union imperialism' as we know it took shape.

The trade unions of the North began to see their external policy as part of that of their respective national governments. Western trade unions, particularly those of the United States, were firm believers and active players in the Cold War. In Western Europe the wartime role of the unions in terms of production and the national war effort was extended to the post-war period, where they played a major role in reconstruction. While internationalist rhetoric might still make an appearance at trade-union congresses, the practice of the unions was not only nationalist but also statist. The labour movements of the West/North were becoming an integral element of the nation-state.

Two significant cases, both involving the British trade unions, exemplify this development.

The relationship between British and Indian trade unions went back to the 1920s when the British Labour Party assisted in forming the All-India Trades Union Congress. What is most interesting is that the British effort to assist the development of trade unions in India had two sides. On the one hand the British Communist Party was assisting its comrades in India. But on the other hand, as Gary Busch shows, British trade unionists were helping their colleagues in India build strong unions, not sent 'by the British Government but by the textile unions of Lancashire' (Busch, 1983: 110), who feared that the Indian textile industry might undercut British prices and cost them jobs. During the Second World War, the British government worked closely with India's (pro-Allies) communists against the pacifist Congress activists in the trade unions. All aspects of the new international labour scene were here: Western unions acting in 'solidarity' but really for protectionist motives, 'communists' acting unscrupulously in the Soviet state's interests, and then some genuine international solidarity as well.

In Africa we see the most clear trade-union imperialism after the Second World War as the British TUC began to act openly as the labour arm of the Foreign and Colonial Offices. As Busch describes it, these British trade unionists seconded by the state

> were sent to the colonies where they kept a close watch over the development of unionism. Their major power lay in their ability to advise the local colonial administrators on which unionists and unions were to be recognised. The labour advisor supervised labour legislation and labour policy. (Busch, 1983: 87)

From apathy and paternalism towards colonial workers, Northern trade unionists had now become active agents of the colonial state and an integral element of imperialist strategy.

At the world level the post-war period was dominated by political splits in the trade-union movement. In 1945, the formation of the World Federation of Trade Unions (WFTU), claiming 65 million members, seemed to signal a fragile unity between communist and non-communist trade unions. However, no amount of diplomacy could hide the rifts and a split soon emerged over the US Marshall Plan for the reconstruction of Europe, opposed by the unions of the East. By

1949, the ICFTU had been formed, led by the now unified US labour movement of the AFL–CIO, which had overcome its own 'communist' problem. From then on, the whole history of international trade union-ism was dominated by the conflict between the ICFTU and the now explicitly pro-Soviet WFTU. Both set up regional organisations in the various regions of the South, where the Cold War was also played out by proxy. In 1949, the ICFTU claimed 48 million members world-wide, a figure which had increased to 67 million by 1979. Hegemonic in the West, the ICFTU also made serious advances in the South through its undoubted power and influence as well as patronage and 'trade-union imperialism'.

For its part the WFTU went on in the 1950s to become an explicitly communist organisation under Soviet tutelage. Apart from significant affiliates in France, Italy and Latin America, it did not make any significant inroads in the West and its claimed 150 million members included many nominal workers, it would seem. Regional affiliates in Latin America, Africa and the Middle East acquired a certain politics of influence in their region but one subordinated to Soviet state interests. Strongly committed to international trade-union unity, WFTU was rebuffed by the ICFTU but had some success at national level. In particular it had reasonably cordial relations with the Christian Trade Union International, which became the much more radical WCL (World Confederation of Labour) in 1968. When this organisation became the WCL it also pledged its opposition to capitalism and argued for the socialisation of the means of production. In his history of the international trade-union movement, Windmuller notes ironi-cally that this organisation, 'which had come into being 50 years earlier as a centre of opposition to the socialist domination of international labour organisations had ended up by adopting the essence of its opponents' original programme' (Windmuller, 1980: 591).

It is important at this stage to stand back and seek to understand the basis of international trade-union activity during this period. Lewis Lorwin has famously advanced the 'ideological' explanation in his classic text, where he argues that 'the ICFTU and the ITS, while helping to improve working and living conditions, also "stand guard for freedom and democracy"'(Lorwin, 1953: 343) in the international arena. Free-world ideology and opposition to the 'communist threat' may have been one factor, but it clearly was not the only one. John Logue, in his brief but thoughtful theorising of trade-union internationalism (as against internationalism), argues that international trade-union action is rational for trade unions (Logue, 1980: 20), which we could call an 'economic' explanation. We would probably need to add a third, specifically 'political', explanation. This would centre on the continued relevance of labour internationalism, however diluted or even perverted. Once their national bases were secured, trade-union and labour leaders would naturally move to develop strategic and political alliances internationally to strengthen their position at home, if for no other reason.

If the immediate post-war period was dominated by British trade-union imperialism, by the 1950s and 1960s US labour imperialism was firmly in the ascendant. There is a vast critical and polemical literature on this topic (e.g. Spalding, 1977), and many of the 'horror stories' are familiar, from US intervention in Allende's Chile, to Central America and elsewhere. Thompson and Larson's *Where Were You Brother? An Account of Trade Union Imperialism* (Thompson and Larson, 1978) provides a clear example of the genre. Their basic thesis is that 'Third World unions have been divided and weakened under the cover of the international trade union movement, in turn making whole-scale oppression more likely' (Thompson and Larson, 1978: 2). The argument is that Western trade unions have become bureaucratised and that their leaders have found a community of interests with their national governments. The international activities of these unions thus simply further the interests of the Northern states and are in direct conflict with the interests of the working classes in the South. However, not only is this account conspiratorial, and wrong in its belief that union leaders are just puppets on a string, but it cannot account for the cases where solidarity actions have taken place (see the section on development solidarity below).

To my mind, we need to unpack the trade-union imperialism thesis. All three international union centres (ICFTU, WFTU and WCL) promoted 'solidarity' actions in Latin America with the objective of 'strengthening' the trade unions. It is a matter of record that the AIFLD (American Institute for Free Labor Development) has promoted coups in Brazil and Chile and subverted legitimate governments in Nicaragua and elsewhere. It has often left in the wake of its 'education and training' programmes weakened unions. Under the cover of 'depoliticising' and professionalising unions it has created a weak business unionism in the image of the AFL–CIO. It has often worked hand in glove with the Central Intelligence Agency in the interests of US imperialism and against democratisation. However, as is much clearer in the present era, it is still in the objective interests of the US trade unions to have strong counterparts in the South to prevent cheap labour undercutting their own jobs. The regulatory function of international trade-union activity demands this, as the British unions realised in colonial India. With the Cold War behind us, much of this debate is now arguably of historical interest only.

Before we conclude this section we need to sound a note of caution. Trade-union imperialism was a fact and many trade unionists in the South in particular suffered its effects. It also had a corrosive moral and political impact on the trade unions of the North. However, it is important to set this period in context. Denis McShane's detailed historical monograph on the International Metalworkers' Federation (McShane, 1992) provides a useful corrective balance on the popular leftist conspiratorial view. Written by a dedicated international trade unionist, this study is a scrupulous account with insider insight and cannot be accused of being apologetic (as indeed many pro-Western trade-union histories have been). McShane makes three general points about international trade unionism during the Cold War on the basis of his case study:

1. The Cold War was not something external to the trade unions but reflected the very real divisions between communists and others.
2. Labour movement strategy internationally followed its experience and interests and cannot be seen as simply imposed by governments.
3. It would be wrong to reduce international trade-union history during the Cold War to devious and far-sighted US manipulation alone (McShane, 1992: 279–81).

Trade-union internationalism could be based on universalist solidaristic principles or on pragmatic self-interest, but in the Cold War era it also became part of the diplomatic dimension of nation-state interactions. Internationalism became a rhetorical cover for a politicised trade-union foreign policy on behalf of Western powers and of the Soviet Union. As McShane puts it, 'national traditions, national demands, and national political culture' (McShane, 1992: 294) could hardly be subsumed under the shallow internationalist rhetoric of conferences. Of course, while the Northern unions were hardly internationalist in the spirit of the First International, their international reach increased dramatically during this period, to some extent at least mirroring the development of capitalism internationally (see Chapter 2). This leads us to the next topic: how trade unions sought to confront capital at the global level. Because, notwithstanding a strategic alliance with the state at the diplomatic level, trade unions still had a job to do in the workplace, still had members to represent and traditional trade-union objectives to pursue.

COUNTERVAILING POWERS

The global economy of the 'Golden Era' was dominated by the multi-national corporations. The international trade unions, from the 1960s onwards, made a concerted effort to build 'countervailing' labour power against the MNCs on a transnational basis. In essence, the theory was that trade unions could develop structures to mirror the reach of the MNCs, with which they could eventually engage in transnational collective bargaining. The key players were to be the ITSs, which were now beginning to come into their own as transnational labour organisations. The most influential ITSs in terms of international outreach were the IMF (International Metalworkers' Federation), the IUF (International Union of Food and Allied Workers) and the ICF (International Federation of Chemical and General Workers Union). Charles Levinson, as assistant general secretary of the IMF, began planning for union regulation by industry as far back as the mid-1950s and then took the concept to fruition as head of the ICF in the 1970s. Levinson went on to popularise the notion of trade-union counter-vailing power across the labour movement.

Charles Levinson, in his popular book on *International Trade Unionism* (Levinson, 1972), argued essentially that 'in terms of inter-national action to develop a new countervailing union response to the multinational companies, the most important thing is that there exist bargaining relations directly with these undertakings' (Levinson, 1972: 106). In what was a very early engagement by a labour intellectual with the internationalisation of capital, Levinson advanced a three-stage model of union responses:

1. Company-wide support for a single union in one country in a dispute with a foreign subsidiary.
2. Multiple negotiations with a company in several countries at the same time.

3. Integrated negotiations across the multinational around common demands (Levinson, 1972: 110).

According to Levinson there were already plenty of examples where unions had shown solidarity with an overseas union in dispute as per stage 1, and he believed the move towards full transnational collective bargaining would come sooner rather than later.

What Levinson was arguing was that transnational collective bargaining was the single most important strategy (the 'best bet' as it were) unions could develop in response to the economic and political internationalisation of capital. Other options included concerted action at the national level (as in the whole Golden Era stage), a more 'political' strategy, or the lobbying of intergovernmental organisations to establish 'codes of conduct' to regulate the multinationals. In some ways these choices are still present today. In practice, the international chemical workers' federation set up a number of bodies similar to the world company councils (see below) in leading industries. In 1969 the council at the French MNC Saint Gobain was one of the first to achieve success at the national level through concerted international action. Though Levinson's work was a landmark in labour thinking and strategy at the transnational level, he inevitably came in for considerable empirical and theoretical criticism, which we will now consider in turn.

A fierce attack on Levinson's whole approach came from two academics, Northrup and Rowan, who spent 580 pages examining 'every' claim of multinational collective bargaining or attempts by unions 'to influence company behaviour or action across national frontiers' (Northrup and Rowan, 1979: 330). They concluded that 'the documentary evidence ... demonstrates beyond a shadow of a doubt that these claims [of Levinson and others] are, at best, figments of a fertile imagination but worked by an extraordinary publicity sense' (Northrup and Rowan, 1978: 331). The fact is that throughout the 1970s there were a number of transnational disputes in Western Europe that were of public record (see TIE, 1985). Other studies, even one commissioned by employers in the early 1970s, concluded for example that 'more than one quarter ... of the largest US and foreign multinationals have already been targets of multinational union action' (Hershfield, 1975: 9). There was undoubtedly a wave of transnational organising in the 1970s. It may have been 'oversold' and tendencies were possibly confused with facts; nevertheless, in spite of its ultimate failure (in terms of its ambitious objectives), it was a significant period for labour internationalism.

An arguably more far-reaching critique of the Levinson thesis came from two German Marxist writers, Werner Olle and Wolfgang Schoeller (1984). They disagreed that the internationalisation of capital through the MNC has provided for the first time an 'objective' basis for labour internationalism. Olle and Schoeller disagreed with the 'implicit attempt [by Levinson and others] to find a superficial *economic* basis for the necessity and possibility of international trade union politics' (Olle and Schoeller, 1984: 70). Given nationally distinct conditions of production, a trade-union-based 'economistic' international can only reproduce competition between national capitals. Indeed, from this angle international trade-union politics can readily be seen as a form of national protectionism. For Olle and Schoeller the choice is a stark one: either 'nationalise' the union strategy explicitly and consciously engage in national competition between workers, or go 'in the direction of a *politicisation* of trade-union activity combining the struggle for ... [better wages] ... with the perspective of developing the power of the proletariat' (Olle and Schoeller, 1984: 71). Though somewhat polarised, this analysis does at least alert us to the contradictions underlying bland calls for 'solidarity'.

Another related critique of 1970s' notions of labour solidarity came from Haworth and Ramsay (1984), who argued for 'grasping the nettle' of the fundamental asymmetry between capital and labour. This analysis flowed from the 'new international division of labour' (see Chapter 5) debates at the time, so that workers in the North and South are literally 'worlds apart'. Capital looks outwards and expands, labour looks inwards and is defensive. To use a military metaphor, as Haworth and Ramsay put it, 'labour and capital are in one sense not even fighting in the same battlefield' (Haworth and Ramsay, 1984: 73). What is interesting is how those two sets of critiques pointed in their 'way forward' to debates of the 1990s. Olle went on to hinge the future of the labour movement on the issue of global development, in keeping with the 'greening' of the German left. Haworth and Ramsay, for their part, pointed to the need to go beyond the realm of production, to accept the multiple identities of workers, and to develop what became known as a 'social movement' unionism which recognised that labour politics did not begin and end on the factory floor and in the union office.

It is important at this stage to provide some concrete evidence of transnational labour organising and action in the 1970s. One of the most significant experiences was that of the IMF World Auto Councils set up at the instigation of the US United Auto Workers (UAW), a leading progressive union in that country. The auto councils consisted of representatives from each trade union in a given company, involving both the parent company and its overseas subsidiaries. These were formed in Ford, Volkswagen, Nissan and other auto industry MNCs. Apart from basic but essential exchange of information, they sought to move towards a harmonisation of conditions in the various plants. The late 1970s was the period when MNCs were beginning to transfer production to low-wage areas, so this was a particularly acute concern. One of the most detailed studies of world auto councils, by Burton Beninder, concluded that the type of action engaged in by those IMF bodies 'was and still is uphill work and often more unsuccessful than successful' (Bendiner, 1977: 71). There were success stories, and examples of labour internationalism did at least have a significant symbolic effect.

It is no surprise that cross-border union organising occurred first and most successfully in the auto industry. Here was the classic 'Fordist' industry, highly concentrated and integrated, with a traditionally well-organised workforce. Well used to militant sectional actions, the auto workers of this period were probably the best suited for this strategy. Even so there were problems involving inter-union rivalries and, of course, where different national union interests were at stake. An economic or collective bargaining common interest was probably not enough for any devolution of authority from the national to the international level that would have been necessary in the long term. In other industries, in spite of some successes by the international food federation, the IUF (for example in Nestlé), things were different. In more decentralised industries, with low-paid, less skilled and less organised workforces, international co-ordination was even less likely to be successful. It was at this stage that it became clear that a broader strategy to regulate the MNCs across the board, and not company by company, was necessary.

We must agree with Rebecca Gumbrell-McCormick that, 'In general, very few of the WCCs [World Company Councils] stood the test of time or achieved the sort of results for which they were intended' (Gumbrell-McCormick, 2000: 381). After some early successes the

MNCs were able to counter a labour strategy on this terrain. The criticisms outlined above (some from a very hostile anti-labour perspective) led to a certain credibility gap. It was almost as if labour leaders knew they were engaging in a game of bluff with the MNCs, aware they did not have the strength to impose something like transnational collective bargaining. Finally, the divisions in the international trade-union movement between the 'free world' ICFTU and the communist-affiliated unions had a debilitating effect. At one point in the mid-1970s Charles Levinson himself attacked rank-and-file leaders in the rubber industry when they organised transnational action in Europe involving the French CGT and the Spanish Comisiones Obreras, both seen as 'communist'. The ITS seemed to share the ICFTU's divisive 'anti-communism', which fundamentally weakened labour unity.

In conclusion, trade unions in the 1970s did make a concerted effort to develop structures and strategies to confront transnational capitalism. There was nothing inevitable about this, and labour structures do not just mirror capital's development. In short, we cannot just see labour's 'subjective' development catching up with capital's 'objective' development, as it were. There is a fundamental asymmetry between capital and labour that needs to be recognised and not just brushed aside. Essentially the policy of transnational collective bargaining was a syndicalist and economistic one. That is to say, its logic was a trade-union one and not necessarily a labour movement, let alone a socialist, one. There are many obstacles to workers organising, let alone taking action across national frontiers. I think finally, though, we need to ponder on Visser's provocative argument that,

> Impressive as they may seem, these obstacles were probably not the main reason why in the past thirty years there was no multinational collective bargaining. The more simple point could be defended that unions paid lip service and did not really need multinational collective bargaining. (Visser, 1998: 246)

DEVELOPMENT SOLIDARITY

What is probably remarkable in terms of the story of labour internationalism is how outstanding episodes of solidarity occurred in spite of 'trade-union imperialism', the Cold War and the general spread of nationalist ideologies. It was a democratic form of solidarity which internationalism manifested but it was also a form of development solidarity in so far as it was most often directed towards countries in the South. In some ways labour concern with development issues springs from the limitations of the 'transnational bargaining' perspective discussed above. In a world which was rapidly internationalising in the 1970s, and at a time the Northern economies were beginning to go into recession (see Chapter 2), a narrowly economistic perspective was clearly inadequate. The international trade unions, and particularly the ICFTU, began to concern themselves actively with global development issues. This missing link allowed the unions to at least understand that there was a world beyond the advanced industrial societies and that 'free collective bargaining' was not a universal model of labour–capital relations.

The high point of the international labour movement's impact on the development debate was probably in the early 1980s with the Brandt Report (Report of the Independent Commission on International Development Issues, 1981) on North–South relations. Since the 1970s, the ICFTU had been waging a consistent campaign in various international fora to achieve some level of regulation over the operations of the MNCs. As Rebecca Gumbrell-McCormick shows,

> the steady work of the ICFTU and the ITSs [International Trade Secretariats] appeared to be having some impact on public opinion and government policies, for example in the use of trade policies to promote human and trade union rights and in some national legislation as in Sweden. (Gumbrell-McCormick, 2000: 395)

This work was consolidated with the Brandt Report, which was highly influential at the time in setting a critical tone in relation to MNC practices. Furthermore, it was probably the first time that a high-level international body of this type had official trade-union representatives. However, this initiative was short-lived as the major Northern economies moved into the era of neo-liberalisation, and 'codes of conduct' for MNCs were for a while relegated in practice.

More recently we have seen a resurgence of international labour movement engagement with development issues. Thus in 1997, SID issued a stirring electronic document, *A New Global Agenda: Labour Visions and Strategies for the 21st Century*, with a significant section on global development. The South was not presented as a cheap labour reservoir waiting to undercut Northern workers' wages and conditions. The tone was principled: 'The lack of solidarity in the world is unacceptable as it will only lead to further poverty, further marginalisation of countries, more conflicts and wars.' International trade negotiations need to be democratised, says the SID, through the participation 'of workers and other sectors of society'. The aim of the international trade-union movement should be global sustainable development and its methods should be based on principles of global solidarity. Neo-liberalism has failed according to the SID, and 'only the labour movement with its basic principles of freedom, equality and solidarity can come up with a global solution that can create a social and sustainable development.'

The long and ultimately successful international trade-union (and others') campaign against the apartheid regime in South Africa clearly went beyond development solidarity. However, it is a landmark in terms of internationalism in both its 'old' and 'new' varieties. Perhaps it can be viewed as a transitional case with 'old' party, trade-union, state politics and Cold War issues prevailing but with a turn towards the 'new' of the social movements and post-Cold War politics. From the 1970s onwards a campaign of solidarity with workers in South Africa was mounted at all levels of the international trade-union movement, from the ICFTU to the ITSs, from national union centres to an array of local unions. Roger Southall, who has carried out an exhaustive study of this chapter in international labour history, concludes that 'The resultant picture of trade-union internationalism which emerges is incoherent, inconsistent, muddied and almost definitely unheroic; nonetheless, although trade-union internationalism may have been distanced from its worthy class base, it could never be entirely disconnected' (Southall, 1994: 167). The moral and material aid provided by the international labour movement to its counterparts in South Africa was of crucial significance.

The ICFTU's Cold War orientation was lessened after 1969 with the departure of the US affiliate, the AFL–CIO. Henceforth, relations with the trade unions in South Africa improved, though tensions remained. The ITSs were also instrumental in taking a stance against apartheid in the unions. The International Metalworkers' Federation (IMF) actually expelled the apartheid-era affiliates in South Africa, which led the independent FOSATU to declare in 1982 that 'It is the first time that a major international body has taken action against South African unions for practising apartheid' (cited in Webster, 1984: 226). Many national trade-union centres also played a key role in isolating the apartheid regime and building up workers' organisations in South Africa. In Britain and Canada, for example, the trade-union centrals were instrumental in mounting a disinvestment campaign and providing financial support for the emerging independent black unions. Though riven by sharp disagreements between different political tendencies both in South Africa and internationally, these campaigns were considered effective.

The international struggle against the apartheid regime in South Africa demonstrated that the spirit of the First International could be rekindled by solidaristic action. Workers across the world, and not just their leaders, took action on behalf of others. Declarations of support at conferences were often followed by real campaigns and actions. Though the campaign was inevitably uneven across time and space, it was sustained over many, many years. It impacted on thousands of workers across the world, for whom it had a watershed politicising effect. It was a genuine workers' solidarity and display of internationalism, untainted by self-interest. Perhaps as important as this aspect, though, is a recognition of the amount of work which went into generating and sustaining this solidarity. We see that internationalism does not just happen spontaneously and requires resources to create. It also shows that a common democratic objective can unite labour, community, religious and political forces around a campaign. Though unique in many ways, the South African solidarity saga still repays detailed study today.

Another major, if more localised, case of internationalism centred around the Coca-Cola factory in Guatemala City in the early and mid-1980s. Attacks on the Coca-Cola union leaders by state violence, with management complicity, led to an effective campaign by the relevant International Trade Secretariat, the IUF, then led by Dan Gallin. After failing to achieve negotiations with the company, the IUF called for a tourist boycott, which was supported by Amnesty International and other human rights organisations. The objective of the international campaign was to secure recognition of a genuine trade union at the Coca-Cola plant and to remove the threat of violence and intimidation by management and the state. In the USA unions and campaigning groups put pressure on the parent company and the European unions indicated that they were willing to go as far as sympathy action to force the company to negotiate. The 1984 campaign was particularly successful, involving religious groups, human rights and solidarity groups in an effective international campaign against the parent company. Eventually, the IUF forced the giant Coca-Cola corporation to behave.

The perspective from Guatemala can be gathered from the account by Miguel Angel Alvisurez, who was one of the Coca-Cola union leaders at the time. For Alvisurez the IUF action and that of its affiliates across the world, 'without saying it or blowing their trumpets, has put into practice *proletarian internationalism*' (Alvisurez, 1985: 73). That the IUF took up a general political position against the dictatorship in Guatemala was even more significant on the ground than any trade-union solidarity as such. The tourist boycott was seen as effective and workers' understanding of the international dimension grew apace. The workers in the plants carried out a succession of factory occupations, one of which lasted over a year. They gathered the support of the broader trade-union movement in Guatemala, itself encouraged by the protective or enabling environment created by the international campaign. At first the giant MNC was able to outmanoeuvre the unions on the international scene, but the learning curve of the international union movement was steep and its gains in terms of organisation and experience were enduring.

We are now back where we started. As it came into being, the labour movement was internationalist by necessity and by belief. That internationalism was due to mutual interest and solidarity based on beliefs about the international 'brotherhood' of 'man'. It was democratic before it was socialist. It was 'Eurocentric' before the colonial revolution brought the majority of the workers of the world onto the scene. Now, as we move on to consider the era of globalisation and the 'new' forms of internationalism it has given rise to, we can first look back at the formative phase. In a broad retrospective of nationalism and the international labour movement, Michael Forman argues for the 1840s that, 'As a class, the proletariat had to be internationalist to achieve its political goals, because the basis of its very existence *as a class* was an international system' (Forman, 1998: 47). I would argue with Forman that this situation is mirrored today: solidarity with the oppressed at home and abroad, unity of the broad working masses in a democratic spirit, international labour organisation to counter that of capital – all these are as necessary today as they were a century and a half ago.

SEVEN

THE 'NEW' INTERNATIONALISM

There is now, across the political spectrum and across the world, a feeling that we are entering a new period of labour internationalism. Global capitalism seems to demand a global labour response, and the divisions of the Cold War are behind us. In a way, this 'new' internationalism is renewing a very 'old' tradition of the labour movement going back to the First International in Marx's day. This chapter begins by examining how labour internationalism has developed in the era of globalisation as, supposedly, we move beyond the nation-state. We find, then, that this new internationalism has moved beyond a conception of transnational collective bargaining, involving a more 'social movement' unionism. This section on 'trade unions and others' is followed by one on 'global development' which provides us with a broader context to reconsider such issues as the 'social clause' (Chapter 5). Finally, this chapter turns to the theoretical and practical issues surrounding the new relationships opening up between the global and the local levels, not forgetting the sometimes overlooked regional and subregional levels of labour activity.

UNIONS IN TRANSITION

Some observers may have been surprised at the Davos 2001 meeting to hear John Sweeney, president of the US AFL–CIO, proclaim that Seattle 1999 and other actions were not a 'backlash' against globalisation but, rather, the 'birth pangs of a new internationalism' (AFL–CIO, 2001). There had already been a shake-out in the AFL–CIO Foreign Affairs Department and an explicit critique of the old 'trade-union imperialism' ways. However, this was now the top leader of the AFL–CIO at a major international forum calling for a renewal of proletarian internationalism. Sweeney declared that 'This movement for a new internationalism is building from the bottom up, not the top down.... Its forum is the public square, not the boardroom' (AFL–CIO, 2001). In this 'new morning dawning', Sweeney sees 'workers, environmentalists, religious leaders and students coming together to call for workers' rights and human rights and consumer and environmental protections in the global economy' (AFL–CIO, 2001). While one must never confuse rhetoric and reality, and Sweeney is seeking to protect AFL–CIO jobs as much as anything else, this discourse does seem to signal a new awareness of the international dimension.

Jay Mazur, Chair of the AFL–CIO International Affairs Committee, contributed in 2000 to the influential US policy-makers' journal *Foreign Affairs* (Mazur, 2000). On the back of the Seattle debacle for the WTO, Mazur sought to develop a reasonable and responsible trade-union view on globalisation. Mazur recalls how, 'not so long ago, a major union's international activity could be carried out by a single person who might even have other organisational responsibilities' (Mazur, 2000: 86). Today, by contrast, many of a union's departments (research, health, legal, safety, corporate affairs, political action, etc.) have a central international dimension, due to the effects of globalisation. Given the perceived 'race to the bottom' in terms of labour rewards and conditions, unions in the rich countries must of necessity concern themselves with the plight of the majority of workers in the South. The transformation of the world economy, and the disruptions caused to the global elite's plans at Seattle, mean, for Mazur, that the time is now ripe for trade unions to demand a 'seat at the table' of global capitalism's board of management.

However remarkable the apparent turnaround of the AFL–CIO and the ICFTU might be, it was of course the ITSs which had been steadily pursuing an internationalist path since the 1960s. Thus the ICEM, for example, organised its Second World Congress in 1999 around the issue of 'Facing Global Power: Strategies for Global Unionism'. In terms of the new concern with the issue of 'global governance', the ICEM poses a stark alternative: the 'globalisation of greed' or the 'globalisation of solidarity' (ICEM, 1999: 34). Neo-liberal globalisation is based squarely on the rule of competition and is inimical to any conception of human solidarity. For the ICEM, some corporations have already acknowledged the integrated nature of their operations and see the advantage of dealing with the ITSs on issues that are intrinsically global, such as the environment. Though the ICEM has to date signed only one fully global collective agreement (with Statoil, the transnational oil and gas group), they were optimistic for the future that 'global corporations need global unions' (ICEM, 1999: 42).

As for the ICFTU, it has finally in recent years begun to take a balanced (as against Cold War) stance towards global capitalism. Having overcome its Cold War divisions, the ICFTU is now better placed to act as general labour interlocutor in the corridors of financial and political power. Much of its philosophy is based on the simple dictum that 'the global economy needs global rules' (ICFTU, 1997b: 57), recalling its classic Golden Age pluralist conception of industrial relations. It was interesting in this regard to see the World Bank 1997 report (World Bank, 1997) giving the trade unions a much more positive role than had ever been the case for such a body before. It seems very hard, though, to envisage how a traditional 'social partnership' approach might work at the international level in today's climate. Nor does the rather contradictory 'social movement' orientation advanced at other times by the ICFTU seem particularly viable politically. The ICFTU should not be seen as a 'slumbering giant' about to awaken to lead the international proletariat. Its recent 'internationalist' turn, however, does create a more favourable environment for labour solidarity actions.

The motivation behind the new global outreach of the ITSs and others is articulated around the slogan 'Global Business – Global Workers' Rights'. For Denis McShane, 'Global action is not now the narrow preserve of big governments, rich banks and multinational companies. We can all act globally to assert humankind's place in the new world economy' (McShane, 1996: 3). If organisations such as the World Trade Organisation exist to safeguard the global rights of capital and intellectual property rights (currently a very contentious area), so should labour seek global representation. Social and environmental rights also require international regulation. The underlying ethos of the global unionism movement is that 'The global economy has to meet its social obligations' (McShane, 1996: 3). In brief, the new international social movements are called on to reverse the 1960s' feminist and ecology slogan 'Think Global, Act Local', with global action now seen as the only way to confront the now firmly globalised capitalist system.

If neo-liberal globalisation provides the main incentive for the new trade-union internationalism, it is the communications/information revolution which provides it with its tools. It is not a form of techno-logical determinism to argue that the Internet is a crucial facilitator and enabler of labour internationalism. Though a sober realist com-pared to some Internet enthusiasts, Eric Lee has proclaimed that, 'Thanks to the Internet, a century-long decline in internationalism has already been reversed. For thousands of trade unionists who log on every day, the International has already been reborn' (Lee, 1997a: 186). It is, indeed, tempting to draw analogies between the brave new world opened up by international labour communications based on the Inter-net and the perspective Marx had as the First International started up. What is particularly interesting is that the present wave of communication-based internationalism really began with Charles Levinson, who developed the notion of 'countervailing power' in the 1970s (see Chapter 6) but who also promoted the use of computers and computer communications through his leading role in the international trade secretariats.

It would seem obvious that instantaneous and cheap communications cannot alone create labour internationalism. However, we can note that the communications or electronic internationalism we see on the rise today does, at least potentially, offer a more democratic way of oper-ating. As Peter Waterman put it early on in this debate, 'In place of hierarchical structure and political competition what we seem to have [in the new labour communications] is the network structure and the principle of co-operation' (Waterman, 1985: 245). Ideas and commu-nications flowing around a web are different from those going up and down a vertical organisation. Certainly in practice, as with the ICFTU's 2000 online international labour conference, we find a mixed state, with networking rhetoric being allied to a verticalist practice not averse to censoring critical views. When all is said and done, the Internet does seem to have the potential to set up a countervailing 'virtual' power (of the imagination) to that of the transnational corporations, cutting across traditional lines of hierarchy, divisions between national movements, and distinctions between strategy, action and education.

We have established that labour has moved, albeit hesitantly and unevenly, beyond the nation-state. What is 'new' about this internationalism is probably mainly its informational nature. We need to consider, then, to what extent global unionism is, indeed, a 'player' in the arena of globalisation. While the global context appears more pressing today than in the heyday of national regulation, we can only really say that global unionism is a tendency more than a social reality. It exists mainly because, as the ICFTU argues, 'Unions at the national level are seeing much of what they have achieved being undermined by global financial and industrial decisions' (ICFTU, 1996: 5). A problem that arises here is that there is an inherent tendency for trade unions simply to replicate their national strategy at the international level. Yet we know from the experience of the 1970s that transnational collective bargaining is unlikely and possibly even nonviable. Andreas Breitenfellner (of the Austrian Federation of Trade Unions), for example, notes that 'The legal basis for transnational industrial action is circumscribed by the different national legislations and labour relations system' (Breitenfellner, 1997: 547).

Taking a broader look at the issue or project of global unionism we can see it in terms of 'regulation' of the global economy. Breitenfellner's analysis is indicative of the mixed level of the debate on global unionism. He argues that global unionism needs to go beyond congress diplomacy and information exchange: 'trade unions should perceive themselves as being part of a global civil society' (Breitenfellner, 1997: 552). There is a feeling that globalisation creates opportunities as well as causing severe problems for labour. New and cheaper communications technologies are seen to provide the basis for better global links. There is a call for strategies and actions at a global level drawing on 'the tradition of labour internationalism' (Breitenfellner, 1997: 552). Yet, when Breitenfellner comes to drawing up the actual mechanisms whereby labour will seek to exercise some social regulation over the global economy he is disappointingly traditional, arguing that 'The ultimate aim of global unionism would be to institutionalise a system of tripartite social partnership' (Breitenfellner, 1997: 522) – that is to say, the tried and failed post-war tripartism of capital, labour and nation-state.

We can usefully sum up this section with a retrospective look at the international labour movement. Nearly fifty years ago, Lewis Lorwin published an influential study of the history and outlook of the international labour movement (Lorwin, 1953). Lorwin concluded that 'Trade unions in all countries ... tend to give increasing attention to *national* economic policies, in disregard of the possibilities of inter-national economic co-operation' (Lorwin, 1953: 334). This was be-cause, according to Lorwin, 'the inner logic of trade unions is to concern themselves more and more with questions of *national* policy, since these impinge directly or indirectly on the basic trade-union function of improving working and living conditions' (Lorwin, 1953: 334). What is most remarkable is that half a century on we can replace the term national by *international* in these quotations and have a relevant statement. Precisely in the same way that the Golden Era (Chapter 4) demanded a national strategy for labour, the Global Era (Chapter 5) demands an international response by trade unions. This helps explain the rationale behind John Sweeney's statements, quoted at the beginning of this chapter, on the birth of a new labour inter-nationalism.

TRADE UNIONS AND OTHERS

If capitalism has changed fundamentally over the last fifty years, so has the nature of the working classes and their collective expressions such as trade unions. The 'new' capitalism is more flexible, more decentred, then the solid centralised bureaucratic capitalist order of the 1950s (see Chapter 4). The 'new' working class is less male, less manufacturing based, than it was. The trade unions that express workers' collective interests cover far less of the workforce than they did once and it is a truism to say that they suffer from an 'identity crisis'. In all three aspects we find a different dispensation today than in 1950. Above all, there is a greater understanding that social identity is both complex and fluid. Workers are also citizens and consumers; they are also divided by gender and ethnicity, for example. Fluidity is also a natural condition and we should not expect consciousness to be fixed. This thumbnail sketch necessarily points towards a possible new mode of internationalism in keeping with the 'postmodern' globalised era in which we live.

We need to be careful in seeking out always what is 'new' (as in the new capitalism, new working class, new internationalism, etc.), as often the label implies a break with the past which is simply not present. However, it would be worth considering the six characteristics Peter Waterman sees as distinguishing the 'new' labour internationalism:

1. Cross-border solidarity activity by or between wage-workers at shop-floor, grassroots or community level.
2. Expressing their daily-life concerns and aspirations.
3. Based on their resources and efforts.
4. In opposition to the major forces or expressions of international exploitation and oppression (e.g. capitalism, statism, patriarchy, racism, imperialism, militarism).
5. Tending to create a global community of interest and activity.
6. Complementary to those of other mass popular and democratic interests, identities and movements (e.g. of women, oppressed national/ethnic communities, human rights, and the environment) (Waterman, 1998: 80).

There is something of a 'wish list' flavour to these characteristics, but the general point is clear. Today, we can expect labour internationalism to have a broader remit than in the past; it cannot be compartmentalised in narrow union and party terms; it is facing global capitalism and not just the factory order. In brief, a complex (even disorganised) capitalism demands a complex internationalism. It is to the various 'new' aspects of internationalism that we now turn.

Practically, the first thing we note when surveying the world of international solidarity is that it is women rather than workers (not necessarily contradictory categories, of course) who are the prime movers on the global stage. The 1970s concept of 'Global Sisterhood' (Morgan, 1984) may have been severely criticised for eliding differences, but it reflected a very real aspiration. This drive to unify women's struggles for emancipation across the globe reached its peak perhaps with the 1995 Beijing Conference. The women's movement has been global in its transnational orientation but also in its holistic approach to the oppression of women. In this way it has, indeed, been exemplary in its practice and its theoretical elaboration of what 'global solidarity' might mean. Furthermore, in recent years the international women's movement has had a significant impact on the labour movement, so that even the ICFTU may refer to 'sexism' and 'oppression', terms once far removed from the traditional trade-union lexicon. Universal 'sisterhood' may have been a white Northern middle-class construct (see Mohanty, 1993) but it did signal a 'new' moral internationalism.

Another prime site for transnational activity today is that of human rights. Certainly the notion of human rights is imbued with individualist and liberal notions of humanity. Since the 1980s, however, we

seem to have witnessed the emergence of a 'new' internationalist conception of human rights. Thus, in Argentina the campaign against the
military dictatorship had as its slogan, 'The defence of human dignity
knows no boundaries'. This transnational conception of human rights
probably peaked in the late 1990s when Chilean dictator General
Pinochet was arrested in London for gross human rights violations.
We found that the argument of 'national sovereignty' was no defence
when the august British Law Lords decided he should answer for
human rights abuses in Chile. There is now a transnational democratic space infinitely more developed than when the United Nations
was created. Specifically, we note with Anthony McGrew 'the extent
to which the traditional notions of sovereign political space and political community are being reconstituted by the nature of the international human rights regime and the activities of the transnational
social movements in the human rights domain' (McGrew, 1995: 46). It
is not surprising, in this context, that the international labour movement has mounted successful campaigns around the slogan 'Workers'
rights are human rights'.

Apart from gender and human rights, it is unquestionably around
environmental issues that some of the most dynamic transnational
activity is to be found today. Organisations such as Greenpeace have
successfully made an impact on global politics because the environment is quite clearly (at least after Chernobyl) a transnational issue,
but also because they have been adept at matching their campaigning
strategies to the nature of the 'new' capitalism. The notion of 'sustainable development' has entered the mainstream since the 1992 Earth
Summit in Rio. Whatever its precise meaning, this concept has acquired considerable legitimacy and can be used by campaigning groups
as a yardstick. Clearly, if a global concept of 'fair labour standards'
was to acquire similar status it would represent a breakthrough for
labour. Of course, as with the notion of 'global sisterhood' or 'universal' human rights, there are huge differences between the dominant
Northern perspective and the 'view from the South'. Campaigners in
the South have argued, against the dominant conception of 'sustainability', that poverty itself is an environmental problem and conspires
against sustainability.

Environmentalism and workers' rights have not always sat well
together, especially when the first is taken to be naturalism or conser-
vationism. The industrialist/productivist ethos of the factory does not

take easily to environmental concerns. Workers do not readily lose jobs to save the environment. As Laurie Adkin puts it in a useful case study of ecology and labour in Canada: 'Union officials try to avoid "choosing sides" in conflicts which put their members' job security against the environment, health, gender or racial equality, peace, or the aspirations of "third world" peoples' (Adkin, 1999: 210). This strategy simply avoids the issue and assumes a zero-sum game where jobs and the environment are concerned (a gain for one is a loss for the other). However, in recent years the discourse of sustainable development has become widely accepted across society. Workers also live on the planet and are interested in its long-term prospects. Practical issues such as waste management, both in the North and in the South, are also now increasingly related to job creation. Seattle 1999, of course, symbolically marked the coming together of labour and environmental activists in a social movement against globalisation.

While gender, human rights and the environment are all aspects of the new labour internationalism (broadly understood), it is the relationship between production and consumption which is the crucial dimension, to my mind. It is a truism to say that capitalism in the North is, indeed, consumerism. For a certain strand of Marxism (and of the international solidarity movement) this is to be lamented; nevertheless, it also opens up new possibilities for labour solidarity across the world. In the mid-1990s there were a series of consumer boycotts in the United States aimed at big 'names', especially in the apparel industry. Carefully nurtured publicity scandals around Gap, Calvin Klein, Levi-Strauss, Reebok and other high-profile companies were successful in forcing them to implement 'codes of conduct' on labour conditions in their overseas plants. In Europe, the 'Clean Clothes' campaign was also very successful in forcing the retail sector and the consumer to examine the 'labour behind the label', exposing oppressive conditions, especially of domestic-based female homeworkers in the South. Not only were some retailers moved to accept ILO-set fair labour standards for their subcontractors, but a general renaissance of transnational consciousness and solidarity resulted from this campaign.

The mid-1990s sweatshop campaigns in the USA, according to Andrew Ross, 'provided a successful model for coalitions between labour, environmental, and social justice interests: local and international, government and non-government, organised labor and community groups ... and targeting the weak links in capital's chain'

(Ross, 1997: 37). In many ways these events were paradigmatic of the new labour internationalism. They cut across the boundaries of national/international, production/consumption, labour/community and so on. A small campaigning organisation, the National Labor Committee, which organised much of this work, exposed a weak link in capital's armoury. It also became a player on the stage of globalisation and effectively changed the terms of struggle. The 'name' of the blue-chip company was only as good as consumer confidence made it. The 'new' capitalism had found a 'new' solidarity movement opposing it, just as adept at trading in images (for example, the media-friendly Walt Disney products campaign), but based on a progressive broad front of worker, study, religious, human rights and community groups.

All the various global social movements (gender, environment, human rights and labour) have had an increasing, if variable, impact on the management institutions of the new global capitalism. In the case of the women's movement the impact on the World Bank has been considerable, although the environmental movement has probably had greater visible effects. Indeed the World Bank nowadays has sustainable and gendered development as articles of faith. Thus the ruling bodies of global governance are subject to pressure from coalitions constructed within global civil society. Global capitalism is not monolithic and has a certain permeability. The shift from the Fordist state to the looser concept of governance, from centralism to the network mode, has opened up a certain space for contestation from below. The international labour movement has not had as great an impact on the managers of global capitalism and is still effectively

TABLE 7.1 LABOUR REPERTOIRES AND ACTIONS, 1650–2000

1650–1850 Parochial/ patronised	1850–1980 National/ autonomous	1980–2000+ Transnational/ solidaristic
Food riots	Strikes	Earth/Women's summits
Machine sabotage	Public rallies	Band Aid concerts
Tax officials' expulsion	Insurrections	Consumer boycotts

Source: Cohen and Rai, 2000: 15.

frozen out in many cases. However, this movement understands that the system is permeable and works at all levels – the World Trade Organisation, the ILO and also the various UN bodies – to make the voice of labour heard.

Finally, we can turn to the useful idea of labour 'repertoires' (Tilly, 1978) to describe the way in which workers may develop ideas and take actions from a 'repertoire' to some extent set by objective conditions. Cohen and Rai have extended this notion to global social movements in a suggestive way. The three types of repertoire they distinguish for broad historical periods are set out in Table 7.1. We need not make too much of this table to get some use from it. If in the national era labour struggles were national, electoral, industrial and autonomous (insurrections being few and far between), in the global or transnational era, gender and environment come to the fore only with international consumer boycott movements, all in the spirit of solidarity. Strictly speaking labour internationalism would thus probably fall somewhere in between the second and third types of repertoire, being workplace based but also expressing some of the broader concerns of the global solidarity era.

GLOBAL DEVELOPMENT

We noted in Chapter 6 that the Brandt Commission of the mid-1970s represented a high point of influence of the international trade-union movement on the global development debate. However, in the cold climate created by the Reagan–Thatcher regimes that followed, there was little space for such notions as 'codes of conduct' for the TNCs. During the 1980s attempts to curb the power of the TNCs wound down, with an end signalled effectively by the closure of the UN Centre on Transnational Corporations in 1993. By the mid-1990s the global development debate had been revived and the ICFTU was to throw its weight behind the 'social clause' campaign. In the interim the ICFTU had come under pressure from some of its affiliates in the South, who complained of ICFTU policy documents' 'bias towards the industrialised countries of the North' (Gumbrell-McCormick, 2000: 505). Voices from labour and women in the South had a considerable impact at the discursive level, so that when the ICFTU did re-engage with global development in the 1990s it was much more attuned to the problems of poverty, unemployment and underdevelopment.

The 1990s international trade-union movement's understanding of global development is exemplified by the ICEM Second World Congress of 1999 held, not insignificantly, in Durban, South Africa. The ICEM explicitly sought to develop a strategy for 'global unionism' to confront 'global power'. There is, by the ICEM, an immediate and blunt recognition that 'The world economy has never been just.... But now the world social economy displays the greatest inequalities since the last century' (ICEM, 1999: 31). There is a clear understanding that mounting socio-economic inequalities drive a wedge between working people within and between nations. There is even a recognition, in trade-union debates, that 'The liberation of the colonies brought improved living conditions for millions and ... assisted countries to escape from the serfdom ... of the last century' (ICEM, 1999: 31). Now globalisation threatens to turn the clock back and recolonise the South. What is particularly interesting about the ICEM analysis is that it poses implicitly the need for a new 'global compact' between the workers of the North and the countries of the South to confront the effects of neo-liberal globalisation.

The North/South or global development conundrum of the international trade-union movement came to revolve around the 'social clause' debate, whose origins could be traced back to the late 1940s but which became a major issue in the 1990s. The international trade-union movement, the ICFTU in particular, has been in the forefront of efforts since the 1980s to build an element of social regulation into the emerging global governance structures. At the first WTO ministerial meeting in Singapore in 1996 the ICFTU (supported by the World Confederation of Labour) proposal for linking trade and labour standards was opposed by a coalition of neo-liberal states and countries such as India claiming an anti-imperialist stance. By the time the third ministerial meeting of the WTO was held in Seattle in 1999 the campaign for a social clause had made considerable progress. On the one hand, US President Clinton seemed to court the labour vote by speaking out loudly in its support. On the other hand, the ICFTU had worked intensively with its affiliates in the South to achieve much greater internal consensus and to dissipate to some extent the opposition from Southern radical NGOs. It is ironic that when the talks at Seattle were suspended there was a document on core labour standards on the table which more countries supported.

The case against the 'social clause' has been argued most clearly and consistently by trade unionists in India (see John and Chenoy, 1996), although these views received support from South African and Brazilian trade unionists as well. There is an undercurrent of economic and cultural nationalism underlying much of the critique of 'linkage', but the real target is simply globalisation. There is also an undoubted alignment by some trade unionists with national capital and the state against the 'world system'. The complaint that protectionism is an underlying motivation of some supporters of 'linkage' does not change the fact that without international labour standards trade liberalisation will tend to drive down labour conditions worldwide. National 'sovereignty' and national 'interests' can, indeed, be used to protect the comparative advantage of low wages in the South, but they can also be used in the North to keep out the goods produced in the South. The argument that labour is not a trade-related issue (which the Chinese government makes particularly forcefully) is simply wrong if we think of the role of labour in producing the goods that are traded. There is, however, a contradiction for those labour movements in the South engaged in fierce struggles against the impact of structural adjustment if they then turn to a body such as the WTO for 'protection'. The ICFTU would argue that its intervention with the WTO was as tactical and struggle-oriented as any daily interaction of trade unionists with employers.

It would appear that some of the debates on the social clause hinge on tactical disagreements. For example, we can question whether it is in the interests of global democracy to strengthen the WTO by getting it to police a social clause in the South. We could argue that the ILO is better placed and more representative to carry out this task, but then its weakness is apparent to all observers and even to itself. We certainly need to recognise that a social clause as part of international trade agreements can only impact on the export sector and thus will not affect the majority of workers, especially those in the informal sector. We could also argue that it would be better to have 'codes of conduct' for transnational companies, rather than an imperialist-dominated 'code of conduct' for countries. However, none of these debates seems to affect the principle of valid core labour standards. In that sense I think we can usefully start with Julio Godio's statement that, 'if the struggle to transform the world is international, the fight for a social clause can mobilise workers on a global scale to regulate the market, renewing thus, this time at an international level, the historic confrontation between capital and labour' (Godio, 1998: 355).

A broader perspective is needed, I believe, to situate the social clause debate properly. We can start with the argument by Silver and Arrighi that, 'contrary to widespread opinion, the so-called North–South divide continues to constitute (as it has throughout the twentieth century) the main obstacle to the formation of a homogeneous world proletarian condition' (Silver and Arrighi, 2000: 53). Indeed, various studies testify to the enduring nature of the global hierarchy of wealth from the Second World War to the end of the century. What this means is that for the international labour movement the issue of what Silver and Arrighi call 'global distributional justice' (Silver and Arrighi, 2000: 69) is inescapable. There can simply be no unified international labour movement while these divisions persist, especially while workers of the North seek to scapegoat those in the South for their own perceived slipping in the global pecking order. No case could be clearer in this regard than the opposition of the AFL–CIO in the USA to the accession of China into the global trading system. The expressed concern for China's workers cannot mask the protectionism, and indeed racism, motivating this stance on an issue crucial to the future of a unified global labour movement.

When faced with a highly uneven global development and deeply entrenched differences it can seem rather glib simply to assert that global problems call for global solutions. The divisions between the economic North and South will not be swept away by cosmopolitan discourses about shared planets. Very often proclamations of universality are a mask for particular interests. What is needed, I would argue, is a holistic approach which does not politely gloss over inequality. Amartya Sen has made a powerful case for an inclusive approach to work and rights in the era of globalisation which recognises that 'Universality means facing difficult questions – *some* perceived conflicts of interest are real – but a comprehensive framework makes it possible to address them' (Sen, 2000: 1). On this realist note we can then move beyond the international to the truly global as a new basis for solidarity. In this spirit, Sen also helps us understand that if capitalist ethics are now truly global, so the world's workers require certain basic global rights that would necessarily transcend national legal recognition.

We can further note that in the era of globalisation the main issue for the ruling elites is the question of governance. Whereas government under national capitalism entailed the orderly capacity to make decisions and enforce them, governance in the era of globalisation points to 'an order which cannot be externally imposed but is the result of the interaction of a multiplicity of ... influencing actors' (Kouiman and Van Vloet, 1993: 64). There is a blurring of boundaries between national and international affairs, as there is in terms of who has responsibility for tackling specific socio-economic issues. The process of global governance today involves a broad range of actors, including the major multilateral agencies such as the IMF, the World Bank and the WTO, but also a series of transnational social movements, including the labour movement. A recent study argues that 'increasing engagement between international institutions and sectors of civil society is producing a new form of global governance' (O'Brien et al., 2000: back cover). The influence of civil society on global governance mechanisms is uneven at best, but it does point towards a possible trend in years to come.

For the working people of the world, the main issue could be said to be the question of citizenship. If global civil society is more imagined than real, then global citizenship can remain only an aspiration at present. However, if, as we have argued repeatedly, workers are also citizens in the era of globalisation, we require at least a conception of what global citizenship might mean. Whereas governance has arguably become less democratic in the era of globalisation, it has encouraged or enabled certain democratic practices. Contact between social groups across frontiers is much easier, quicker and cheaper. The world really has shrunk in a social sense. If it is the particular form of globalisation that has led to the democratic deficit of our era, then a stronger mode of social regulation could strengthen democracy. Anthony McGrew argues in this regard that, contrary to the negative developments caused by globalisation which are usually focused on in progressive circles, it 'is also associated with processes of political empowerment and democratisation' (McGrew, 1997: 238). This point brings us back to the issue of agency and the way workers can shape their future.

Having set some broad parameters for the discussion of labour futures in terms of global development, we can now be more specific. One strategy for international labour could be along the lines of the Global Compact signed by the ICFTU with the United Nations in

2000. This peak organizations agreement (springing from the World Economic Forum meetings in Davos) is a purely voluntary arrangement bringing labour, environmental and business representatives together under UN auspices. A sceptical view of the Global Compact would indicate, however, that its main function is simply to give an ethical cover to the TNCs. At the opposite end of the spectrum we have strategies which advocate a local perspective and focus against the ravages of globalisation. The notion that the local is stable while the global is fluid is problematic, however. A sceptical view of this strategy would point towards the failed strategies of 'disengagement' from the world economy in the 1970s and the pitfalls of protectionist strategies for all concerned. To break out of this glib global-versus-local debate over strategies for labour we need to unpack the terms.

THE LOCAL AND THE GLOBAL

If the 'new' internationalism of the era of globalisation is to be seen as distinctive it might also involve a new understanding of the 'architecture' of human society. To pose the local against the global as a simple binary opposition with nothing 'in between', as it were, lacks credibility. It is as though a house had just a foundation and a roof with nothing in between. At the very least we need to consider the national, regional and subregional 'levels' (although that architectural image lacks fluidity). One of the most striking features of the current phase of globalisation is precisely the intermingling of all these 'levels' in a multiplex and 'hybrid' form of interconnectedness. From this perspective, the local–global 'paradox' to which some writers refer is misconceived if by that we mean simply that 'while economic relationships have become ever more *global* in scope and nature, political responses to economic globalisation are becoming more *localised*' (Jonas, 1999: 325). This posits a links between the local and the global that is too simple and unidirectional, and ignores the issue of agencies through which people, social groups and cities, for example, interact with the global.

The regional level of labour internationalism is relatively neglected, for two reasons. The first is that in the globalisation literature the regional tends to be seen as a subordinate and uncomplicatedly complementary level. Thus while it is recognised that the 'new regionalism' is a response to globalisation, it is seen as playing a supportive role in the neo-liberal drive for competitiveness. At this stage it may be useful to introduce the distinction between regionalisation and regionalism in so far as it may add some nuance to our understanding. Regionalisation, following Grugel and Hout, usually refers to 'the regional expression of the global processes of economic integration and the changing structures of production and power' (Grugel and Hout, 1999: 10). This process would appear to be the regional 'moment' of the globalisation process. Regionalism, on the other hand, following Gamble and Payne, can be taken to be 'a type of state project which can be distinguished from other types of state projects such as globalism' (Gamble and Payne, 1996: 250). This state project may flow with, but may also flow against (or be in contradiction with), the historic process of globalisation.

Regional trade-union activity is of central importance to the labour movements of the North. One of the most developed examples of transnational trade unionism is in relation to the European Union. During the flourishing of transnational collective bargaining enthusiasm in the 1960s and 1970s, Western Europe was often considered a crunch case. There was a layer of enlightened trade unionists for whom there was little sense in bargaining separately with different arms of the same TNC in each country. Though the ETUC was formed in 1970 it has not been a particularly representative body although it meets regularly with the employers' umbrella organisation and has a certain EU legitimacy at the level of social policy. The European Works Councils (EWCs) have begun to operate in the 1990s, representing the most ambitious aspect of the social charter in so far as they could lead to transnational industrial relations within the TNCs operating in the EU. Overall, however, 'national trade unions may well prove reluctant to field the necessary authority and resources to European-level organisation to enable them to pursue transnational negotiations' (Marginson and Sisson, 1996: 44–5). To my mind, the European experience demonstrates the limits of a syndicalist (i.e. exclusively trade-union-oriented) international strategy.

The regional dimension is also of growing importance for transnational labour activity in the South. It is notable that MERCOSUR (Common Market of the Southern Cone) in Latin America is the fourth most significant trade bloc in the world, with a GDP of nearly US$1,000 billion. While the main dynamic of this regional free-trade zone set up in 1991 is to facilitate integration with neo-liberal globalisation, it does seem to contain an alternative dynamic. Economic integration in the Southern Cone of Latin America is also a defensive strategy vis-à-vis globalisation and reflects the lingering *desarollista* (developmentalist) strategy of some industrial sectors. When the socialist president of Chile, Ricardo Lagos, visited Argentina in 2000 he declared that in a world of 'globalisers' and 'globalised' the MERCOSUR approach was 'the formula to confront the challenges of globalisation' (*Clarin*, 10 July 2000: 5). Brazil's leading role in relation to MERCOSUR places that country in de facto leadership of a Southern bloc in opposition to the US project of a Free Trade of the Americas Zone. The trade unions' active role within MERCOSUR is a good example of regional transitional activity. It also shows that the labour movement cannot abstain from regional integration projects.

Finally, we have the most interesting case of North–South regional transnationalism with NAFTA, formed in 1994. The conflictual, but ultimately productive, interaction between Mexican, US and Canadian trade unions over NAFTA may yet prove to be a watershed in terms of labour transnationalism between North and South. Nationalist and protectionist responses were the first reaction by labour, but these shifted, albeit unevenly and hesitantly, towards a common position on this major exercise of capitalist rationalisation. Establishing a community of interests among the workers of North America was not easy and, of course, did not eliminate national interest. It was noticeable that the Canadian (and particularly Quebecois) unions played a role in mediating between the quite opposed US and Mexican positions (see Bakvis, 1998). The mixed result of these debates can be gauged in a statement by Lane Kirkland, veteran president of the AFL–CIO at the time, for whom 'You can't be a trade unionist unless you are an internationalist', the reason being that 'substandard conditions anywhere' (read Mexico) were 'a threat to good conditions anywhere' (read the USA) (cited in French et al., 1994: 1). This, of course, just shows that internationalism and self-interest are not incompatible.

Transnational labour activity can now be seen in slightly more complex terms: it is not just labour 'going global' to match capital's globalising strategy. Nor is it a simple localist strategy to compensate for labour's weakness at the international level. Local and global labour activity cannot be seen as mutually exclusive; nor are they in a hierarchy of importance. The local and the global can only be understood in relational terms, in a 'dialectical' relationship as it were. Ash Amin rejects, correctly in my mind, 'the *territorial* idea of sequestered spatial logics – local, national, continental and global – pitted against each other' (Amin, 1997: 133). These are not separate 'places' but, rather, intermixed social relations. Thus labour cannot really pursue a progressive strategy of transformation based on territorial units; rather, it needs to take account of the hybrid and interdependent social logic of globalisation/regionalisation/localisation.

There are problems with any simple understanding of labour solidarity as 'going global' to match capital. Indeed, it may actually be demoralising to propose a strategy that cannot be achieved. Perhaps linked-up local struggles may be another way to 'go global'. Andrew Herod mentions in this regard the successful 1998 General Motors dispute in the USA where two plants in one community successfully brought the giant auto company to a standstill (Herod, 2001). Herod is undoubtedly correct to conclude that, 'in an increasingly interconnected planetary economy a locally focused campaign against a TNC may sometimes prove highly effective, particularly if such local disputes target crucial parts of that corporation's global operation' (Herod, 2001: 412). This would thus be a truly global strategy, in so far as it is well attuned to the nature of globalisation, but one applied locally. If we recall that globalisation is a discourse as much as a strategy, we can see how this type of approach may counter the demoralisation created by neo-liberal globalisation, which fosters the belief across the world that 'There is no alternative' (TINA).

There are, however, also problems with any 'localist' strategy for labour in the era of globalisation. During the 1998 strike by Liverpool dockers there was considerable international solidarity activity. Undoubtedly this occurred to some extent because the local and national levels for labour advancement were hostile, if not closed down. However, some commentators constantly sought to return the struggle to its local context to pursue 'class action' as in the 1970s dockers' disputes. Here we detect a localism that in its blind denial of the complexity of globalisation (seen only as a block) constricts labour's options. Put more generally, the local cannot be seen as a stable island in the stormy seas of globalisation. There is even a certain reactionary tinge to this localism, which can all too easily lead to protectionist demands and chauvinist sentiments. As Hardt and Negri put it, 'this 'localist' position is misleading in so far as it rests on a false dichotomy between the global and the local, assuming that the global entails homogenisation and undifferentiated identity whereas the local pre-serves heterogeneity and difference' (Hardt and Negri, 2000: 44). Local differences are not 'natural', and in fact can be seen to be 'produced' by globalisation.

An abstract labour 'global solidarity' strategy may in fact be dis-empowering, as we saw above. Nor can localisation – empowering the local – be an adequate response to globalisation. Certainly trade unions need to develop a strategy attuned to the particularities of their locality. They also require a broad social movement orientation, bringing in the whole community where possible, if they are not to be limited to syndicalism. But globalisation will not be threatened by a sum of many little localisms. Macro-level responses are necessary and the demand for a 'social clause' is where at present the main impetus for reform lies. Contesting global governance at this level is also necessary and there is little point in accusing the ICFTU of 'reformism' in this regard. Bridging the apparent gulf between local and global strategies can be achieved, I believe, through what Brecher, Costello and Smith call 'linking the nooks and crannies' (Brecher et al., 2000: 23) where labour activity takes place across the world, and thus 'developing a common vision and program' (Brecher et al., 2000: 25) to contest neo-liberal globalisation effectively.

Do we, then, have a 'new' internationalism today? To some extent previous examples of internationalism, such as that against the apart-heid regime in South Africa, prefigured present practice. Official labour internationalism, such as that articulated by the ICFTU, appears to be in transition (see Moody, 1997: ch. 10), with considerable hangovers from the old bureaucratic practices. The 'official' left perspective also seems to be caught up in the old nation-statist perspective. Thus a special issue of *Monthly Review* (Monthly Review, 2000) on the 'new internationalism' after Seattle seemed more keen to dismiss globalis-ation as a framework of analysis and simply repeat timeless Marxist nostrums than to develop a transnational labour strategy adequate to the needs of the time. Even 'globalisation from below', although attractive as a slogan, lacks concrete purchase in the new situation, in so far as it neglects the North/South dimension. What we can be confident of is that the new era of globalisation is creating a novel and complex terrain for labour internationalism, where local, regional and global levels interact, and where community, consumption and pro-duction 'levels' are also all present.

EIGHT

RESULTS AND PROSPECTS

Even as this conclusion was being written the world of labour and globalisation had moved on in the nine months or so since the introduction was taking shape. What were tendencies towards an international orientation by labour leaders, for example, are now established practices. This chapter examines the results of our enquiry into labour in the era of globalisation and looks at its prospects in the era to come. We begin by re-examining the brave new world created by neo-liberal globalisation and consider the role that labour and other social movements may play. The next section considers the options once we move 'beyond competition' and realise that there is an alternative to the unsustainable status quo. For example, the 'social clause' is considered, but also the issue of labour benchmarking. This is followed by a consideration of Working Future, the new patterns of work which are emerging and the new strategies for resistance they have generated. Finally, we look at how labour has virtually been reinvented in the last decade or so. A new, more internationalist, as well as objectively 'globalised', labour movement is emerging with a strong social movement or community orientation.

THE NEW ORDER

Friedrich von Hayek's *The Road to Serfdom* (Hayek, [1944] 1955), which was to inspire Margaret Thatcher and the rest of the neo-liberal counter-revolutionaries, was published towards the end of the Second World War. Its gospel of free markets and rolling back of the state came into its own in the last quarter of the twentieth century.

State intervention – be it economic regulation, financial controls, welfare states, social protection or even the existence of such bodies as trade unions – was held to be the road to 'serfdom'. The new world order still subscribes to von Hayek, but a revised or muted version. A genuine alternative vision of a world order derives from the work of another Austrian economist, whose book also appeared towards the end of the Second World War. Karl Polanyi's *The Great Transformation* (Polanyi, [1945] 1957) is now coming back into fashion in some International Political Economy (IPE) circles, but is generally quite unknown, especially by comparison with von Hayek. As already intimated in Chapter 1, I believe Polanyi's work provides a useful general framework for both understanding the new world order and developing labour's strategy in the era of globalisation.

Karl Polanyi was writing at the mid-point of the last century about the 'Great Transformation' which resulted from England's 'Industrial Revolution' in the eighteenth and nineteenth centuries. Yet it can also be argued that the 'Great Transformation' really referred to the cataclysmic institutional transformation after the 1930s (see Goldfrank, 1990). In their different ways, the New Deal in the USA, Nazism in Germany and Stalinism in the USSR were examples of the 'double movement' which Polanyi saw as establishing social control over market mechanisms. In terms of our object of analysis here – the conflictual and multidirectional relationship between globalisation and a social-movement democratisation – Polanyi's problematic in the 1950s may well inspire and provide direction (and historical context) to our enquiries. To begin with we may consider Polanyi's definition of the 'double movement':

> It can be personified as the action of two organising principles in society ... The one was the principle of economic liberalism, aiming at the establishment of a self-regulating market ... using largely laissez-faire and free trade as its methods; the other was the principle of social protection aiming at the conservation of man and nature ... using protective legislation, restrictive associations, and other instruments of intervention as its methods. (Polanyi, 1957: 132)

In 'translating' Polanyi from mid-twentieth century to early twenty-first century we can start with globalisation, which, if it is nothing else, is the worldwide application of laissez-faire principles. If Polanyi would write about how 'markets spread all over the face of the globe and the amount of goods involved grew to unbelievable proportions'

(Polanyi, 1957: 76), this is doubly true today, even for those who believe that globalisation is only a tendency and that what we are witnessing is mainly internationalisation. Yet, and this is why Polanyi is so contemporary, the counter-movement(s) through which society protects itself are equally inevitable. Wherever there was, as with the Industrial Revolution or now with the 'Globalisation Revolution', 'an unparalleled momentum to the mechanism of markets', there was also 'a deep-seated movement [which] sprang into being to resist the pernicious effects of a market-controlled economy' (Polanyi, 1957: 76). As distinct from both liberalism and orthodox Marxism, Polanyi argued that this was 'the one comprehensive feature in the history of the age' (Polanyi, 1957: 76). There is nothing inevitable about this process but it certainly does seem to cut across the intense pessimism of much anti-globalisation literature, for whom we are simply 'all doomed'.

For Polanyi a major characteristic of the market society was that it had become 'disembedded' socially; that is to say, it was uprooted or divorced from its social and political institutions. What a disembedded and self-regulating market economy produces in people is insecurity and social anxiety. Protective counter-movements by society and the state must also seek to block the total disembedding of the market by re-embedding it through state intervention and social legislation. Of course, in the era of globalisation that re-embedding, must also occur at an international level to be effective, even more than was the case in the 1930s. As well as re-embedding, what occurs, or should occur, is de-commodification of the 'factors of production' and in particular that peculiar commodity of labour. Polanyi reveals, in his seemingly naïve assumption that 'Labour is only another name for a human activity which goes with life itself.... The commodity description of labour ... is entirely fictitious' (Polanyi, 1957: 72). He goes on to argue, quite sensibly, that if trade unions or social legislation did not 'interfere' with the mobility of labour they would 'have entirely failed in their purpose' (Polanyi, 1957: 177), which was precisely to cut across the 'laws' of supply and demand to remove human labour from the orbit of the market.

This argument leads up to a well-grounded understanding of globalisation and democracy in terms of a 'double movement' akin to that described and analysed by Polanyi. Stephen Gill has argued persuasively that Polanyi's 'double movement' can be seen as a metaphor for the 'socio-political forces which wish to assert more democratic control over political life' (Gill, 1995: 7). In this way, Polanyi can be seen as a theorist of counter-hegemonic movements, a tradition given its founding statements by Antonio Gramsci and renewed today in critical globalisation studies. Of course these can take various forms, from a strategy of working mainly within the parameters of globalisation to achieve some degree of regulation (with many critical globalisers now joining this camp), to the all-out opposition of the anti-globalisers in the streets of Seattle and beyond, through the various permutations in between where there is a growing body of 'revolutionary reformist' and strategic thinking now going on. That this may find an echo in far-sighted thinking by the global elite is no bad thing and simply reflects the fact that the 'Polanyi problem' is now being recognised.

The 'double movement' at the heart of the 'great transformation(s)' also points us towards the issue of agency. Both orthodox Marxists and uncritical globalists tend to collapse tendencies – towards self-regulating markets and globalisation – into essences. The necessary counter-movements of regulation, decommodification and re-embedding provide us with a less necessitarian view of the world. Contemporary counter-movements will not, in all likelihood, lead to a revival of the post-Second World War settlement and social contract, because the world has indeed gone through a 'great transformation' since the collapse of state socialism and the acceleration of capitalist globalisation. Undoubtedly, however, if global anarchy is to be avoided, new global social modes of regulation will emerge. What is also certain is that Polanyi, as a precursor of the theory of radical democracy, would be looking to ordinary people for democratic alternatives to current forms of globalisation.

It would seem to be indicative of a new mood among the organic intellectuals of the new global order that *The Economist* should dedicate a special issue to 'The Case for Globalisation' (23–29 September 2000). This austere and sober organ of finance capital made the strange admission that the protestors at Seattle (and subsequently) 'are right that the tide of 'globalisation', powerful as the engine driving it may be, can be turned back' (19). The mighty forces driving globalisation are not just 'pandering' to street protests, as *The Economist* sees it. We need to ask why 'Governments are apologising for globalisation and promising to civilise it' and why the anti-globalisation protests 'are meeting no intellectual resistance from official quarters' (19). It may, indeed, simply be the case that the hour of von Hayek is gone and the hour of Polanyi has arrived. The hegemony of a 'straight' neo-liberalism inspired by von Hayek is tarnished even among the ruling elite. Street protests would hardly affect a hegemonic global order unless it was already undermined from within. If governments are 'apologising' (an overstated term perhaps) over neo-liberal globalisation, it might be because they perceive the urgency of the 'Polanyi problem' (see Chapter 1), namely the need to regulate capitalism if it is to survive.

A useful case study of capitalism's current contradictions is provided by the issue of so-called 'corporate responsibility'. One leading transnational corporation took up the mantle of 'corporate citizenship' because 'Companies are part of society. They enjoy certain rights to trade freely but, like individuals, they also have certain responsibilities for the wider public good' (cited in Sklair, 2001: 171). Why do TNCs feel they need to (or at least be seen to) be 'responsive' to governments, consumers and even pressure groups? Of course the Shell corporation would wish to burnish an image tarnished by the Brent Spar disaster in the North Sea and by its tragic involvement in Nigeria. While the public discourse may refer to balancing private profit and the public good, the simple fact is that a company's reputation is a weapon in business competition, and reputations are constructed socially and subjectively through perceptions. This means that the TNCs are susceptible to social and political pressure, not that they have been reinvented as good citizens. With financial objectives being at least moderated by social, environmental and ethical criteria, we can at least see a Polanyian problematic at play which is a long way from the full-blown rampant neo-liberalisation of the 1980s.

As Marx said long ago, every economic system has limits, and that applies to capitalism as much as to any other mode of production. It seems hard to believe but until early 2001 many analysts professed to believe that the US stockmarket had 'broken the mold' and would henceforth only go up. Not only is capitalism still subject to cycles but it may be approaching limits in terms of the natural resources and further open space to conquer for the market. As Leslie Sklair puts it, the transnational capitalist class are 'globalising as they struggle to come to terms with the contradictions of the global capitalist system they themselves have been instrumental in creating' (Sklair, 2000: 761). The new order exploits workers, disrupts communities and disappoints consumers, all of which may fight back separately or through variously configured coalitions of interests. For each victory of the transnational capitalist class, there is a new blow struck from below through a strike, a consumer boycott or a legal challenge to their hegemonic role. It is the role of democracy to unify these diverse activities. This takes us back to the Polanyi-inspired notion of counterposing globalisation with democracy, which would of course include labour as an agent of democratisation.

The stability of global governance is now contested in a whole series of different ways. International organisations – and the World Bank is a particular case in point – are not the monoliths they were once thought to be, or at least that they were portrayed as by radical critics. Over the last twenty years international organisations of capitalism have increasingly engaged with global social movements and shown a certain permeability. Governance is moving away from an exclusively state-based mode of operation to embrace elements of civil society. The study by O'Brien et al. of multilateral economic institutions and global social movements goes so far as to argue that we are witnessing a 'transformation in the nature of governance' (O'Brien et al., 2000: 206) at a global level due to the encounter. This 'complex multilateralism' they identify should not be confused with some naïve unilinear move towards democratisation of global governance. Indeed, much of the 'dialogue' with civil society on the part of these international organisations is motivated by a desire to neutralise or co-opt social and democratic opposition to their hegemonic aspirations. It is just as well to recognise that contradictions are opening up and not just assume that globalism has already won the day.

To understand better the hegemony of the new world order it would be well to recall that Gramsci's celebrated concept of 'hegemony' had an economic component: 'though hegemony is ethico-political, it must also be economic, must necessarily be based on the decisive function exercised by the leading group in the decisive nucleus of economic activity' (Gramsci, 1971b: 161). While most commentators think of hegemony as a political or cultural 'consent' type of notion, for Gramsci it was clearly also 'structural'. In his analysis of the national and international levels, for example in relation to Fordism, Gramsci always analysed social classes and forces in this integrated way. This points us towards the importance of the transnational capitalist class, for example, but also towards the way in which production is an integral element of the world order. If Fordism can now be seen in its full national/international, production/consumption, political/economic moments, so can the globalism of the new world order. As capitalism reorganises on a global scale and seeks to impose a new hegemonic order, so the political economy of global labour must be an integral element, for its understanding as much as for its critique from a democratic standpoint.

In his *Producing Hegemony*, Mark Rupert (Rupert, 1995) has pointed towards a new approach based on Gramscian IPE (International Political Economy). This is a study of the Fordist era showing how a 'historic bloc' (which included US labour as a junior partner) created a productivity-based political consensus in the North and generalised this vision across the world. This era has now come to an end and the neo-liberal era (the Washington consensus) has already run into difficulties. The 'historic bloc' between the transnational capitalist class and the labour movement has been shattered. The hegemony of neo-liberalism – its ability to be seen as a popular 'common sense' – has expired and few conflate it with universal aspirations, as once Fordism and popular consumption were equated. This analytical perspective allows us to see a space for transformative politics opening up, even if their precise manifestation is still unclear. Rupert is cautious but opens up the analysis when he argues that, 'Under the pressure of late Fordist transnational capitalism, the common sense of industrial workers is once again being contested and reconstructed: ... the identity of interest between workers and their corporate employer – presumed by neo-liberal ideology ... – is being opened to question' (Rupert, 1995: 195). In that questioning the various parts of the international labour movement are undoubtedly playing their part.

BEYOND COMPETITION

Gradually since the heyday of neo-liberalism in the 1980s the world has been moving 'beyond' competition, once seen as the driving spirit of the era. Even the very notion of 'corporate citizenship', referred to above, points towards a different conception of the world than one where competition rules supreme. What has happened, in part, is that Margaret Thatcher's famous war cry 'There is no alternative' (TINA) has simply been rendered obsolete. In theoretical terms, we have moved beyond what Roberto Unger calls 'false necessity' and now understand that 'the institutional arrangements of contemporary society are the outcomes of many loosely connected sequences of social and ideological conflict rather than of irresistable and determinate functional imperatives' (Unger, 1998: 24). An anti-necessitarian perspective allows us to see that history is open-ended and not predetermined, and that we are not puppets but, rather, have the possibility to resist and also to reconstruct our lives and the world around us. For a while, though, 'competition' seemed irresistible.

In the course of the 1980s, 'competitiveness' became the mantra and the 'way forward' for capital and the state to such an extent that even profitability became demoted to being a long-term objective. To 'compete' in the global economy was the watchword of national political leaders, business associations, the media and even trade unions. As globalisation reconfigured the capitalist system, so 'competitiveness' became the one best way to play the new game. In a context of liberalisation of market forces and deregulation of capitalism, to 'compete' was the way to survive. For the believers 'Competition is a powerful instrument for innovation. It stimulates the search for cheaper and better processes, products, and services.... In principle, competition makes the pull of demand the driving force of economic innovation' (Group of Lisbon, 1995: 91). Fair competition is a reasonable enough criterion for producers and it may, indeed, ensure that the consumer has a greater choice and better goods and services to choose from. Yet in practice the notion of 'competitiveness' is flawed at every level. Ultimately it is a philosophy for war at the global level, fuelling the notion that nations should become stronger to 'beat' others.

The Lisbon Group of thinkers and policy-makers made a powerful case in the mid-1990s for the 'limits to competition' (Group of Lisbon, 1995). Their conclusion was that 'Competitiveness fundamentalists are aggressive in their theory, blind in their approach and sectarian in their judgement' (Group of Lisbon, 1995: 99). The market simply does not represent the only factor determining economic success and social well-being. Nor can it deal with social inequality, representing the interests, as it does, of very rich individuals and nations. Even more, it is flawed in that a purely competitive drive would ultimately lead to its opposite as protectionism seeks to keep competitors out of established markets. Paul Krugman – no radical – argues, furthermore, that not only is competitiveness 'a meaningless word when applied to national economies' (it is firms that compete, not countries) but also that 'Thinking in terms of competitiveness leads directly and indirectly to bad economic policies on a wide range of issues, domestic and foreign, whether it be in health care or trade' (Krugman, 1994: 35). In sum, 'competitiveness' is flawed conceptually as well as being a totally inadequate way to plan long-term for global governance.

A new global regulatory order simply cannot be constructed around the principle of competition. The new spatial disorder created by globalisation does, however, require some form of regulation. The old problem of uneven development is taking new, more accentuated forms which need to be dealt with if globalisation is going to be sustainable even in its own terms. For Tickell and Peck, 'There is as yet no mechanism in place for regulating [uneven development in] global capitalism. Without one there can be no basis for the formation of a new regime of accumulation' (Tickell and Peck, 1995: 370). The much-vaunted 'glocalisation' process, whereby the global and the local merge in a new synergy, is seen to be inherently unstable and, in fact, as reflecting the new contradictions of capitalism. In the vacuum left behind by the demise of the Fordist social mode of regulation, the nation-state, let alone the local state, has few powers of regulation. While locally labour has created coalitions of interest with local capital and the state, this is not a path which can escape the rule of 'competition', this time between cities seeking to attract outside investment.

One particular aspect of global regulation where labour can perhaps play an important role is the regional level. We have seen how, in the North and in the South, new regional transnational coalitions of labour have formed. Regional co-operation is also, however, part of the 'double movement' detected by Polanyi whereby social regulation is imposed on an ever-expanding capitalism. In a little-known article from 1945 Polanyi argued that the 'universal capitalism' which was then emerging might be countered by 'regional planning' (Polanyi, 1945). He saw the West 'committed to restore free markets where they have disappeared' (Polanyi, 1945: 89) in the East. He believed Yugoslavia had got it right by going for a regional solution – 'no longer market-ridden' – and that 'tomorrow Europe as a whole may yearn for the Balkan cure, and regionalism will be supreme'. Though well aware that 'regionalism is not a panacea', Polanyi makes a plea that may be relevant again today in another post-war era, that beyond the Cold War (Polanyi, 1945: 89). New reciprocal regional structures are indeed emerging with a redistributive component, which will fit in better with global competitiveness, as well as establish a potentially different, more regulatory, dynamic.

The labour movement is active at local, national, regional and global levels, seeking to impose some form of social regulation on global capitalism. At present the 'social clause' is the main platform that the official labour movement advances to obtain respect for basic labour rights. However, as we have seen at various points above, the 'social clause' is viewed by many in the South as a Northern protectionist measure. Though these divisions are being overcome, to some extent, by a strong internal campaign within the ICFTU, a supplementary approach based on the concept of 'benchmarking' would be conceivable. The notion of 'benchmarking' is currently used by the TNCs in a way which 'is normally defined as a system of continuous improvements derived from systematic comparisons with world best practice' (Sklair, 2001: 115). Benchmarking is a logical element in global competition because to survive firms must compare themselves with best practice everywhere in the world. Yet it is not only the new global management consultants who practise benchmarking, and it is not always synonymous with mindless competitiveness.

The Canadian Automobile Workers (CAW) began in the mid-1990s to contest management's 'Japanese' work methods with an independent strategy of their own. This involved intensive research among their members on the impact of the new work organisation models, but also a process of comparative 'benchmarking [of] the quality of working life' (Lewchuck and Robertson, 1999: 59). This approach does not treat workplaces in isolation and believes in an independent labour strategy on all issues concerning workers. The setting of workers' benchmarks, on key issues from wages and conditions to health and safety but also including an equality agenda and issues of social responsibility, could be a new way of formulating international labour standards. Much as the world of the TNC has as its horizon certain international benchmark companies, so workers, trade unions and the broader labour movement can set comparative benchmark standards. Mirrored on the practice of capital, and with a certain legitimacy gained by its association with the 'quality control' philosophy, this strategy would also give labour an independent horizon of possibilities, not set by capital and the state and not guided by the now discredited principles of competitiveness.

Finally, in considering a world 'beyond' competition it is well to recall the embeddedness of social and economic institutions. They are not the free-floating rational actors which a pure competition theory would assume them to be. Market transactions are not simply imper-sonal processes. Economic and social co-ordination mechanisms in any society entail an element of trust and are necessarily 'constrained by the social context within which they are embedded' (Hollingsworth and Boyer, 1996: 11). Markets are simply not the ideal means to co-ordinate transactions in an atmosphere of uncertainty. In the globalised postmodern era this is doubly so, as transactions are speeded up and are often virtual in nature. To uncertainty we can now add complexity (disorganised versus organised capitalism) as an argument for em-beddedness against market principles. Today's 'flexible' systems of production, based on highly skilled labour, require a minimum of co-operation between employers and their employees, as much as co-ordination with suppliers and customers. The workplace is embedded in social, political, cultural, gender and moral relationships that cannot be subsumed within market categories or overruled by calls to 'compete'.

Trade unions are also 'embedded' social organisations. It is a con-stant theme in Polanyi's writings that trust, reciprocity and long-term relationships are necessary to build a sustainable social and economic system. The 'embeddedness' hypothesis (see Granovetter, 1992) simi-larly argues that these 'non-capitalist' logics are necessary for capital-ism and even for the market system itself. Trade unions, in so far as they tend to become a social movement and not a merely formal organisation, are sustained by communities, associations and even families at the end of the day. The unions and the broader labour movement are made up of, and indeed themselves create, a dense network of social relations. They cannot be reduced to the individual actor of rational choice theory who takes decisions in a social and moral vacuum. The 'moral economy' of the labour movement, and in particular the principle of 'solidarity', will conceivably play a significant role in designing a social system 'beyond' competition. An alternative social system of production, which does not rely on blind market mechanisms, will necessarily be based around the political economy of labour.

FUTURE WORK

In the new capitalist order the nature of work is changing fast, but there have also been many myths constructed around this transforma-tion process. We have not witnessed the 'end of work' and we are not all ICT workers. If we take the global workforce as our focus we see that it actually doubled in numbers between 1965 and 1998. David Coates points to an obvious conclusion, which is often missed in the literature: 'Globalisation in its modern form is a process based less on the proliferation of computers than on the proliferation of proletarians' (Coates, 2000: 256). Massive proletarianisation is at least as much a feature of globalisation as the increased mobility of capital. Another feature often missed in media and academic emphases on the 'new' in terms of 'teleworkers', 'cyberworkers' and so on is the survival and indeed expansion of 'old' forms of work. While the new informational economy is having profound effects on the world of work, it is well to recall that fully two-thirds of the world's workers still work in the fields of the South (and of the North for that matter). Development is always uneven but it is also combined, in terms of labour development as much as in economic development.

For the vast majority of the world's workers the much-vaunted informational economy has had only a negative effect. For every worker who benefits from the 'knowledge economy' there are many more still being super-exploited in a paddy field or at McDonald's. It is worth taking India as an example because it is that country's government, employers and some trade unions who have led the campaign against the 'social clause'. Why they take the stance becomes clearer when we realise that 60 per cent of India's GDP is contributed by that country's massive unorganised sector. A third of the working population and two-thirds of the landless agricultural workers live below the official fairly basic nutrition-based poverty line (Harriss-White and Gooptu, 2000: 90). When referring to an 'unorganised' sector, we need to be clear what this means. There is a distinction between the 'organised' capitalism of the early twentieth century and the 'disorganised' capitalism of the late twentieth century. For India, Harriss-White and Gooptu make clear that while 'most work may be unregulated by the state ... the markets for their labour are far from "unstructured"' (Harriss-White and Gooptu, 2000: 90). In fact the workers and their labour are closely regulated by the reconstituted 'traditional' structures of class, caste and gender.

The situation of those not benefiting from the 'new' global economy has been taken up by the ILO with its 'Decent Work' campaign. For a whole historical period, the ILO had focused mainly on male workers in formal economic institutions. At the turn of the century, however, it began to reorient towards the broad mass of the working poor and took up a strong gender stance. The ILO recognises that 'The agenda for 'decent work', resting as it does on complementarities and new synergies between the social and economic aspects of development, requires new analytical frameworks' (ILO, 1999: 3). They advocate a concept of 'social efficiency' to match or balance the economic logic of globalisation. The informal sector is recognised as a crucial area where organised labour needs a strategy, particularly in the South. Women workers are made more visible through its new perspective, and the particular situation of migrant and child workers can be prioritised. The concept of 'decent work' is, of course, a social construction and varies across cultures. What the ILO has done is to introduce an ethical element into the 'jobs debate', recognising that the quality of employment is as important as quantity.

At the other end of the work continuum is the new(ish) 'teleworker', the networkers and innovators of globalisation, the workers of 'turbo-capitalism'. These highly skilled, self-sufficient new employees are seen as the harbingers of future work practices and a categorical break with the traditional workers of capitalism. These 'symbolic analysts' are the flip side of the McDonald's worker in the North, with whom they are more or less on a par in terms of numbers. They represent the beginnings of a true global labour market. They are, indeed, different from the industrial worker who actually 'made' things, in so far as they 'think' about things. However, it is less clear that this form of work represents any sort of break with the 'traditional' capital/ wage-labour relationship based on exploitation. Ursula Huws writes that 'It is apparent that a new cybertariat is in the making' (Huws, 2000: 20), referring to the new front-line information workers of the North (and parts of the South) who are rapidly becoming proletarianised. There is, indeed, no certainty that the labour process of the new 'teleworker' is any more worker-friendly (in essence, as against image) than that of their 1950s' counterparts who wore grey suits to the office and had a job for life, however boring it might have been.

There is a common conception that these 'new' workers cannot be organised by the 'old' labour movement. This problem is recognised acutely by the trade unions, and thus a British trade union leader declared in 2000 that 'The whole future of trade unions depends on us demonstrating our value in [the] new sectors. We cannot just rest on our traditional heartlands of manufacturing and the public sector'

(Morgan, 2000: 5). The new ICT professionals are much younger than the average trade-union member and their memory is of the neo-liberal era and not of the Golden Era in which the unions had a certain social weight. Nevertheless, the 'flexibility' of the new labour regime spells insecurity for its workers, and its much-vaunted speed of operations leads directly to stress for its operatives. This is creating some inroads for the unions, particularly when 'old' unionised companies set up 'new' economy offshoots. There is still a feeling that it is not only employer resistance that unions face but the perceived irrelevance of traditional trade unionism for the 'new' workers. Sitting in the dot.com sector with a good salary, tempting share options and even employee 'chill-out zones', why would you need a union?

In practice, the trade unions have begun to make considerable inroads into the 'new' economy. This is hardly surprising if one recalls an earlier 'new' capitalism when office workers came on the scene. They were considered 'different' from their factory-floor counterparts, but by the mid-twentieth century white-collar workers were one of the bastions of the labour movement in many countries. For Seumus Milne, the initial skirmishes between managers and union organisers in the dot.com sector 'suggest the workings of the new economy may turn out to be more familiar than previously imagined' (Milne, 2000: 7). In short, the new economy still suffers from old problems. So the famous Amazon online bookshop was the site of a fierce unionisation battle in 2000, led by the Communication Workers of America for the customer-service representatives and by the United Food and Commercial Workers Union for those who parcel up the books ordered on the Internet. And it is the Internet which has been the logical place to organise for many computer programmers. Thus in France the UbiSoft video games producer employees set up the first 'virtual trade union' in 2000 to defend their working conditions in a sector which does not believe in human-relations departments let alone trade unions.

The 'new' knowledge workers may not seem so novel if a long-term view of the changing nature of the labour process is taken. Workers have nearly always used knowledge as well as physical effort to get the job done. The early car workers had precisely such a knowledge of the labour process that Taylorism had to separate the tasks of conception and execution to create white-collar employees and blue-collar workers, respectively. Today, for every 'upmarket' flexibilised knowledge worker there are three 'downmarket' flexibilised workers. What is technically possible in terms of 'future work' is unlikely to materialise in a social system still (or even more than ever) dominated by private profit and social divisions. As Guy Standing points out, 'In terms of work, the growth areas of the late twentieth century have been care and voluntary and paid work in non-governmental service organisations, usually non-profit, welfare-oriented groups' (Standing, 1999a: 395). Yet this work is not socialised; it has not become part of the mainstream of society. The denigration of nonprofitable activities will probably diminish in the decades to come as the obsession with 'social capital' increases.

We perhaps need to reconsider at this point the relationship between work and technology, in so far as it is crucial to all debates on the future of work. In the sociology of work there is a long tradition of technological determinism going back to Marx, who once said that 'The handmill gives you society with the feudal lord; the steam mill gives you society with the industrial capitalist' (Marx, 1976: 166). Marx may well have regretted this statement, and indeed elsewhere broke with this type of determinism, but the tradition lingers on. So, from at least the 1960s there has been a tendency to argue that 'computers give you a post-industrial society'. All work will be carried out by computers and robots, and this will spell the end of work as we know it. In the real world, however, technology is mediated by social and political structures which make this scenario unlikely. New communications technology may soon mediate all economic transactions, but the underlying social structure is still a divided one. Tilly and Tilly argue persuasively that 'Most technically possible futures [for work] will not materialise' (Tilly and Tilly, 1998: 263). While technological innovation will most certainly impinge dramatically on the world of work, this will be mediated by capitalist organisational imperatives, and, for that matter, by the nature of workers' responses to them.

Another crucial relationship is that between work and culture, without which we inevitably end up with a form of economism. Even the labour market, beloved of neo-classical economists, cannot be understood divorced from the historical and cultural context in which it is embedded. There is nothing natural or universal about a labour market or work itself in so far as they are profoundly shaped by local, national or socially produced cultural frameworks. As Amartya Sen once put it, the *homo economicus* of neo-classical economic theory 'is close to being a social moron' (Sen, 1981: 99). Workers are set in a social and cultural context that is far more complex than this hyper-individualist theoretical construction. Cultures have different conceptions of work – what is desirable, what is effective, what is fair. 'A fair day's pay for a fair day's work' means something different in each phase of human history and for different cultures. The culture of the workplace and the traditions of the labour movement are every bit as much a part of material work practices as the machine or the tool. Work cultures and labour 'traditions' are constantly being remade, and are likely to remain a crucial element in 'future work'.

Finally, when considering the future of work we should also recall with Tilly and Tilly that 'Future work will continue to depend on struggle – muted, routinised or openly contentious' (Tilly and Tilly, 1998: 264). The repertoires of action in the diverse workplaces of capitalism have always been shaped by the continuous interplay between employers and employees. This is a dance which always has two partners, even though one or the other may lead at specific points in time. Class struggle has certainly changed in its format and its modalities since the early days of capitalism but there is nothing to indicate that struggle has vacated the contemporary workplace. Indeed, there is every indication that globalisation is proving to be as powerful an agglutinating factor as classical capitalism was in terms of unifying different social struggles against a common enemy. The repertoires of contention deployed by today's future workers may be different – and an element of individualism is undoubtedly more important than in the heyday of collectivist ideologies – but they are emerging and helping to shape the future of the globalised 'new economy' as well.

LABOUR REINVENTED

There is widespread agreement that the international labour movement has suffered serious setbacks over the last twenty years. However, there is a growing feeling that labour either is (or at least should be) 'reinventing' itself. To give just one example, Bruno Trentin (a leading Italian trade unionist) declares that, 'To engage the union with the new realities entails carrying out a genuine cultural revolution, because the union needs to abandon a conception of representativity it has held throughout its history' (Anderson and Trentin, 1996: 61). This is a specific point about whom trade unions represent and how they do this, but the underlying ethos is a general one. Trade unions at the start of the twenty-first century are facing a different reality due to globalisation, and the 'flexibilisation' of work in particular, which demands a 'cultural revolution' if they are to meet the challenge. Manuel Castells, from an academic perspective, also argues that the labour movement needs to 'reinvent' itself as capitalism has, 'becoming conscious of the new historical situation and through a broad debate in the factories and community [*barrio*]' (Castells, 1999: 5). These are calls for change, but to what extent has this transformation of labour actually occurred?

Academic models of labour's transformation to match those of capital tend to be evolutionist. Thus, for Alain Touraine the history of trade unionism takes an organic or biological form: 'Movements such as unionism have a life history: infancy, youth, maturity, old age and death' (Touraine, 1988: 153). Another leading sociologist, Manuel Castells, simply does not mention trade unions in his three-volume analysis of the new globalised information society (Castells, 1996a, 1997, 1998). Touraine works with a simple chronological model of trade unionism:

1. A business unionism focused on economic objectives.
2. A more radical class-conscious phase.
3. A turn towards political bargaining based on success in the previous phase.
4. The current defensive phase based on de-industrialisation and the crisis of the working class (based on Touraine, 1996).

Certainly this schema captures something, particularly in relation to Western Europe. However, not only is it Eurocentric, but it fails to capture the dynamic nature of the capital–labour relation. Just like capitalism, trade unions as a *social* movement are capable of mutation, transformation and regeneration. This process may be delayed and it is usually uneven, and it does not simply 'mirror' capital's transformation, but there is nothing to be gained from mooting a simple evolutionary schema that proclaims the trade unions dead or dying.

Another perspective, developed by Peter Fairbrother among others, is the 'trade-union renewal' thesis. As Fairbrother defines it, 'renewal is about the way unions reorganise and recompose themselves to meet the problems of work and employment ... it is in the workplace that unions organise, sustain and renew themselves' (Fairbrother, 1989: 3–4). This is a perspective which brings the labour process into focus and which understands that workers can be active agents. Trade unions are not just formal organisations but social movements with tensions and struggles – for example, over the issue of union democracy. Perhaps Fairbrother is somewhat idealistic in arguing that 'any movement towards union renewal must and will come from the bottom up' (Fairbrother, 1989: 6), but it is important to reintroduce union politics into the debate. Trade unions can (and do) become bureaucratic, as well as conservative in their methods, and they can be co-opted by the state and capital. Trade unions can (and do) go through a process of renewal – in terms of organisation, strategy and methods – and combat routinisation. At least some trade unions have begun to reinvent themselves to represent workers better in the era of globalisation.

At a national level, many trade unions have gone through a process of 'renewal' (if not reinvention) in the past five to ten years. No change is more dramatic, perhaps, than that in the US labour movement, once the paradigm of union bureaucracy and labour imperialism overseas. The AFL–CIO, under new leadership since the watershed elections of 1995, recognises the challenges it faces if it is to survive (let alone prosper) in the new era. Its new leaders ask openly: 'Why did a labor movement that was so vibrant, massive and capable of bringing about fundamental change in the 1930s and 1940s become virtually moribund in the 1980s and 1990s?' (Mantsios, 1999: xv). The US unions now have half the membership they had in the mid-twentieth century and they only 'represent' one in seven US workers. The AFL–CIO now sees itself going 'back to basics', asking itself about its purpose, its representativity, its strategy and its organisation. While remaining staunchly pro-market in many ways, the AFL–CIO has realised the limitations of a Washington-based lobbying approach and is rediscovering its roots as a vigorous, campaigning social movement. Whether better organisation and more militancy will 'renew' the US labour movement is, of course, an open question.

The point is that the process of trade-union renewal can be assessed in different ways depending on one's perspective. An attitude of *plus ça change...* is common among radical critics. Thus Peter Meiksins writes of the 1995 change of guard at the AFL–CIO that in the absence of a 'class project' it runs the risk of falling prey to divisions 'both by retreating further from the use of class as an organising principle and by relying on a variety of vague formulations which create the illusion of unity rather than its reality' (Meiksins, 1997: 42). The new organising drive of the AFL–CIO is, indeed, also fairly neglectful of the new workplace regimes and the need for union democracy. Yet it seems somewhat abstract to declare that, 'To really overcome the divisions within the working class, organised labour would have to create an alternative "model" for the organisation of production' (Meiksins, 1997: 41). It is maybe time to overcome the old critical distinction between reform and 'really' revolutionary measures which this type of analysis depends on. I am persuaded by Roberto Unger's deceptively simple definition of 'radical reform' as a species of transformative politics: 'Reform is radical when it addresses and changes the basic arrangements of society: its formative structure of institutions and enacted beliefs. It is reform because it deals with one discrete part of this structure at a time' (Unger, 1998: 18–19).

At an international level, the ICFTU has, significantly, recently engaged in a Millennial Review of its organisation, capacities and strategy. Even its most fervent critics recognise that the ICFTU is changing from the Cold War, pro-imperialist, narrowly bureaucratic organisation it once was. After its Millennium Conference in Durban (significant in itself) ICFTU General Secretary Bill Jordan declared that, 'In periods of revolutionary change, and we are in one now, we must be able to think and act outside the straight-jacket of our traditions ... The trade-union movement, once again, needs new ideas for the needs of new workers, new occupations, new forms of work organisation, new employment relationships' (Jordan, 2000: 2). The Millennial Review was designed to meet precisely these challenges. The policy review has already broken with a number of traditions, and the face of the labour movement has begun to reflect the gender and geographical spread of its membership much more. It has become a more inclusive and more accessible organisation than it once was. However, its organisational capabilities are still extremely limited in terms of finances and personnel, in spite of better links with the ITSs.

Again, how we assess the ICFTU 'renewal' depends on our perspective. It is probably good all round (for critics and supporters alike) to have a more sober appraisal of the ICFTU's capabilities, rather than view it as a 'slumbering giant'. In terms of the politics of the ICFTU it would not, perhaps, be unkind to see it in terms of Bill Jordan's old British TUC politics writ large. The TUC also had its phase of 'new unionism' in the 1990s as it sought to come to terms with declining membership and the new 'flexible' labour market conditions. We should not exaggerate the radicalism of a turn towards a more realistic and engaged trade-union politics. However, I am not sure about the comment by Stevis and Boswell that, 'On balance, the ICFTU has adopted a regulatory rather than a reformist internationalist strategy' (Stevis and Boswell, 2001: 25). The 'social clause' is certainly a less radical strategy than Levinson's vision in the 1970s of trade unions establishing a countervailing power to that of the MNCs, with its echoes of Leninist 'dual power' strategies. Yet if, in the current mood of triumphant globalism, the international trade-union movement can play a role in terms of social regulation, through the 'social clause' and other means, it would still be a revolutionary reform.

If we were to derive one key issue for labour renewal at a national level it might be that of working-class unity and articulation. Solidarity starts at home in a sense, and trade unions have always had a problem in maintaining unity across gender, racial, ethnic, religious, age and skill divides. Globalisation exacerbates national differences as the drive for 'competitivity' reaches down into every workplace. So capitalism accentuates differences, and in its present 'speeded up' form takes this to a new pitch. Unity among workers was never a given of course, and the myth of working-class solidarity in a past Golden Age was often based on an exclusivist male-manual-skilled-permanent employee. A related aspect is that of union 'articulation', defined by Waddington as 'cohesive and coherent interrelationships between workplace, regional and national levels of organisation' (Waddington, 1999: 3). If a labour movement does not achieve a degree of articulation it is prone to damaging internal conflict between its various levels of organisation. Finally, in the era of globalisation, union articulation is required at the international level to meet the new challenges, but this adds a whole new level which requires articulation.

At the international level the main issue in labour renewal terms is the emergence of a new sense of global solidarity. The drive for an international trade-union strategy in the 1970s may have failed, but it was renewed in the 1990s in possibly more propitious circumstances. Reconsidering the earlier debate in terms of the new context of globaisation, Harvie Ramsay found that 'the *incentives* for unions to pursue internationalism have grown in the last decade', even if 'the *capacities* of unions to organise themselves internationally are more problematical' (Ramsay, 2000: 214). International economic integration and the methods of lean production push the drive towards international labour solidarity. Greater harmonisation of capitalist structures and procedures (the 'one right way' of neo-liberalism) also presents an easier target for labour. Certainly the obstacles to a successful international strategy still exist, and the trade unions have been severely weakened by the era of neo-liberalism. It is well worth recalling, as a Ford executive once supposedly did, that employers are at a disadvantage vis-à-vis the unions at the international level in so far as they lack the equivalent international institutions and traditions of solidarity (Ramsay, 2000: 217).

In conclusion, has the process of trade-union renewal/reinvention created a new global labour movement capable of confronting the effects of globalisation? I would say that the international trade-union movement is, at one and the same time, a 'new' transnational social movement and a representative organisation that is 'more' than the transnational advocacy groups, promoting gender, environmental and human rights issues. By necessity the ICFTU has had to reconsider its Cold War past and, however unevenly or hesitantly, move towards a united and democratic approach to globalisation. In doing so it has learned much from the 'new' social movements and from NGOs' way of working. However, trade unions, as always, advocate on behalf of their members, and, whatever the problems with 'representativity' they are more democratic than, say, Greenpeace. The international trade-union movement certainly has the motivation to 'go global' (even if it is just to survive) and it has the 'technology' (Internet, cheaper travel) to do so. It will, if the analysis in this book is at all sound, play a central and increasing role in achieving a degree of social regulation over the worldwide expansion of capitalism in the decades to come.

REFERENCES

Adkin, L. (1999) 'Ecology and Labour: Towards a New Societal Paradigm', in R. Munck and P. Waterman, eds, *Labour Worldwide in the Era of Globalisation*. London: Macmillan.

AFL–CIO (2001) 'Remarks by AFL–CIO President John J. Sweeney, World Economic Forum, Davos, Switzerland'. 28 January, <www.aflcio.org/pub/speech2001/sp0128.htm>.

Aglietta, M. (1979) *A Theory of Capitalist Regulation*. London: Verso.

Aglietta, M. (1998) 'Capitalism at the Turn of the Century: Regulation Theory and the Challenge of Social Change', *New Left Review* 232, November–December, pp. 41–90.

Agnew, J. and Corbridge, S. (1995) *Mastering Space: Hegemony, Territory and International Political Economy*. London: Routledge.

Althusser, L. (1971) 'Ideology and Ideological States Apparatuses (Notes Towards an Investigation)', in L. Althusser, *Lenin and Philosophy and Other Essays*. London: Verso.

Altvater, E. (1992) 'Fordist and Post-Fordist International Division of Labor and Monetary Regimes', in M. Storper and A. Scott, eds, *Pathways to Industrialization and Regional Development*. London: Routledge.

Alvisurez, M.A. (1985) *Tiempo de sudor y lucha*. San Salvador, El Salvador: Edición Local.

Amin, A. (1997) 'Playing Globalisation', *Theory, Culture and Society*, vol. 14, no. 2, pp. 123–37.

Anderson, L. and Trentin, B. (1996) *Trabajo, derechos y sindicato en el mundo*. Caracas: Nueva Sociedad.

Anner, M. (2001) *Evaluation Report: IFCTU for Core Labour Standards in the WTO*. Oslo: Norwegian Federation of Trade Unions (ILO–Norway).

Antunes, R. (1980) 'Por un novo sindicalismo', *Cadernos de Debate* 7.

Appadurai, A. (1996) *Modernity at Large: Cultural Dimensions of Globalisation*. Minneapolis and London: Trocaire.

Armstrong, P., Glyn, A. and Harrison, J. (1984) *Capitalism Since 1945*. London: Methuen.

Aronowitz, S. and Di Fazio, W. (1994) *The Jobless Future*. Minneapolis: University of Minnesota Press.

Arrighi, G. (1996) 'Workers of the World at Century's End', *Review*, vol. 19, no. 3.

Bakvis, P. (1998) 'Free Trade in the Americas: The Perspective of Québec Labour and Popular-Sector Organizations', *Labour, Capital and Society*, vol. 31, no. 1–2, pp. 153, 165.

Barnes, H. (1996) 'Mollycoddled', *Foreign Affairs*, vol. 75, no. 4, July–August, pp. 173–4.

Beck, U. (2000) *The Brave New World of Work*. Cambridge: Polity Press.

Bendiner, B. (1977) 'World Automotive Councils: A Union Response to Transnational Bargaining', in R. Banks and J. Stieber, eds, *Multinationals, Unions and Labor Relations in Industrialised Countries*. Ithaca: Cornell University Press.

Berger, S. and Dore, R., eds (1996) *National Diversity and Global Capitalism*. Ithaca, NY: Cornell University Press.

Bienefeld, M. (1994) 'Capitalism and the Nation State in the Dog Days of the Twentieth Century', in R. Milliband and L. Panitch, eds, *Socialist Register 1994*. London: Merlin Press, pp. 94–129.

Blyton, P., Lucio, M.M., McGurk, J. and Turnbull, P. (1998) *Contesting Globalisation: Airline Restructuring, Labour Flexibility and Trade Union Strategies*. London: International Transport Workers' Federation.

Boyer, R. (1988) 'Defensive or Offensive Flexibility', in R. Boyer, ed., *The Search for Labour Market Flexibility*. Oxford: Clarendon Press.

Boyer, R. (1995) 'Capital–Labour Relations in OECD Countries: From the Fordist Golden Age to Contrasted National Trajectories', in J. Schor and J.-I. You, eds, *Capital, the State and Labour: A Global Perspective*. Aldershot: Edward Elgar.

Boyer, R. (2000) 'Is a Finance Growth Regime a Viable Alternative to Fordism?', *Economy and Society*, vol. 29, no. 1, pp. 111–45.

Boyer, R. and Drache, D., eds (1995) *States Against Markets: The Limits of Globalisation*. London: Routledge.

Boyer, R. and Hollingsworth, J.R. (1996) 'From National Embeddedness to Spatial and Institutional Nestedness', in J.R. Hollingsworth and R. Boyers, eds, *Contemporary Capitalism: The Embeddedness of Institutions*. Cambridge: Cambridge University Press.

Brecher, J., Costello, T. and Smith, B. (2000) *Globalization from Below: The Power of Solidarity*. Cambridge, MA: South End Press.

Breitenfellner, A. (1997) 'Global Unionism: A Potential Player', *International Labour Review*, vol. 136, no. 4, pp. 531–54.

Brenner, R. (1998) 'The Economics of Global Turbulence', *New Left Review* 229, May–June.

Bryant, C. (1994) 'Economic Utopianism and Sociological Realism: Strategies for Transformation in East-Central Europe', in C. Bryant and E. Mokrzycki, eds, *The New Great Transformation? Change and Continuity in East-Central Europe*. London: Routledge.

Buketov, K. (1999) 'The Russian Trade Unions: From Chaos to a New Paradigm', in R. Munck and P. Waterman, eds, *Labour Worldwide in the Era of Globalisation*. London: Macmillan.

Burawoy, M. and Lukács, J. (1992) *The Radiant Past: Ideology and Reality in Hungary's Road to Capitalism*. Chicago: Chicago University Press.

Busch, G. (1983) *The Political Role of International Trades Unions*. London: Macmillan.

Castells, M. (1996a) *The Information Age. Volume I: The Rise of the Network Society*. Oxford: Blackwell.

Castells, M. (1996b) 'Empleo, trabajo y sindicatos en la nueva economía global', *La Factoría* 1.

Castells, M. (1997) *The Information Age. Volume II: The Power of Identity*. Oxford: Blackwell.

Castells, M. (1998) *The Information Age. Volume III: End of Millennium*. Oxford: Blackwell.

Castells, M. and Portes, A. (1989) 'World Underneath: The Origins, Dynamics and Effects of the Informal Economy', in A. Portes, M. Castells and L.A. Benton, eds, *The Informal Economy: Studies in Advanced and Less Developed Countries*. Baltimore, MA: Johns Hopkins University Press.

Chesnais, F. (1997) *La Mondialisation du Capital*. Paris: Syros.

Chhachhi, A. and Pittin, R. (1996) Introduction, in A. Chhachhi and R. Pittin, eds, *Confronting State, Capital and Patriarchy*. London: Macmillan.

Clarke, S. (1992) 'Privatization and the Development of Capitalism in Russia', *New Left Review* 196, November–December, pp. 3–28.

Coates, D. (2000) *Models of Capitalism:Growth and Stagnation in the Modern Era*. Cambridge: Polity Press.

Cohen, R. (1991) *Contested Domains: Debates in International Labour Studies*. London: Zed Books.

Cohen, R. and Rai, S. (2000) 'Global Social Movements: Towards a Cosmopolitan Politics', in R. Cohen and S. Rai, eds, *Global Social Movements*. London and New Brunswick: Athlone Press.

Coriat, B. (1992) 'The Revitalization of Mass Production in the Computer Age', in M. Storper and A. Scott, eds, *Pathways to Industrialisation and Regional Development*. London: Routledge.

Cox, R. (1996) *Approaches to World Order*. Cambridge: Cambridge University Press.

Crouch, C. and Streek, W., eds (1997) *Political Economy of Modern Capitalism: Mapping Convergence and Diversity*. London: Sage.

Dalton, G., ed. (1971) *Primitive, Archaic and Modern Economies*. Boston, MA: Beacon Press.

DeMartino, G. (1991) 'Trade-Unions, Isolation and the Catechism of the Left', *Rethinking Marxism*, vol. 4, no. 3.

Diller, J. (1999) 'A Social Conscience in the Global Marketplace? Labour Dimensions of Codes of Conduct, Social Labelling and Investor Initiatives', *International Labour Review*, vol. 138, no. 2, pp. 99–130.

Drache, D. (1999) *Globalisation: Is There Anything to Fear?* Centre for the

Study of Globalisation and Regionalisation, University of Warwick, Working Paper no. 23.

Elger, T. and Smith, C. (1994) 'Global Japanisation? Convergence and Competition in the Organisation of the Labour Process', in T. Elger and C. Smith, eds, *Global Japanisation? The Transnational Transformation of the Labour Process*. London: Routledge.

Elson, D. (1996) 'Appraising Recent Developments in the World Market for Nimble Fingers', in A. Chhachhi and R. Pittin, eds, *Confronting State, Capital and Patriarchy*. London: Macmillan.

Elson, D. and Pearson, R. (1981) 'The Subordination of Women and the Internationalisation of Production', in K. Young et al., eds, *Of Marriage in the Market: Women's Subordination in International Perspective*. London: CSE Books.

Emmanuel, A. (1972) *Unequal Exchange: A Study of the Imperialism of Trade*. London: Verso.

Fairbrother, P. (1989) *Workplace Unionism in the 1980s: A Process of Renewal*. London: Workers Educational Association.

Fairbrother, P. (1999) 'The Changing State and Implications for Trade Unions', ESRC Labour Seminar, University of Warwick.

Falk, R. (1999) *Predatory Globalisation*. Cambridge: Polity Press.

Featherstone, M. (1995) *Undoing Culture: Globalisation, Postmodernism and Identity*. London: Sage.

Featherstone, M., ed. (1990) *Global Culture: Nationalism, Globalisation and Modernity*. London: Sage.

Fine, J. (1999) 'Moving Innovation from the Margins to the Centre', in G. Mantsios, ed., *A New Labor Movement for the New Century*. New York: Monthly Review Press.

Forman, M. (1998) *Nationalism and the International Labour Movement*. University Park: Penn State University Press.

Freeman, R. (1994) 'Comments', in R. Ehrenberg, ed., *Labor Markets and Integrating National Economies*. Washington DC: The Brookings Institution.

French, J., Cowie, J. and Littleham, S. (1994) *Labor and NAFTA: A Briefing Book*. Durham, NC: Duke University Press.

Fröbel, F., Heinrichs, J. and Kreye, U. (1980) *The New International Division of Labour*. Cambridge: Cambridge University Press.

Frundt, H. (1998) *Trade Conditions and Labor Rights*. Gainsville: University Press of Florida.

Fukuyama, F. (1992) *The End of History and the Last Man*. New York: Oxford University Press.

Fukuyama, F. (1996) *Trust: The Social Virtues and the Creation of Prosperity*. New York: Free Press.

Gallin, D. (2000) 'Organised Labour as a Global Social Force', in R. Munck, ed., *Globalisation: The Challenge of Labour*. Liverpool: GSEU. <www.globdem.org.uk>.

Gamble, A. and Payne, A. (1996) 'Conclusion: The New Regionalism', in A.

Gamble and A. Payne, eds, *Regionalism and World Order*. London: Macmillan.

Gibson-Graham, J.K. (1996) *The End of Capitalism (As We Knew It)*. Oxford: Blackwell.

Gill, S. (1995) 'Theorising the Interregnum: The Double Movement and Global Politics in the 1990s', in B. Hettne, ed., *International Political Economy: Understanding Global Disorder*. London: Zed Books.

Gills, B. (2000) 'Globalisation and the Politics of Resistance', in B. Gills, ed., *Globalisation and the Politics of Resistance*. London: Macmillan.

Glasman, M. (1994) 'The Great Deformation: Polanyi, Poland and the Errors of Planned Spontaneity', in C. Bryant and E. Mokrzycki, eds, *The New Great Transformation? Change and Continuity in East-Central Europe*. London: Routledge.

Glyn, A. (1999) 'Internal and External Constraints on Egalitarian Policies', in D. Baker, G. Epstein and R. Pollin, eds, *Globalisation and Progressive Economic Policy*. Cambridge: Cambridge University Press.

Godio, J. (1998) 'La cláusula social como herramienta del desarollo integrado en los países de America Central y el Canbe', in M.S. Portella de Castro and A. Wachendorfer, eds, *Sindicalismo y globalización*. Caracas: Nueva Sociedad.

Goldfrank,W. (1990), 'Fascism and the Great Transformation', in K. Polanyi-Levitt, ed., *The Life and Work of Karl Polanyi*, Montreal: Black Rose Books.

Gorz, A. (1982) *Farewell to the Working Class*. London: Pluto Press.

Gough, I. (1979) *The Political Economy of the Welfare State*. London: Macmillan.

Gramsci, A. (1971a) 'Americanism and Fordism', in Q. Hoare and G. Nowell Smith, eds, *Selections from the Prison Notebooks of Antonio Gramsci*. London: Lawrence & Wishart.

Gramsci, A. (1971b) 'Some Theoretical and Practical Aspects of "Economism"', in Q. Hoare and G. Nowell Smith, eds, *Selections from the Prison Notebooks of Antonio Gramsci*. London: Lawrence & Wishart.

Granovetter, M. (1992) *The Sociology of Economic Life*. Boulder, CO: Westview Press.

Group of Lisbon, The (1996) *Limits to Competition*. Cambridge, MA: MIT Press.

Grugel, J. and Hout, W. (1999) 'Regions, Regionalism and the South', in J. Grugel and W. Hout, eds, *Regionalism Across the North–South Divide*. London and New York: Routledge.

Gumbrell-McCormick, R. (2000) 'Facing New Challenges: The International Confederation of Free Trade Unions (1971–1990s)', in M. van der Linden, ed., *The International Confederation of Free Trade Unions*. Berne: Peter Lang.

Hale, A., ed. (1999) *Trade Myths and Gender Realities*. Uppsala: Global Publications Foundation.

Hardt, M. and Negri, A. (2000) *Empire*. Cambridge, MA: Harvard University Press.

Harriss-White, B. and Gooptu, N. (2000) 'Mapping India's World of

Unorganised Labour', in L. Panitch and C. Leys, eds, *Socialist Register 2001: Working Classes: Global Realities*. London: Merlin Press, pp. 89–118.

Haworth, N. and Ramsay, H. (1984) 'Grasping the Nettle: Problems with the Theory of International Trade Union Solidarity', in P. Waterman, ed., *The New Labour Internationalism*. The Hague: ILERI.

Hayek, F.A. von ([1944] 1955) *The Road to Serfdom*. London: Routledge.

Held, D. (1995) *Democracy and the Global Order*. Cambridge: Polity Press.

Held, D., McGrew, A, Goldblatt, D. and Perraton, P. (1999) *Global Transformations: Politics, Economics and Culture*. Cambridge: Polity Press.

Hensman, R. (2001) 'World Trade and Workers' Rights: In Search of an Internationalist Position', *Antipode*, vol. 33, no. 3, pp. 427–50.

Herod, A. (ed) (1998) *Organizing the Landscape: Geographical Perspectives on Labor Unionism*. Minneapolis: University of Minnesota Press.

Herod, A. (2001) 'Labor Internationalism and the Contradiction of Globalization: Or, Why the Local is Sometimes Still Important in a Global Economy', *Antipode*, vol. 33, no. 3, pp. 407–26.

Hershfield, D.C. (1975) 'The Multinational Union Challenges the Multinational Company', *The Conference Board Report*, no. 658.

Hirst, P. and Thompson, G. (1996) *Globalisation in Question*. Cambridge: Polity Press.

Hirst, P. and Zeitlin, J., eds (1989) *Reversing Industrial Decline? Industrial Structure and Policy in Britain and Her Competitors*. London: Berg.

Hobsbawm, E. (1988) 'Working Class Internationalism', in F. van Holthuan and M. van der Linden, eds, *Internationalism in the Labour Movement 1830–1940*. Leiden: E.J. Brill.

Hobsbawm, E. (1994) *Age of Extremes: The Short Twentieth Century 1914–1991*. London: Michael Joseph.

Hollingsworth, J.R. and Boyer, R. (1996) 'Coordination of Economic Actors and Social Systems of Production', in J.R. Hollingsworth and R. Boyer, eds, *Contemporary Capitalism: The Embeddedness of Institutions*. Cambridge: Cambridge University Press.

Hollingsworth, J.R. and Boyer, R., eds (1996) *Contemporary Capitalism: The Embeddedness of Institutions*. Cambridge: Cambridge University Press.

Hölmstrom, M. (1984) *Industry and Inequality: The Social Anthropology of Indian Labour*. Cambridge: Cambridge University Press.

Huws, B. (2000) 'The Making of a Cybertariat? Virtual Work in a Real World', in L. Panitch and C. Leys, eds, *Socialist Register 2001: Working Classes: Global Realities*. London: Merlin Press, pp. 1–24.

ICEM (1996) *Power and Counterpower: The Union Responses to Global Capital*. London: Pluto Press.

ICEM (1999) *Facing Global Power: Strategies for Global Unionism*. Durban, South Africa, Second World Congress.

ICFTU (1990) *On Organising Workers in the Informal Sector*. Brussels: ICFTU.

ICFTU (1997a) *Sixteenth World Congress of the ICFTU. The Global Market: Trade Unionism's Greatest Challenge*. Brussels: ICFTU.

ICFTU (1997b) *The Global Market: Trade Unionism's Greatest Challenge*. Brussels: ICFTU.

ILO (1995) *World Employment 1995*. Geneva: ILO.

ILO (1997) *World Employment Report 1996–7: Industrial Relations, Democracy and Stability*. Geneva: ILO.

ILO (1999) 'Conference on Organised Labour in the 21st Century', <www. ilo.org/public/english/130inst/research/network.htm>.

Jameson, F. (1998) 'Notes on Globalisation as a Philosophical Issue', in F. Jameson and M. Miyoshi, eds, *The Cultures of Globalisation*. Durham, NC and London: Duke University Press.

Jhabvala, R. (1994) 'Self-Employed Women's Association: Organising Women by Struggle and Development', in S. Rowbotham and S. Mitter, eds, *Dignity and Daily Bread*. London: Routledge.

John, J. and Chenoy, A.M., eds (1996) *Labour, Environment and Globalisation*. New Delhi, India: Centre for Education and Communication.

Johnston, W. (1991) 'Global Work Force 2000: The New World Labor Market', *Harvard Business Review*, March–April, pp. 115–27.

Jonas, A. (1999) 'Investigating the Local–Global Paradox', in A. Herod, ed., *Organising the Landscape: Geographical Perspectives on Labor Unionism*, Minneapolis: University of Minnesota Press.

Kalecki, M. (1943) 'Political Aspects of Full Employment', in M. Kalecki (1971) *Selected Essays on the Dynamics of the Capitalist Economy*. Cambridge: Cambridge University Press.

Kapstein, E. (1996) 'Workers and the World Economy', *Foreign Affairs*, vol. 27, no. 3, May–June, pp. 14–37.

Knudsen, K. (1988) 'The Strike History of the First International', in F. van Holthuan and M. van der Linden, eds, *International in the Labour Movement 1830–1940*. Leiden: E.J. Brill.

Köllö, J. (1995) 'After a Dark Golden Age in Eastern Europe', in J. Schor and J.-I. You, eds, *Capital, the State and Labour: A Global Perspective*. Aldershot: Edward Elgar.

Kouiman, J. and van Vloet, M. (1993) 'Government and Public Management', in K. Elliasen and J. Kouiman, eds, *Managing Public Organisations*. London: Sage.

Krugman, P. (1994) 'Competitiveness: A Dangerous Obsession', *Foreign Affairs*, vol. 73, no. 2, March–April.

Krugman, P., et al. (1996) 'Workers and Economists. The Global Economy Has Left Keynes in its Train', *Foreign Affairs*, vol. 27, no. 24, July–August, pp. 164–81.

Lagos, R. (1994) 'Labour Market Flexibility: What Does it Mean?', *CEPAL Review* 54, December, pp. 81–95.

Lambert, R. (1999) 'An Emerging Force? Independent Labour in Indonesia', *Labour, Capital and Society*, vol. 32, no. 1, pp. 70–106.

Lee, E. (1996) 'Globalisation and Employment: Is anxiety justified?', *International Labour Review*, vol. 135, no. 5, pp. 485–97.

Lee, E. (1997a) *The Labour Movement and the Internet: The New Internationalism*. London: Pluto Press.

Lee, E. (1997b) 'Globalisation and Labour Standards', *International Labour Review*, vol. 136, no. 2, pp. 173–90.

Lester, R. (1997) *Citizenship: Feminist Perspectives*. London: Macmillan.

Levinson, C. (1972) *International Trade Unionism*. London: Allen & Unwin.

Lewchuck, W. and Robertson, D. (1999) 'The Canadian Automobile Workers and Lean Production: Results of a Worker-Based Benchmarking Study', in J. Waddington, ed., *Globalisation and Patterns of Labour Resistance*. London: Mansell.

Lipietz, A. (1982) 'Towards Global Fordism?', *New Left Review* 132, March–April.

Lipietz, A. (1987) *Mirages and Miracles: The Crises of Global Fordism*. London: Verso.

Lipietz, A. (1995) 'Capital–Labour Relations at the Dawn of the Twenty-first Century', in J. Schor and J.-I. You, eds, *Capital, the State and Labour*. Aldershot: Edward Elgar.

Lister, R. (1997) *Citizenship: Feminist Perspectives*. London: Macmillan.

Logue, J. (1980) *Towards a Theory of Trade Union Internationalism*. Gothenburg: University of Gothenburg.

Lorwin, L. (1953) *The International Labor Movement*. New York: Harper & Brothers.

McGrew, A. (1995) 'World Order and Political Space', in J. Anderson et al., eds, *A Global World?* Oxford: Oxford University Press.

McGrew, A. (1997) 'Democracy Beyond Borders? Globalisation and the Reconstruction of Democratic Theory and Practice', in A. McGrew, ed., *The Transformation of Democracy? Globalisation and Territorial Democracy*. Cambridge: Polity Press.

McMichael, P. (2000) *Development and Social Change: A Global Perspective*. Thousand Oaks, CA: Pine Forge Press.

McShane, D., et al. (1984) *Power! Black Workers, Their Unions and the Struggle for Freedom in South Africa*. Nottingham: Spokesman.

McShane, D. (1992) *International Labour and the Origins of the Cold War*. Oxford: Clarendon Press.

McShane, D. (1997) *Global Business: Global Rights*. Fabian Pamphlet no. 575. London: Fabian Society.

Mann, M. (1987) 'Ruling Class Strategies and Citizenship', *Sociology*, vol. 21, no. 3, pp. 339–54.

Mantsios, G. (1998) *A New Labor Movement for the New Century*. New York: Monthly Review Press.

Marginson, P. and Sisson, K. (1996) 'The Structure of Transnational Capital in Europe: The Emerging Euro-Company and its Implications for Industrial Relations', in R. Hyman and A. Ferner, eds, *New Frontiers in European Industrial Relations*. Oxford: Blackwell.

Marglin, S. (1990) 'Lessons of the Golden Age: An Overview', in S. Marglin and J. Schor, eds, *The Golden Age of Capitalism*. Oxford: Clarendon Press.

Marglin, S. and Schor, J., eds (1990) *The Golden Age of Capitalism: Reinterpreting the Postwar Experience*. Oxford: Clarendon Press.

Marshall, T.H. (1950) *Citizenship and Social Class*. Cambridge: Cambridge University Press.

Martin, H.-P. and Schumann, H. (1998) *The Global Trap: Globalisation and the Assault on Prosperity and Democracy*. London: Zed Books.

Marx, K. (1976) *Capital* Volume 1. Harmondsworth: Penguin.

Mazur, J. (2000) 'Labor's New Internationalism', *Foreign Affairs*, vol. 79, no. 1, January–February, pp. 79–93.

Meiksins, P. (1997) 'Same as it Ever Was? Structure of the Working Class', *Monthly Review*, vol. 49, no. 3, pp. 31–45.

Mendell, M. and Salée, D. (1991) 'Introduction', in M. Mendell and D. Salée, eds, *The Legacy of Karl Polanyi: Market, State, and Society at the End of the Twentieth Century*. New York: St. Martin's Press.

Milne, S. (2000) 'Unions Aim to Swallow Amazon', *Guardian*, Online Section, 7 December, p. 7.

Mintz, S. (1974) *Caribbean Transformations*. Chicago: Aldine.

Mitter, S. (1994) 'On Organizing Women in Casualised Work: A Global Overview', in S. Rowbotham and S. Mitter, eds, *Dignity and Daily Bread: New Forms of Economic Organising among Poor Women in the Third World and the First*. London: Routledge.

Moghadam, V. (1995) 'Gender Aspects of Employment and Unemployment in a Global Perspective', in M. Simai, ed., *Global Employment: The Future of Work*, Volume One. London: Zed Books.

Mohanty, C.T. (1993) 'Under Western Eyes: Feminist Scholarship and Colonial Discourse', in P. Williams and L. Chrisman, eds, *Colonial Discourse and Post-Colonial Theory*. Hemel Hampstead: Harvester Wheatsheaf.

Monthly Review (2000), 'After Seattle: A New Internationalism?' *Monthly Review*, July–August.

Moody, K. (1997) *Workers in a Lean World*. London: Verso.

Morgan, D. (2000) 'An Open Shop in the New Economy', *Observer*, 10 September, p. 5.

Morgan, R., ed. (1970) *Sisterhood is Powerful*. New York: Vintage Books.

Morgan, R., ed. (1984) *Sisterhood is Global*, Harmondsworth: Penguin.

Nash, B. (1998) 'Forum: Problems and Prospects for a Global Labor Movement', *Journal of World-Systems Research*, vol. 4, no. 1, Winter, pp. 3–9.

Northrup, U.R. and Rowan, R. (1979) *Multinational Collective Bargaining Attempts*. Pennsylvania: University of Pennsylvania Press.

O'Brien, R., Goetz, A.M., Scholte, J.A. and Williams, M. (2000) *Contesting Global Governance: Multinational Economic Institutions and Global Social Movement*. Cambridge: Cambridge University Press.

OECD (1996) *Trade, Employment and Labor Standards: A Study of Core Workers Rights and International Trade*. Paris: OECD.

Ohmae, K. (1990) *The Borderless World*. London: Collins.

Olle, W. and Schoeller, W. (1984) 'World Market Competition and Restrictions upon Trade Union Policies', in P. Waterman, ed., *The New Labour Internationalism*. The Hague: ILERI.

Peck, J. (1996) *Work-Place: The Social Regulation of Labor Markets*. New York and London: Guilford Press.

Piore, M. and Sabel, C. (1984) *The Second Industrial Divide*. New York: Basic Books.

Polanyi, K. ([1944] 1957) *The Great Transformation: The Political and Economic Origins of Our Time*. Boston: Beacon Press.

Polanyi, K. (1945) 'Universal Capitalism or Regional Planning?', *London Quarterly of World Affairs*, January, pp. 86–91.

Pollert, A. (1998) 'Dismantling Flexibility?', *Capital and Class* 34, Spring, pp. 42–75.

Portes, A. (1985) 'Latin American Class Structures: Their Composition and Change During the Last Decade', *Latin American Research Review*, vol. 20, no. 3, pp. 7–39.

Ramsay, H. (1999) 'In Search of International Union Theory', in J. Waddington, ed., *Globalization and Patterns of Labour Resistance*. London: Mansell.

Reich, R. (1992) *The Work of Nations*. New York: Vintage Books.

Report of the Independent Commission on International Development Issues (1981) *North–South: A Programme for Survival*. London: Pan Books.

Rifkin, J. (1996) *The End of Work*. New York: Putnam.

Roldan, M. (1996) 'Women Organising in the Process of Deindustrialisation', in A. Chhachhi and R. Pittin, eds, *Confronting State, Capital and Patriarchy*. London: Macmillan.

Rosa, K. (1994) 'The Conditions and Organisational Activities of Women in Free Trade Zones: Malaysia, Philippines and Sri Lanka, 1970–1990', in S. Rowbotham and S. Mitter, eds, *Dignity and Daily Bread: New Forms of Economic Organising among Poor Women in the Third World and the First*. London: Routledge.

Ross, A. (1997) 'Introduction', in A. Ross, ed., *No Sweat: Fashion, Free Trade, and the Rights of Garment Workers*. London: Verso.

Rowbotham, S. and Mitter, S., eds (1994) *Dignity and Daily Bread: New Forms of Economic Organising among Poor Women in the Third World and the First*. London: Routledge.

Roxborough, I. (1984) *Unions and Politics in Mexico*. Cambridge: Cambridge University Press.

Rubery, J. and Fagan, C. (1994) 'Does Feminisation Mean a Flexible Labour Force?', in R. Hyman and A. Ferner, eds, *New Frontiers in European Industrial Relations*. Oxford: Blackwell.

Rupert, M. (1995) *Producing Hegemony: The Politics of Mass Production and American Global Power*. Cambridge: Cambridge University Press.

Schoenberger, E. (1989) 'Multinational Corporations and the New International Division of Labour: A Critical Appraisal', in S. Wood, ed., *The Transformation of Work? Skill, Flexibility and the Labour Process*. London: Allen & Unwin.

Scholte, J.A. (2000) *Globalisation: A Critical Introduction*. London: Macmillan.

Schor, J. and You, J.-I., eds (1995) *Capital, the State and Labour: A Global Perspective*, Aldershot: Edward Elgar.

Scott, A.M. (1994) *Divisions and Solidarities: Gender, Class and Employment in Latin America*. London: Routledge.

Seidman, G. (1994) *Manufacturing Militance: Workers' Movements in Brazil and South Africa, 1970–1985*. Berkeley: University of California Press.

Sen, A. (1981) *Poverty and Famines: An Essay in Entitlement and Deprivation*. Oxford: Clarendon Press.

Sen, A. (2000) 'Work and Rights', *International Labour Review*, vol. 139, no. 2, pp. 119–28.

Shailor, B. and Kourpias, G. (1998) 'Developing and Enforcing International Labor Standards', in G. Mantsios, ed., *A New Labor Movement for the New Century*. New York: Monthly Review Press.

Shiva, V. (1996) 'Social and Environmental Clauses: A Political Diversion', in J. John and A. Chenoy, eds, *Labour, Environmentalism and Globalisation*. New Delhi: Centre for Education and Communication.

SID (General Workers' Union, Denmark) (1997) *A New Global Agenda: Visions and Strategies for the 21st Century*. <www.antenna.nl/~waterman/visions.htm>.

Silver, B. and Arrighi, G. (2000) 'Workers North and South', in L. Panitch and C. Leys, eds, *Socialist Register 2001. Working Classes: Global Realities*. London: Merlin Press, pp. 53–76.

Simai, M., ed. (1995a) *Global Employment: An International Investigation into the Future of Work*, Volume 1. London: Zed Books.

Simai, M. (1995b) 'The Politics and Economics of Global Employment', in M. Simai, ed., *Global Employment: An International Investigation into the Future of Work*, Volume 1. London: Zed Books.

Singh, A. (1994) 'Global Economic Change, Skills and International Competitiveness', *International Labour Review*, vol. 133, no. 2, pp. 135–48.

Sklair, L. (2001) *The Transnational Capitalist Class*. Oxford: Blackwell.

Soros, G. (1998) *The Crisis of Global Capitalism*. London: Little, Brown.

Southall, R. (1994) 'The Development and Delivery of "Northern" Worker Solidarity to South African Trade Unions in the 1970s and 1980s', *Journal of Commonwealth and Comparative Politics*, vol. 32, no. 2, pp. 166–99.

Spalding, H. (1977) *Organised Labor in Latin America*. New York: Harper & Row.

Stallings, B. (1995) 'The New International Context of Development', in B. Stallings, ed., *Global Change, Regional Response: The New International Context of Development*. Cambridge: Cambridge University Press, pp. 349–87.

Standing, G. (1989) 'Global Feminization through Flexible Labor', *World Development*, vol. 17, no. 7, pp. 1077-95.

Standing, G. (1992) 'Alternative Routes to Labour Flexibility', in M. Storper and A. Scott, eds, *Pathways to Industrialisation and Regional Development*, London: Routledge.

Standing, G. (1999a) *Global Labour Flexibility*. London: Macmillan.

Standing, G. (1999b) 'Global Feminisation Through Flexible Labor', *World Development*, vol. 17, no. 7, pp. 1077–95.

Stevia, D. and Boswell, T. (2001) 'International Labor Organising, 1864-2000', International Studies Assocaition, 42nd Annual Convention, Chicago.

Sweeney, J. (2001) 'Adressing the Backlash against Globalisation', Labour Leaders @ Davos.

Tabb, W. (1999) 'Labor and the Imperialism of Finance', *Monthly Review*, vol. 51, no. 5, October.

Taylor, R. (1999) *Trade Unions and Transnational Industrial Relations*. Labour and Society Programme, DP/99/1999, Geneva: ILO.

Thelen, K. and Kume, I. (1999) 'The Effect of Globalisation on Labor Revisited: Lessons from Germany and Japan', *Politics and Society*, vol. 27, no. 4, pp. 477–505.

Thomas, H., ed. (1991) *Globalisation and Third World Trade Unions: The Challenge of Rapid Economic Change*. London: Zed Books.

Thompson, D. and Larson, R. (1978) *Where Were You Brother? An Account of Trade Union Imperialism*. London: War on Want.

Tickell, A. and Peck, J. (1995) 'Social regulation *After* Fordism: Regulation Theory, Neo-liberalism and the Global–Local Nexus', *Economy and Society*. vol. 24, no. 3, pp. 357–86.

Tichelman, F. (1988) 'Social "Internationalism" and the Colonial World', in F. van Holtuan and M. van der Linden, eds, *Internationalism in the Labour Movement 1830–1940*. Leiden: E.J. Brill.

TIE (1985) *Meeting the Corporate Challenge*, TIE Report No 18/19. Amsterdam: Transnational Information Exchange.

Tilly, C. (1978) *From Mobilization to Revolution*. Reading, MA: Addison-Wesley.

Tilly, C. (1995) 'Globalisation Threatens Labor's Rights', *International Labor and Working Class History* 47, Spring, pp. 1–23.

Tilly, C. and Tilly, C. (1998) *Work Under Capitalism*. Boulder, CO: Westview Press.

Tomlinson, J. (1999) *Globalisation and Culture*. Cambridge: Polity Press.

Touraine, A. (1986) 'Unionism as a Social Movement', in S.M. Lipset, ed., *Unions in Transition*. San Francisco, CA: ICS Press.

Unger, R.M. (1998) *Democracy Realised: The Progressive Alternative*. London: Verso.

Van der Linden, M. (1988) 'The Rise and Fall of the First International', in F. van Holthuan and M. van der Linden, eds, *Internationalism in the Labour Movement 1830–1940*. Leiden: E.J. Brill.

Van Dijk, M.P. (1995) 'The Internationalisation of the Labour Market', in M. Simai, ed., *Global Employment: An International Investigation into the Future of Work*. London: Zed Books.

Van Holthuan, F., and Van der Linden, M., eds, *Internationalism in the Labour Movement 1830–1940*. Leiden: E.J. Brill.

Visser, J. (1998) 'Learning to Play: The Europeanisation of Trade Unions', in P. Pasture and J. Verberckmoes, eds, *Working-Class Internationalism and the Appeal of National Identity: Historical Debates and Current Perspectives*. Oxford: Berg.

Waddington, J., ed. (1999) *Globalization and Patterns of Labour Resistance*. London: Mansell.

Walker, R. (1999a) 'Foreword', in A. Herod, ed., *Organizing the Landscape:*

Geographical Perspectives on Labor Unionism. Minneapolis: University of Minnesota Press.

Walker, R. (1999b) 'Putting Capital in its Place: Globalisation and the Prospects for Labor', unpublished paper.

Wallerstein, I. (1983) *Historical Capitalism*. London: Verso.

Warren, B. (1980) *Imperialism: Pioneer of Capitalism*. London: Verso.

Waterman, P., ed. (1985) *For a New Labour Internationalism*. The Hague: ILERI.

Waterman, P. (1998) *Globalisation, Social Movements and the New Internationalisms*. London: Mansell.

Waters, M. (2001) *Globalization*. London: Routledge.

Webber, M. and Rigby, D. (1996) *The Golden Age Illusion: Rethinking Postwar Capitalism*. New York: Guilford Press.

Webster, E. (1984) 'The International Metalworkers Federation in South Africa (1974–1980)', in P. Waterman, ed., *The New Labour Internationalism*. The Hague: ILERI.

Weiss, L. (1997) 'Globalisation and the Myth of the Powerless State', *New Left Review* 225, September–October, pp. 3–27.

Weiss, L. (1999) 'Managed Openness: Beyond Neoliberal Globalism', *New Left Review* 238, November–December, pp. 126–40.

Williams, K., et al. (1992) 'Against Lean Production', *Economy and Society*, vol. 6, no. 4, pp. 517–55.

Wills, J. (2001) 'Uneven Geographies of Capital and Labour: The Lessons of the European Works Councils', *Antipode*, vol. 33, no. 3.

Windmuller, J.P. (1980) *The International Trade Union Movement*. Antwerp: Kluwer.

Womack, J., et al. (1990) *The Machine That Changed the World*. New York: Rawson Associates.

Wood, A. (1994) *North–South Trade, Employment and Inequality: Changing Fortunes in a Skill-driven World*. Oxford: Clarendon Press.

Wood, E.M. (1997) 'Labor, the State, and Class Struggle', in E.M. Wood, ed., *Rising From the Ashes? Labor in the Age of 'Global' Capitalism, Monthly Review*, vol. 49, no. 3.

World Bank (1995) *Workers in an Integrating World: World Development Report 1995*. Oxford: Oxford University Press.

World Bank (1996) *From Plan to Market: World Development Report 1996*. Oxford: Oxford University Press.

World Bank (1997) *World Development Report 1997: The State in a Changing World*. Washington, DC: World Bank.

Wright, E.O. (1985) *Classes*. London: Verso.

You, J.-I. (1995) 'Changing Capital–Labour Relations in South Korea', in J. Schor and J.-I. You, eds, *Capital, the State and Labour: A Global Perspective*. Aldershot: Edward Elgar.

Young, B. (2000) 'The "Mistress" and the "Maid" in the Globalised Economy', in L. Panitch and C. Leys, eds, *Socialist Register 2001. Working Classes. Global Realities*. London: Merlin Press, pp. 315–28.

INDEX

INTERNET RESOURCES

Increasingly, the student of labour in the era of globalisation will be turning to the Internet for news and analysis of latest developments. To update on many of the themes analysed in the text above, the following websites will be invaluable. It is not fully comprehensive but with the links included in most of these sites you are likely to find what you want.

Congress of South African Trade Unions

<http://www.cosatu.org.za/>
COSATU pioneered the new social movement unionism and now plays a key role in post-apartheid South Africa.

The Global Compact

<http://www.unglobalcompact.org/>
A UN-sponsored campaign where labour, environmental and human rights issues are brought together to seek a new 'global compact'.

Global March Against Child Labour

<http://www.globalmarch.org/>
Reports on the worst forms of child labour. A campaigning site but linked to many resources on this key issue.

Global Solidarity

<http://www.antenna.nl/~waterman/>
A social-movement-oriented labour site promoting 'global solidarity' and seeking alternatives to capitalist globalisation.

Global Unions

<http://www.global-unions.org/>
Jointly owned and managed by a number of international trade union organisations, this site is basically a directory.

International Centre for Trade Union Rights

<http://www.ictur.labournet.org/>
Focused on labour rights across the globe, ICTUR is accredited with the UN and the ILO, bringing together trade unionists, labour lawyers and other concerned parties.

International Confederation of Free Trade Unions

<http://www.icftu.org/>
The key labour 'player' in terms of the struggles around globalisation. A very institutional site but nonetheless useful for information.

International Federation of Chemical Energy, Mine and General Workers' Unions

<http://www.icem.org/>
The ICEM has been a leading force in promoting international trade union action. Check out international trade unionism in practice here.

International Labour Organisation

<http://www.ilo.org/>
The long-standing international tripartite (trade unions, business and government) organisation. Of late it has developed interesting campaigns (e.g. Decent Work) and ran the first 'Interactive Conference on Organised Labour in the 21st Century'.

International Labour Solidarity Web Site

<http://www.labournet.org/>
Promotes links between trade unions across the globe. Activist-oriented but includes valuable resources.

International Transport Workers' Federation

<http://www.itf.org.uk/>
The ITF has a long history on international trade unionism, from the dockers to the airline workers today. A good working site.

Labour Start

<http://www.labourstart.org/>
Billed as 'Where trade unionists start their day on the net'. Effectively run by Eric Lee who wrote the first book on labour and the Internet.

Sindicato Mercosul

<http://www.sindicatomercosul.com.br/>
The site of the trade unions of Latin America's Southern Cone Common Market (Mercosur). Very active in promoting a regional response to globalisation.

Women Working Worldwide

<http://www.poptel.org.uk/women-ww/>
A UK-based organisation supporting the struggles of women workers across the globe. Promotes the 'Labour Behind the Label' campaign.

World Social Forum (Brazil)

<http://www.forumsocialmundial.org.br/>
While the global elite gather at Davos, the unions, peasant organisations and women's organisations meet in Porto Alegre, Brazil. This is 'globalisation from below' in practice.

ZED TITLES ON GLOBALISATION

The ongoing headlong rush towards an economically much more integrated world – usually referred to as globalisation – is intimately connected to the changing nature of capitalism and to one strand of economic theory and policy which is currently dominant, neoliberalism. Zed Books has published an extensive and growing list of titles that explore these processes and changes from a variety of perspectives.

Samir Amin, *Capitalism in the Age of Globalization: The Management of Contemporary Society*

Robert Biel, *The New Imperialism: Crisis and Contradictions in North–South Relations*

Walden Bello, Nicola Bullard, Kamal Malhotra (eds), *Global Finance: New Thinking on Regulating Speculative Capital Markets*

Christian Comeliau, *Impasses of the Market Society*

Carlos M. Correa, *Intellectual Property Rights, the WTO and Developing Countries: The TRIPS Agreement and Policy Options*

Peter Custers, *Capital Accumulation and Women's Labour in Asian Economies*

Bhagirath Lal Das, *An Introduction to the WTO Agreements*

Bhagirath Lal Das, *The WTO Agreements: Deficiencies, Imbalances and Required Changes*

Bhagirath Lal Das, *The World Trade Organization: A Guide to the New Framework for International Trade*

Diplab Dasgupta, *Structural Adjustment, Global Trade and the New Political Economy of Development*

Wim Dierckxsens, *The Limits of Capitalism: An Approach to a Globalization Without Neoliberalism*

Graham Dunkley, *The Free Trade Adventure: The WTO, the Uruguay Round and Globalism: A Critique*

Terence Hopkins and Immanuel Wallerstein et al., *The Age of Transition: Trajectory of the World-System, 1945–2025*

Francois Houtart and Francois Polet (eds), *The Other Davos: The Globalization of Resistance to the World Economic System*

Arthur MacEwan, *Neo-Liberalism or Democracy? Economic Strategy, Markets, and Alternatives for the 21st Century*

Hans-Peter Martin and Harald Schumann, *The Global Trap: Globalization and the Assault on Prosperity and Democracy*

Jan Nederveen Pieterse (ed.), *Global Futures: Shaping Globalization*

James Petras and Henry Veltmeyer, *Globalization Unmasked: Imperialism in the 21st Century*

Saral Sarkar, *Eco-Socialism or Eco-Capitalism? A Critical Analysis of Humanity's Fundamental Choices*

Harry Shutt, *The Trouble With Capitalism: An Enquiry into the Causes of Global Economic Failure*

Kavaljit Singh, *The Globalisation of Finance: A Citizen's Guide*

Kavaljit Singh, *Taming Global Financial Flows: Challenges and Alternatives in the Era of Financial Globalisation*

Amory Starr, *Naming the Enemy: Anti-Corporate Social Movements Confront Globalization*

Bob Sutcliffe, *100 Ways of Seeing an Unequal World*

Oscar Ugarteche, *The False Dilemma: Globalisation: Opportunity or Threat?*

David Woodward, *The Next Crisis? Foreign Direct and Equity Investment in Developing Countries*

For full details of this list and Zed's other subject and general catalogues, please write to: The Marketing Department, Zed Books, 7 Cynthia Street, London N1 9JF, UK or email Sales@zedbooks.demon.co.uk

Visit our website at: http://www.zedbooks.demon.co.uk